D0312819

OTHER BOOKS BY AMITAI ETZIONI

The New Golden Rule: Community and Morality in a Democratic Society (1996)

The Spirit of Community: The Reinvention of American Society (1993)

A Responsive Society (1991)

The Moral Dimension: Toward a New Economics (1988)

Capital Corruption: The New Attack on American Democracy (1984)

An Immodest Agenda: Rebuilding America Before the Twenty-First Century (1983)

Genetic Fix: The Next Technological Revolution (1973)

The Active Society: A Theory of Societal and Political Processes (1968)

Political Unification: A Comparative Study of Leaders and Forces (1965)

Modern Organizations (1964)

A Comparative Analysis of Complex Organizations (1961)

THE LIMITS OF PRIVACY

AMITAI ETZIONI

A Member of the Perseus Books Group

Published by Basic Books, A Member of the Perseus Books Group

Library of Congress Cataloging-in-Publication Data
Etzioni, Amitai.
The limits of privacy / Amitai Etzioni.
p. cm.
Includes index.
ISBN 0-465-04089-6 (cloth); ISBN 0-465-04090-X (pbk.)
1. Privacy, Right of—United States. 2. Public interest—United States. 3. Common good. I. Title.
JC596.2.U5E79 1999
323.44'8'0973—dc21 98-47082
CIP

The paper used in this publication meets the requirements of the American National Standard for Permanence of Paper for Printed Library Materials Z39.48-1984.

10 9 8 7 6 5 4 3 2 1

For the youngest members of the family,
Noa Etzioni and Margaret Kellogg.

Contents

INTRODUCTION

Accompanied by his wife and nine-year-old son, John Becerra moved to Farmington, New York, in December 1995 to start a new life. Becerra had pleaded guilty to sexual abuse, served his time, and quietly begun his probation. In the spring of 1997, however, the Becerra family found themselves in the crosshairs of a neighborhood campaign to drive them out of town. Picketers rallied outside the family's home; a brick was thrown through their car window; a shot was fired through a window of their house; and anonymous calls were made to Mr. and Mrs. Becerra's workplaces. All this happened when members of the community found out about Becerra's past.[1]

One afternoon in late July 1994, seven-year-old Megan Kanka didn't come home. Earlier a neighbor had offered to show her his new puppy. Once inside his home, the man sexually assaulted Megan, then strangled her with a belt and wrapped her head in a plastic bag. Her body was eventually found buried in a nearby park, blood trickling from her mouth and her shorts cut to pieces. Investigation led to the arrest of Jesse Timmendequas, a man who had served six years in prison for two sex offense convictions and who lived with two other child molesters. No one in the neighborhood knew about his past. Especially the Kankas.[2]

No one needs to read a book—let alone a philosophical tract or an extensive policy analysis—to be reminded that the right to be let alone is much cherished, that without privacy no society can long remain free. And unless one has been denied access to all forms of communication and media, one has been fairly and repeatedly warned that privacy is not so much nibbled away as stripped away by every manner of new technology. Hardly a week passes without alarming headlines warning Americans that their cell phone conversations are not secure, employers read their e-mail, mutual funds sell details of their financial records to marketers, and their medical records are an open book. Public opinion polls show that Americans are appropriately agitated.[3] And Congress as well as state legislatures are at least claiming that new legislation to protect privacy is imminent.[4] Also, as the abundance of clichés about cyberspace indicates, new technologies have made invasion of privacy so much easier that we are justified in asking what remains of privacy and how it is to be saved in the new cyberage.[5]

This is a book largely about the other side of the privacy equation. It is about our investment in the common good, about our profound sense of social virtue, and most specifically about our concern for public safety and public health. Although we cherish privacy in a free society, we also value other goods. Hence, we must address the moral, legal, and social issues that arise when serving the common good entails violating privacy.

When I mentioned the subject of this book to audiences of friends, students in my classes, and members of the public, initially they were all taken aback. Privacy, they pointed out, is under siege, if not already overrun. Given privacy's great importance to a free people, my listeners stressed, one should seek new ways to shore it up, not cast more aspersions on it.

To begin a new dialogue about privacy, I have asked these and similar audiences if they would like to know whether the person entrusted with their child care is a convicted child molester. I mention that when such screening is done, thousands are found to have criminal records, ones that include pedophilia.[6] I further ask: Would they want to know whether the staff of the nursing home in which their mother now lives have criminal records that include abusing the elderly? I note that 14 percent of such employees are found to have criminal records, some of which include violent acts against senior citizens.[7] And should public authorities be entitled to determine whether drivers of school buses, pilots, or police officers are under the influence of illegal drugs? Should the FBI be in a position to crack the encrypted messages employed by terrorists before they use them to orchestrate the next Oklahoma City bombing? Addressing such concerns raises the question of if and when we are justified in implementing measures that diminish privacy in the service of the common good.

We may be tempted for a moment to employ a double standard, to seek to enshrine our own privacy while denying that of others, perhaps on the grounds that "we" are innocent but "they" are suspect. However, such a position is too cynical to be seriously entertained. That all of us are subject to the same law is a principle at the heart of democratic government. Nor can we ethically lay claims on others from which we exempt ourselves. In principle and in practice, there is no escaping the basic tension between our profound desire for privacy and our deep concern for public safety and public health.

In my view, a good society does not automatically privilege one core value over another—that is, accord it the special standing of a basically unmitigated good. Although a privileged value may not be treated with the ultimate reverence accorded to an absolute value, it is assumed that it might not be curbed out of consideration for the claims of other values, and that the burden of proof is assumed to be on those who speak for other concerns. When a value is strongly privileged, any other claims are initially suspect and made to jump over numerous hurdles (lawyers speak here of "strict scrutiny") before they are taken into account.

Privacy is treated in our society (more than in any other) as a highly privileged value. The questions this book grapples with are: Under which moral, legal, and social conditions should this right be curbed? What are the specific and significant harms that befall us when we do not allow privacy to be compromised?

The Common Good Defined

When I refer to the "common good" (or to the good society), the reader may fear that I am about to stray into some vague or preachy realm. We all view some rather specific matters as shared concerns of society at large, whatever our terminology—defending ourselves from nuclear attack, for instance. And practically all Americans agree that protecting the environment is a common good, although we differ regarding the scope and specifics of this commitment.

The common goods this book focuses on, public safety and public health, are not two among many, but the mainstays of what are considered practically uncontested common goods. Indeed, when courts and common parlance cite "the public interest," very often the reference is to matters that fall into one of these two pivotal categories. Without questioning the basic virtue of privacy, this book shows that in several important matters of public safety and health, the common good is being systematically neglected out of excessive deference to privacy.

Moreover, I shall try to demonstrate in the following pages that what is called for are not some limited, ad-hoc concessions to the common good, extended if and when a specific and strong case can be presented that privacy must be curbed. What is required is a fundamental change in civic culture, policymaking, and legal doctrines. We need to treat privacy as an individual right that is to be balanced with concerns for the common good—or as one good among others, without a priori privileging any of them.[8]

Discussions about privacy (and other rights) often center on a particular new technology or social measure that violates privacy and hence, it is argued, should be rejected. For example, when civil liberties groups learned recently that parents at work now may watch their children play in child care centers on their desktop computers, these groups objected on the ground that the cameras violate the privacy of the staff.[9] However, as I see it, this claim is merely the beginning of a necessary dialogue on the subject. The next step is to ask whether the gains to the children, the parents, and the community justify whatever loss in privacy is entailed. (Note that the staff are informed about the presence of the cameras.) Even the First Amendment, often considered the most absolute right of them all, does not trump all other considerations; shouting "Fire!" in a crowded theater is not a protected form of speech—unless, of course, there is indeed a fire, as the American Civil Liberties Union (ACLU) reminds us. Privacy should be treated with similarly high, but not unbounded, respect. We must recall that both ethics and public policies often entail not a choice between good and evil or right and wrong, but rather the much more daunting challenge of charting a course when faced with two conflicting rights or goods. This book seeks to contribute to that effort by sorting out the conflicting claims of the right to privacy and the needs of public safety and public health.

ONE SIDE AND THE OTHER: THE NEED FOR BALANCE

My approach is nourished by a social philosophy: communitarian thinking. Communitarianism holds that a good society seeks a carefully crafted balance between individual rights and social responsibilities, between liberty and the common good, a position I have written about elsewhere in some detail.[10] This book applies this approach to the often tense and confused relationship between the right to privacy and specific societal concerns.

If we take as our starting point the general principle that a good society crafts a careful balance between individual rights and the common good, the next step is to apply this principle to actual societies. We can then ask whether a particular society, in a given period, leans too far in one direction or the other. In a society that strongly enforces social duties but neglects individual rights (as does Japan, for instance, when it comes to the rights of women, minorities, and the disabled), strenuously fostering the other side in order to achieve balance would entail the expansion of autonomy. Indeed, even in the West, when John Locke, Adam Smith, and John Stuart Mill wrote their influential works, and for roughly the first 190 years of the American republic, the struggle to expand the realm of individual liberty was extremely justified, and there was little reason to be concerned that social responsibilities would be neglected. However, as communitarians have repeatedly noted, the relationship between rights and responsibilities drastically shifted in American society between 1960 and 1990 as a new emphasis on personal autonomy and individualism gradually overwhelmed other societal considerations. As a result, recognition of the need to rein in the excesses of individualism has grown in the 1990s.[11] I show in this book that this much needed social correction—this balancing of rights with a fresh emphasis on responsibilities—has yet to be brought to bear on privacy issues.

Two reasons stand out for the strong reluctance to face this issue. First, it is widely believed in American society that privacy, far from being excessively indulged, is endangered. The ACLU, for example, claims that "Americans' right to privacy is in peril."[12] Popular magazines have run cover stories about the "death" of privacy.[13] Scholars such as Brian Serr have argued, more carefully but still to the same effect, that "the [Supreme] Court's means of promoting law enforcement interests has tipped the balance unnecessarily further and further away from individual freedom, significantly diminishing the realm of personal privacy," and that "government investigatory techniques threaten to intrude more and more on the privacies of everyday life."[14] David Brin put it mildly, in a book entitled *The Transparent Society:* "Privacy is under siege."[15]

Scott E. Sundby chronicles his colleagues' concern over the "loss of privacy":

> The Supreme Court's recent Fourth Amendment decisions have drawn sharp criticism from the legal academy. Article after article documents the Court's transgressions . . . [how the Court] has suffocated individual privacy through an all-encompassing reasonableness standard. . . . If ever a united cry of warning has been made that a basic civil liberty was in danger, this chorus of law review laments is it.[16]

Indeed, as Richard Spinello writes in "The End of Privacy," "The title of this article may sound ominous, but it is intended to convey the stark reality that our personal privacy may gradually be coming to an end."[17]

These statements by opinion makers and scholars have left their mark on the American public, many of whom are rather alarmed about threats to privacy. A 1996 Harris/Equifax poll of more than 1,000 Americans found that nearly 80 percent of them were "somewhat" or "very" concerned about threats to personal privacy, the highest percentage ever recorded by the polling agency on this subject.[18] A 1997 Harris-Westin poll found a still larger number of Americans troubled about the state of privacy in America. Ninety-two percent of respondents were "concerned" about "threats to their personal privacy"; 64 percent were "*very* concerned."[19]

Effectively summarizing the alarmist position about the loss of privacy, Sundby writes:

> To maintain privacy, one must not write any checks nor make any phone calls. It would be unwise to engage in conversation with another person, or to walk, even on private property, outside one's house. If one is to barbecue or read in the back yard, do so only if surrounded by a fence higher than a double-decker bus and while sitting beneath an opaque awning. The wise individual might also consider purchasing anti-aerial spying devices if available (be sure to check the latest Sharper Image catalogue). Upon retiring inside, be sure to pull the shades together tightly so that no crack exists and to converse only in quiet tones. When discarding letters or other delicate materials, do so only after a thorough shredding of the documents (again see your Sharper Image catalogue); ideally, one would take the trash personally to the disposal site and bury it deep within. Finally, when buying items, carefully inspect them for any electronic tracking devices that may be attached.[20]

Champions of privacy also oppose the idea of adapting conceptions of privacy to contemporary social conditions—even when faced with evidence of specific and significant public safety and public health deficits—because of a widely shared belief that our emphasis on maintaining privacy has no negative consequences. The courts, these advocates hold, far from neglecting the public interest, have regularly included careful attention to it in their deliberations. The same is sometimes said about policymakers, federal and state administrations and legislatures, and regulatory bodies. To put it in the terms of the reference employed here, they would argue, strong advocacy of privacy has not unbalanced the societal scales, and there is thus no need to right them.

THE IMPACT OF STRONG PRIVACY ADVOCACY

In the studies of public policies and related matters of civic culture and legal doctrines that follow, my first call is to demonstrate *that immoderate champions of privacy have not merely engaged in rhetorical excesses but that these excesses have had significant and detrimental effects.* Specifically, I show that the champions of privacy (1) have been successful in delaying for years needed public actions by bottling them up in the courts, even if a balanced view ultimately prevailed; (2) have blocked altogether the introduction of other needed public policies that entail some new limitations on privacy; (3) have had a chilling effect on the consideration of other public policies that would advance the common good, preventing them from being seriously examined because public authorities fear lawsuits by the ACLU or others, and making such considerations politically costly (in the court of public opinion, on the campaign trail, in various legislatures, and in the White House); and (4) have for years sidetracked the introduction of new devices that could enhance both privacy and public health.[21] As we shall see, individualistic public philosophies, policies, and legal doctrines have often had all these effects simultaneously, each effect enforcing the others.

I support these claims by examining in detail five public policies: the issues raised by violation of the privacy of mothers following HIV testing of their newborn children (Chapter 1); the pros and cons of Megan's Laws, which attempt to protect children from repeat sex offenders by notifying the community about the offenders' presence (Chapter 2); the conflicting views on whether the government should be able to examine privately encrypted communications, a sort of phone-tapping of the Internet (Chapter 3); the dangers and opportunities posed by the development of powerful biometric ID systems, which in effect constitute national ID cards (Chapter 4); and the new measures needed to protect the privacy of medical records, measures that go beyond those based on the libertarian doctrine of relying on the consent of patients for each specific use of the information about them (Chapter 5).

Several other public policy measures not examined here reflect the same tension between privacy and the common good: the drug testing of those directly responsible for the lives of others (police, pilots, air traffic controllers, school bus drivers, train engineers); the implementation of antiterrorist measures[22]; the placement of surveillance cameras in public places to deter criminal activity[23]; searches of public school lockers for firearms and drugs; searches for firearms in public housing[24]; the establishment of sobriety checkpoints and antidrug checkpoints; and government-fostered but voluntary HIV testing and contact tracing.[25]

The tension between privacy rights and the common good is also faced by the thirteen states that have *not* set up sobriety checkpoints.

(Indeed, the Michigan Supreme Court has declared them unconstitutional.) Similarly, antidrug checkpoints, which have proven to be surprisingly effective in closing open drug markets, eliminating drive-by shootings, and reducing violent crime, have been challenged in the courts.[26] Some of these challenges have led to temporary removal of the checkpoints; in others, barriers have been permanently dismantled. In some locales such checkpoints have not been erected at all because public authorities fear being sued.

The treatment of HIV stands out among the major public policies, laws, regulations, and court cases in which privileging privacy has had considerable impact. Privacy advocates and their allies have prevented HIV from being treated like other dangerous communicable diseases (a trend referred to among experts as "HIV exceptionalism"). Government-encouraged (but not coerced) HIV testing and contact notification, which does entail some violation of privacy, is still blocked—although several major gay leaders who opposed such measures in the past now favor them.[27] In short, one cannot reasonably claim that privileging privacy has had no ill effects.

The question that needs to be addressed is: How can the common goods at issue be better served without unnecessarily undermining privacy? What, specifically, are the "harms" that privileging privacy entail, and what specific public policy remedies can be introduced that would minimize the diminution of privacy that treating these harms might entail? Finally, how should we address the moral, legal, and social concerns raised by the suggested remedies?

THE PRIVACY PARADOX

Although in several of the policies I examine here in detail, as well in those just cited, I find that privacy often is privileged over the common good, examination of one major area of public policy, that of medical records, shows that privacy is very much endangered, often without serving any significant common good (or one that could not be served in ways much less injurious to privacy). However, I find that this threat to privacy arises not from the state, the villain that champions of privacy traditionally fear most, but rather from the quest for profit by some private companies, privacy merchants. Indeed, I find that these corporations now regularly amass detailed accounts about many aspects of the personal lives of millions of individuals, profiles of the kind that until just a few years ago could be compiled only by the likes of the East German Stasi or other major state agencies, with huge staffs and budgets.

Moreover, I find a pattern: Although our civic culture, public policies, and legal doctrines are attentive to privacy when it is violated by the state, when privacy is threatened by the private sector our culture, policies, and doctrines provide a surprisingly weak defense. Consumers, employees, even patients and children have little protection from marketeers, insurance companies, bankers, and corporate surveillance. If privacy is to be better protected from commercial intrusions, a new approach needs to be developed. As I aim to show, this approach should rely in part on new technological and social devices and in part on a more benign view of the state taking an active role in the protection of privacy. Totalitarianism has deeply concerned people in the twentieth century; its dangers can hardly be ignored in the twenty-first century. However, renewed attention will have to be paid to the ill effects of the new unfettering of market forces. Privacy advocates will not make progress in this area, I will show in the following pages, until they break out of the privacy paradox: Although they fear Big Brother most, they need to lean on him to protect privacy better from Big Bucks.

CRITERIA FOR CORRECTIVE ACTION

The challenge of carefully crafting a balance between the common good and individual rights, between public health, public safety, and privacy, is particularly keen if the balance sought is to be achieved not merely within the context of some abstract theory or model, but in the context of specific historical and social conditions of a real, existing society. The question I raise in practically every lecture I deliver on the subject is: How is one to determine whether the existing relationship between privacy and the common good (or between privacy as one good and other common goods) is out of kilter, and if it is, what ought to be done to correct the imbalance?

In the following pages I suggest four criteria that can help to determine whether an imbalance exists, in which direction society is tilting, the scope of corrective action called for, and the specific qualities of the correctives to be employed. They are applied to each of the five public policies under review here. Even those who do not share the approach to privacy advanced in this book may well find these criteria of interest in the study of other matters of public policy, legal doctrine, and civic culture. (Previous presentations and applications of these criteria have been received favorably.[28]) Indeed, even if the common good could somehow overnight be well protected in all the areas under study—if there were no more pedophiles, no infants born with HIV, no criminals hiding behind false IDs, and no terrorists exchanging unbreakable encrypted messages—the following analysis would still apply. The specific studies of public policy, aside from whatever light they cast on the measures needed to improve the ways we protect public safety and health, also seek to illustrate a mode of policy analysis that encompasses ethical, legal, and practical considerations in the quest for a better society.

Much of the discussion reflects a pivotal fact about society: Unlike ideologies, which can be centered on one core value, society cannot but serve multiple needs and wants. This fact has an important consequence that deserves much more attention: Societies typically *cannot make perfect choices*, because often they must sacrifice some measure of one good for the sake of another. Indeed, much of what is under discussion here concerns trade-offs between privacy and the common good. I like to observe, however, that trade-offs are not always necessary. Indeed, the discussion of most privacy issues should start with a quest for policies or laws that could enhance both goods.

One brief example: A kit that allows individuals to determine their HIV status in the privacy of their own home was developed in 1985. The kit entails no visit to a doctor's office or clinic, no filling out of forms or computer entries. Users can mail in a few drops of blood and a code name and then call for the results. Aside from providing more privacy than had been previously available, the kit also advances public health by offering those reluctant to be tested in a less private place an opportunity to learn their HIV status. One notes with some sadness that the politics of privacy are such that even this very simple kit was bottled up in the Food and Drug Administration (FDA) for seven years before it was finally approved.[29]

The four criteria for determining whether privacy concerns and the common good are out of balance are presented sequentially; only policies and social actions that satisfy the first criterion need to be analyzed in light of the second one, and so on.[30]

First, a well-balanced, communitarian society will take steps to limit privacy only if it faces a *well-documented and macroscopic threat* to the common good, not a merely hypothetical danger. (The phrase "clear and present danger" comes to mind, but for those who are legal minded it implies a standard that is too exacting for the purposes at hand.) Policymakers and the general public are bombarded with dire warnings that society is about to face this or that danger that is so grave (e.g., flesh-eating bacteria, chicken-derived super-flu, brain disease courtesy of mad cows, gaping holes in the ozone layer, El Niño, the extinction of swordfish[31]) that it provides grounds for curtailment of privacy and other individual rights. If a society were to respond to every such warning by curbing rights, they would erode rapidly, often without serving any true common good.

Before limiting privacy, a well-balanced, communitarian society first determines how well documented various reported dangers to the common good are and how encompassing their expected consequences will be. When many thousands of lives are lost and many millions more are at risk, as with HIV, we face a clear and major threat. The effects of abusing marijuana are real but of a much lower magnitude, and hence do not justify the same kind of response. Still other dangers are highly hypothetical and hence usually do not merit public action. (I say "usually" because in situations where the probability of major ill effects is low but the magnitude of possible disutility is very high—for instance, a nuclear attack by terrorists—some privacy-limiting measures might be justified.)

The second criterion is to look at how carefully a society acts to counter a tangible and macroscopic danger without *first resorting to measures that might restrict privacy*. For instance, when medical records are needed by researchers and epidemiologists, the data are collected and utilized in a communitarian society as much as possible without identifying individuals. Because such measures often entail changes in mores, institutions, or habits of the heart rather than laws or constitutionally protected rights, I refer to them in the following discussion as "second-criterion *treatments*."

Third, to the extent that privacy-curbing measures must be introduced, a communitarian society makes them as *minimally intrusive* as possible. For example, many agree that drug tests should be conducted on those directly responsible for the lives of others, such as school bus drivers. Many employers, however, resort to highly intrusive visual surveillance to ensure that the sample is from the person who delivers it when in fact the less intrusive procedure of measuring the temperature of the sample immediately after delivery would suffice. To distinguish these kinds of measures—often undertaken by the government, and typically entailing changes in legal doctrine—from second-criterion treatments, I refer to them as "third-criterion *interventions*."

The principle of limiting the intrusiveness of privacy-curbing measures is further illustrated by the example of a national database that contains the names of medical practitioners who have been sued, sanctioned, or otherwise penalized for crimes, misconduct, or incompetence. The National Practitioner Data Bank allows hospitals that are considering whether to grant "privileges" (the right to practice in the hospital) to a physician to conduct limited background checks on him or her. However, the data bank discloses only that a physician has been subject to malpractice litigation or has been a party to an out-of-court settlement or adverse action (which might include revocation of license to practice or removal of privileges, for acts such as substance abuse), but it stops short of providing details of the violation. Because it is known that, as a rule, physicians are disaffiliated only for major violations, this information suffices for hospitals who seek to protect the public.[32]

Lastly, measures that *treat undesirable side effects* of needed privacy-diminishing measures are to be preferred over those that ignore these effects. Thus, if more widespread HIV testing and contact tracing are deemed necessary to protect public health, efforts must be made to enhance the confidentiality of the records of those tested. These records need to be particularly well protected to ensure that individuals testing positive will not lose their insurance, employment, or housing or otherwise suffer discrimination. For the same reasons, a communitarian society may have to increase penalties for such violations of privacy.

Although the criteria for corrective action have been introduced with examples in which the public good may need to be given priority over privacy, it should be stressed that the same criteria also provide guidance when the societal balance has tilted too far in the opposite direction, that is, when privacy is endangered and the concern for the common good must be scaled back. A case in point is the abuse of medical records. Information in personal medical records that is shared with health insurance companies is sometimes transmitted to other parties, such as employers (who may use the information to fire those with problems such as cancer or the "wrong" genes), banks (who may call in the loans of the sick), and even tabloids.[33]

Drawing on the four criteria to determine whether the spread of personal medical information should be curbed and the privacy of medical records strengthened, we would first seek to establish whether a significant common good is served by spreading such information to third parties. Finding little or none, we would then determine whether these privacy-endangering transmissions can be curbed without altering the law—perhaps by changing patient consent forms (which now require patients to almost totally relinquish control over their medical information and history), installing more advanced safeguards in computer information systems (e.g., audit trails that allow for the tracking of all those who access a file, thus enabling administrators to determine whether there has been unauthorized access), or other such actions. If these measures are deemed insufficient, legal remedies might be considered. A society might, for instance, introduce new penalties for the unauthorized transmission of medical information. Finally, those who have suffered from undue violations of their privacy—for instance, by losing a job as a result of such actions—might be entitled to receive compensation. In short, the four criteria can be used as much to determine whether privacy is deficient as to determine whether it is excessive, as well as to determine what actions should be taken to shore up privacy or to limit the sway of the common good.

The following analysis proceeds on two levels: It seeks to determine which of our public philosophies, policies, and legal doctrines are in need of major modification when it comes to the balance between privacy and the common good, and it illustrates extensively the merit of relying on the four criteria as a way to sort out changes of direction in almost any matter of public concern.

A word about methodology: Knowledge is often either analytical and specialized (the kind basic research generates) or synthesizing and encompassing (the kind policy analysis requires).[34] In this study I draw on sociology, psychology, ethics, and jurisprudence (and occasionally other bodies of knowledge) to cobble together a coherent policy analysis. I recognize that this approach inevitably prevents me from doing justice to any of these disciplines; it is an imperfect choice, but one that I believe policy analysis cannot avoid making.

Toward a New, Communitarian Conception of Privacy

The detailed analysis that follows serves a significant purpose beyond examining major instances in which new limits must be set on privacy (or the common good) and finding ways to ensure that corrective measures are not excessive. It points to a rather different concept of privacy—developed in detail in the last chapter—one that systematically provides for a balance between rights and the common good. The argument unfolds in response to a series of questions: What has been the impact of the sociohistorical conditions under which privacy was fashioned on the concept of privacy that prevails today, one that plays such an important role in our current civic culture, public policies, and legal doctrines? What led to the blending of privacy as an exception from scrutiny ("informational privacy") and privacy as the right to control one's own acts ("decisional privacy")? Has this blending outlived its usefulness, and if so, what would a more clearly delineated conception of privacy entail? A closely related question is: What is the relationship between two elements of the right to be let alone—privacy and autonomy?

I realize that there are those who will immediately condemn any such undertaking as an assault on a sacred American value. I hope to engage as many of them as possible in a reasoned and moral dialogue on a set of crucial issues.

1

HIV Testing of Infants

Should Public Health Override Privacy?

The citizens of forty-nine states and the District of Columbia must come to terms with the question of whether it is acceptable to violate the privacy of mothers in order to save the lives of some of their children. Can mothers, in effect, be tested for HIV and informed of their HIV status, without their consent, so that they can properly treat their infants? So far only New York State has acted on this vital matter. Congress walked away from it by asking the Institute of Medicine (IOM) to study the matter.[1] IOM released its conclusions in October 1998. Congress has yet to take notice.

This specific context for HIV testing should be seen within the larger context of the treatment of AIDS in general. Few public health issues have raised more emotional confrontations and policy disputes than the way AIDS has *not* been treated. The stigma that surrounded AIDS until very recently led gay activists and others to oppose some very basic public health efforts. These activists feared that those who contracted HIV might face loss of jobs, housing, and insurance.[2] At the same time, various public health advocates denounced the "exceptionalism" with which AIDS was treated; the prevention measures that have worked well to contain other dreaded diseases, such as tuberculosis and syphilis, have rarely been deployed to slow the spread of AIDS.[3] In this confrontation between the individual rights of people at risk to contract HIV and the needs of public health, one issue has garnered much less attention but deserves much more: The fate of infants born to mothers who have HIV.

Few matters of public concern offer a better opportunity to explore the thesis that there is a pro-privacy bias in contemporary American society than that of the opposition to mandatory testing of newborns for HIV antibodies and disclosure of the results to their mothers. The main arguments for testing infants are that if mothers of infants who are found to have been exposed to HIV are properly informed and counseled, hundreds of infants could be spared severe suffering and major illness, and often death. Also, mothers would be spared much grief, and significant public costs could be avoided.[4]

The main objection to such disclosure is that it violates the privacy of the mother by revealing her HIV status without her consent. As a result of such privacy violation, proponents of privacy argue, many mothers may be stigmatized or lose their health insurance, livelihood, and in some cases even their home. Opponents of disclosure also argue that alternative ways of serving the same public health goal—preventing the spread of HIV from pregnant women to their infants—are more effective and judicious, such as testing *pregnant* women only after gaining their consent (voluntary testing).

As with many of the issues discussed in this book, the debate about HIV testing of infants is often highly charged; each side demonizes the other by accusing it of seeking to subvert fundamental rights, discriminating against the poor or against gay people, or causing numerous, preventable infant deaths. My attempt here is to advance a civil dialogue. I presume that the motives of all parties to the debate are beyond reproach; disagreements reflect differences of values and goals and conflicting interpretations of the evidence.

A word about terminology. "Proponents" is used in the following examination to refer to those who support unblinded testing, and "opponents" refers to those who oppose such testing. "Unblinded testing" refers to disclosing the results of HIV tests of infants to their mothers and the health care personnel who treat them. In "blind" testing the same tests are conducted but for aggregated, statistical purposes only; information about individual infants is *not* disclosed to any party, parent or otherwise.

BASIC FACTS ABOUT HIV TESTING OF INFANTS

Since 1987 the Centers for Disease Control and Prevention (CDC), in conjunction with local health authorities in forty-four states and the District of Columbia, has arranged and paid for blind testing of all newborn infants for the presence of HIV antibodies. The CDC has used the resulting data to assess the level of HIV in the populations studied, both infants and mothers. The information was initially used only for epidemiological purposes.

In 1993 New York State Assemblywoman Nettie Mayersohn introduced a bill that mandated HIV testing for all infants born in the state and required that mothers be informed of the results. The bill, which would be called the Baby AIDS Law, was drafted in response to reports estimating that as many as 60 percent of the infants who tested positive for HIV were leaving hospitals unidentified and untreated.[5]

It should be noted that, technically speaking, standard HIV antibody tests, the ELISA and the Western Blot, do not determine a newborn's HIV status. Rather, these tests indicate the presence of the mother's HIV antibodies in the newborn's blood. *The test of infants thus reveals whether the mother is infected with HIV,* a discovery that in turn raises ethical, legal, and policy issues. It is also firmly established that a significant number of the infants whose mothers have the disease will develop HIV and ultimately AIDS.[6]

Although the number of infants infected with HIV by their mothers has been declining, the number of new pediatric AIDS cases reported in the United States in just one year alone, from July 1996 to June 1997, was still a troublesome 609.[7] By December 1997 the total number of cases due to perinatal transmission totaled 8,086.[8]

It is crucial for the analysis that follows to realize that the number of children born to mothers who have HIV is much larger than the number who will actually develop HIV, roughly four times so. It is estimated that, without proper treatment, approximately 25 percent of infants born to HIV-positive mothers will contract HIV from their mothers during pregnancy or birth (perinatally), while the other 75 percent will eventually clear their systems of their mothers' HIV antibodies and remain HIV-negative, under special conditions to be discussed shortly.[9]

The fate of the infants is deeply affected by the treatments administered—or not—by their mothers and by health care personnel. Those newborns who have not contracted HIV before or during birth (75 percent) are put at risk if they are breast-fed; a given percentage of them will acquire HIV from their mother after birth in this manner. The CDC estimates that "breastfeeding may increase the [overall] rate of [HIV] transmission [from mother to infant] by 10%–20%,"[10] and the World Health Organization (WHO) suggests that "up to one-third of HIV-infected infants are infected through breastfeeding."[11] In a meta-analysis of the findings of several studies that examined some infants who were breast-fed and others who were not, the risk of transmission of HIV through breast-feeding was found to be 14 percent for infants who otherwise would not have developed the illness. For mothers who developed HIV infection during the postpartum period, the risk of transmission through breast-feeding was 29 percent.[12] These infants will develop full-blown AIDS, suffer the full course of the disease, and die. Their illness and death could have been prevented if the mothers had merely been warned not to breast-feed their infants and had heeded the warning.[13] *This fact alone is an argument for unblinded testing.*

Moreover, there is significant evidence that the lives of the 25 percent born with HIV could be greatly improved and prolonged if mothers and health care personnel were informed of the condition of the infants. Caregivers would be able to provide AZT (and possibly newer drugs) to these infants to reduce their viral loads and provide many corollary benefits. Citing various antiretroviral studies, Leonardo Renna notes: "Studies indicate that ZDV [AZT] treatment improves children's appetites, weight gain and CD4 cell counts. Most importantly, ZDV significantly improves the mental and cognitive development of children."[14]

Health care personnel who know that the infants they are treating have HIV can also provide prophylaxis against the opportunistic infections these infants are particularly prone to getting. These illnesses include, among others, tuberculosis, varicella, meningitis, mycobacterium avium complex, thrush, and particularly pneumocystis carinii pneumonia (PCP). Indeed, according to the CDC, PCP occurs in 37 percent of all HIV-infected infants; of these, 53 percent acquire PCP between three and six months of age. The CDC also reports that the median survival time after infection with PCP is nineteen months.[15]

It should be noted that, at the time of this writing, the benefits of *post*natal treatment of infants with AZT, in terms of *preventing* the development of HIV, are not fully documented. Most trials that have been publicly reported have focused on AZT provided to women during pregnancy, during delivery, and for six weeks after birth. Hence AZT's effectiveness when given only after birth is not clearly established.[16] However, the U.S. Public Health Service recommends that if AZT treatment is not begun before or during delivery, such therapy should be "initiated as soon as possible after birth, preferably within 12–24 hours," and should continue for six weeks.[17]

Furthermore, a 1997 study conducted by the AIDS Institute of the New York Department of Health indicates that "initiation of ARV [antiretroviral] prophylaxis in the newborn period (within 48 hours of birth) may be associated with an intermediate decline in transmission." Among the initial group studied, postpartum administration of ARV prophylaxis resulted in a transmission rate of 8.9 percent, a significant improvement over the 26.5 percent transmission rate from mothers to their infants when no prophylaxis was provided.[18] It should be noted that this study examined only seventy-nine infants who were treated in this fashion. Additional studies are necessary before the benefits of postpartum prophylaxis can be fully assessed.[19] However, if these findings hold up, AZT given within forty-eight hours of birth—which can be done only if it is known which infants are at risk—saves lives by preventing transmission.

Early identification of possible HIV infection also allows physicians to tailor immunization schedules, an important consideration for children with HIV infection.[20] For example, HIV-infected infants should receive flu and measles vaccines more frequently than uninfected children, and some infected babies may need one of the different types of vaccines available rather than another.[21] Finally, test disclosure makes possible "close nutritional monitoring, an essential component of care" for HIV-positive infants.[22]

As these facts about the beneficial effects of postnatal treatment became widely known, public support for unblinding tests increased to the point that, in June 1996, Nettie Mayersohn's legislation was passed in New York State, despite strong and prolonged objections by the American Civil Liberties Union (ACLU), the Gay Men's Health Crisis (GMHC), and the New York chapter of the National Organization for Women (NOW), among others.[23]

As is often the case, opponents have raised both principled and practical objections to this legislation. Principled objections focus on the violation of the rights of the mothers caused by involuntary disclosure of the test results. The New York ACLU argues that, "in effect, mandatory legislation is mandating every new mother in New York State to be tested for HIV. The testing of newborns is an underhanded way of testing mothers and circumventing their rights to consent to the test."[24] Jeffrey Reynolds, deputy director for the Long Island Association for AIDS Care, states that newborn testing "amounts to mandatory testing by proxy, and without informed consent or counseling requirements, for all pregnant women in New York—a sharp departure for a state that mandates coercive testing for no other population." He calls Mayersohn's bill "misguided," adding that "above all, HIV testing after birth is simply too late to reduce the chances of perinatal transmission."[25] The Gay Men's Health Crisis adds:

> Concern over the health of the city's infants does not require that the state ignore their mothers' right to privacy and impose the mandatory newborn HIV testing program you [*Newsday* editorial] advocate. . . . Testing newborns for HIV antibodies . . . is tantamount to testing their mothers. . . . New York State law appropriately prohibits testing any individual for HIV antibodies against his or her will; the fact that you ignore pregnant women's absolute right to the same privacy as all other adults is disturbingly reminiscent of the current trend among conservative policymakers to consider women and their health only in relation to their role—or potential role—in childbearing.[26]

Turning to more emotive and practical objections, when asked, "Is freedom that important that you might allow 15,000 babies' lives to be poured down the drain?" Ruth Macklin, a bioethicist at the Albert Einstein College of Medicine in New York, replies, "At a certain point, one balances freedom against lives, indeed. We fight wars to preserve our freedom, knowing that a certain number of people are going to die."[27]

Terry McGovern, director of the HIV Law Project, has argued that "information is often not kept confidential. . . . I can't tell you how many heartbreaking cases we see where women are thrown out by their families, where children are thrown out of schools."[28] The executive director of the National Women's Health Network claims that "mandatory testing of newborns and their mothers will not save lives and will do nothing to stem the spread of HIV."[29] In the face of these strong objections, other states, as of 1998, have declined to follow New York's lead.

On the federal level, Representatives Tom Coburn (R-Okla.) and Gary Ackerman (D-N.Y.) introduced *draft* legislation in 1995 that would have required all states to follow the New York State example or lose the sizable federal funds they receive under the Ryan White Care Act of 1990. However, the bill raised strong objections from many of the same groups that had objected to it in New York. In response to this initial opposition, the law that was eventually enacted in 1996 reflected a compromise: All states will be required to meet certain goals for pediatric AIDS prevention within five years.[30] By the year 2000 states must reduce their number of pediatric AIDS cases by 50 percent or, through counseling, test 95 percent of pregnant women for HIV. States that do not meet these goals will have to implement unblinded mandatory newborn testing for all mothers who do not receive a prenatal HIV test or lose their Ryan White Care Act funds.[31] The Institute of Medicine was charged with the task of conducting a study of the states' testing procedures and the results they obtained. Thus, through this bill, Congress delayed any final vote on the unblinding of infant tests for a period of close to five years.

Mayersohn's bill, as well as Coburn and Ackerman's congressional bill, also faced opposition from the CDC, which canceled its newborn testing efforts in 1995, shortly after the New York law was enacted and just as the congressional bill was being drafted.[32]

Applying the four evaluative criteria laid out in the introduction, we have seen so far that there is a serious problem: The lives and well-being of a considerable number of infants are at stake. Would second-criterion treatments (which are voluntary and do not involve changes in the law) suffice, or do we need to initiate third-criterion interventions (which entail mandatory acts)?

THE PUBLIC POLICY DEBATE

Opponents of unblinded testing argue that from a medical viewpoint there is a more effective alternative that does not raise the legal and ethical issues, especially the violation of privacy, invoked by unblinded testing. This alternative policy, *voluntary testing of pregnant women* as part of prenatal care or a special program, is said to be capable of achieving the same public health goals as unblinded testing. The ACLU, the Gay Men's Health Crisis, and the CDC, which have all adopted this position,[33] feel that it is supported by the results of a 1994 study: If AZT treatment is administered to HIV-positive pregnant women during pregnancy and delivery, and to infants for six weeks after birth, the risk of infection for the infants is reduced by two-thirds, from 25 percent to 8 percent.[34] In the light of these findings, the CDC issued guidelines in 1995 calling for the voluntary testing of all pregnant women for HIV.[35] Thereafter, there has been a significant reduction in the number of sick infants.[36]

It is correctly argued that voluntary testing of mothers during prenatal care would also dispose of the ethical and legal issues raised by unblinding test results in which mothers' privacy is violated. If mothers were tested instead of infants, their consent would first have to be obtained. And if the proper funds were allocated, health care staff could provide mothers with counseling before the test and help them cope with a positive result if the test's findings were in fact positive. Furthermore, many health care professionals argue for prenatal as opposed to postnatal testing because prenatal treatment is believed to be more effective.

As I see it, the issue is not properly framed when put in terms of choosing between voluntary testing of pregnant women and mandatory infant testing followed by disclosure of the results; *both alternatives are needed*, for reasons spelled out shortly.

Long experience has taught me that whenever one party argues for policy A and against policy B, and the other party for both policy A and policy B, the debate soon makes it sound as if the second party favors B but not A. Hence I repeat: I fully grant that testing pregnant women, counseling them, and encouraging them to take proper medications and undergo appropriate care is a highly desirable public health policy. (Note that this policy requires that considerable resources be allocated and that physicians, other health care personnel, hospitals, and clinics include HIV testing and counseling in their prenatal care programs and make efforts to find the mothers who do not present themselves for prenatal care.) However, successful implementation of this policy does not obviate the need to learn from tests of infants' blood—tests that are already conducted to check for other illnesses, especially phenylketonuria (PKU)—whether they have been exposed to HIV, most notably because many pregnant women do not present themselves for prenatal care despite concerted efforts to encourage them to do so. Many of them can be found and persuaded to provide treatments to their infants only if their infants are tested. One does not choose between seat belts and airbags, both of which are mandated, to protect oneself from auto accidents; similarly, the effectiveness of one policy in reducing HIV transmission to infants does not invalidate another policy.

True, some believe that unblinded infant testing would undermine programs aimed at counseling and testing pregnant women. Alan Fleischman, a physician with the New York Academy of Medicine who strongly opposes unblinded newborn testing, has suggested that if newborn testing is universally conducted, doctors who provide prenatal care may stop advising pregnant women to be tested for HIV under the mistaken assumption that newborn testing eliminates the need for such counseling. This possibility is highly speculative and quite unlikely, especially given current knowledge regarding the benefits of prenatal counseling and testing. A physician who so conducts herself would not discharge her elementary duty to her patient, the woman in her care. Although it is possible that some physicians would conduct themselves in this manner, there seems to be no evidence that more than a very few would do so.

There are several other reasons why infant testing is needed, beyond the very important fact that many pregnant women, including those most likely to develop HIV, do not present themselves for prenatal care. Some pregnant women who do seek prenatal care do not consent to be tested for HIV. And pregnant women who have tested negative may develop HIV after they have been tested but before delivery. It should be noted here that research suggests that the greatest risk of infection occurs during birth.[37] To put it bluntly: Voluntary testing of pregnant women is highly commendable, but numerous infants will still fall through the cracks, so to speak, and need to be "caught" so that they can be helped.

Finally, given that symptoms may take many months or even years to develop, it is quite conceivable that an HIV-positive mother, unaware of her infection, could give birth to yet another child without the benefits of appropriate ARV prophylaxis. This child would also run a significant chance of contracting HIV.

These concerns are supported by the fact that voluntary counseling and testing programs have failed to identify numerous HIV carriers. In New York a study that gathered data from July 1993 through September 1993 determined that only 53 percent of infected infants were identified through prenatal testing and counseling.[38] Although subsequent figures have been more favorable,[39] champions of unblinded testing point out that in New York the improved results were achieved largely after Mayersohn's bill unblinding test results was enacted. (That is, after pregnant women learned that, regardless of whether they decided to undergo prenatal testing, their infant would be tested and the results provided to them.)

Those who favor testing only mothers and not infants also point to the success of voluntary prenatal testing and counseling at one hospital, the Harlem Hospital. This program convinced 90 percent of pregnant women to be tested for HIV. However, as Elaine Abrams, director of pediatric AIDS care at Harlem Hospital notes, "Isn't it troublesome that only this one program has been successful? Counseling has worked in one place and failed everywhere else, and they want to duplicate it?"[40] And Mark Rapoport, a former Westchester

County public health commissioner, notes that although voluntary testing works in "the best circumstances, as at Harlem Hospital ... overall, less than half of women know their infant's status and, therefore, their own status when the baby's born."[41]

It is theoretically possible that if more and more resources are invested in locating, counseling, and testing pregnant women, a point may be reached where only a very few would transmit the disease to their children. *The best way to establish that this day has arrived is to continue to collect data from tests conducted on the infants.* Efforts to reach such a goal are not advanced by canceling infant tests.

Far from being wasteful, the initial results of the New York Baby AIDS Law have been encouraging. Data collected by the New York Department of Health's AIDS Institute and Wadsworth Laboratories indicate that nearly 100 percent of HIV-exposed infants are being identified, and that follow-up efforts have linked 98.8 percent of these infants with care.[42] In the first twelve months of the program, 102 exposed infants were identified whose mother's HIV status had not been known at the time of delivery.[43]

Finally, opponents argue that by the time the results of infant tests are available, mother and child have typically long since left the hospital and some are difficult to locate. However, since 1992 a test has been available that can provide results within ten minutes. This test is rarely used owing to concerns over interpretation of the results, and previous CDC recommendations have suggested that confirmatory tests be performed for all HIV tests before patients are informed of the results. However, the CDC recently changed this policy, urging doctors to make greater use of the rapid test and to inform patients immediately of the results while confirmatory tests are performed.[44]

RELATIVE COSTS OF NEWBORN TESTING

Some objections have been raised to infant testing and disclosure on the grounds that such measures would be too costly. At the Institute of Medicine's Second Perinatal Transmission of HIV Committee Meeting in 1998, Ellen Mangione of the Colorado Department of Public Health and Environment argued that her state's total HIV prevention budget was limited, and that dedicating dollars to unblinded infant tests was thus unacceptable. Another opponent asserted at the meeting that in the first nine months after enactment of the New York Baby AIDS Law, 185,000 infants were tested and "only" 60 infants who tested positive were born to mothers who had not themselves been tested during pregnancy. (The actual figure is 69.)[45]

Actually, the costs of the test are very small because the blood of babies delivered in the health care system in most states is already collected and tested to determine whether the infant has PKU, hypothyroidism, or galactosemia.[46] Testing for HIV is done on "residual" blood specimens, that is, "specimens collected and tested for other reasons that were temporarily stored prior to being discarded."[47]

Dr. Guthrie Birkhead of New York's AIDS Institute has reported that blood-testing is highly automated and that adding an initial HIV test to the existing battery of tests raises the cost only minimally. Birkhead estimates that the change would require two additional technicians, along with a few other nominal expenses.[48] (It should be noted that confirmatory tests and counseling occur only if the first test is positive, and so these costs are incurred by a much smaller number of people.) In short, the costs of testing infants in addition to pregnant women are surprisingly modest.

Opponents who base their objections on cost should also be reminded that the HIV budget is not a zero-sum game; if additional measures were proposed that would directly save or improve lives, added funds might well be made available. Moreover, the costs could be reduced if testing were concentrated in those areas where more than a given number of HIV infections per capita prevails, a proposal the CDC itself considered at one point for another HIV testing measure.[49] This approach, however, could lead to complaints that the testing is focused on certain minorities or socioeconomic groups. One can look at universal testing as a means to avoid even the appearance of discrimination, surely a goal worthy of some added expenditure.

One last point: Because counseling and testing pregnant women is more costly than testing infants, someone guided by cost alone would be compelled to eliminate or restrict these efforts first—certainly an unacceptable solution.

I am not suggesting that costs are irrelevant to this issue. However, given how nominal any added costs would be, such considerations do not seem to justify opposing unblinded testing and forgoing its very considerable benefits.

OTHER ARGUMENTS AGAINST UNBLINDED TESTING

Opponents of unblinded, mandatory testing of infants argue further that such a program would scare women away from the health care system, forcing them to avoid prenatal care and hospital deliveries. For instance, the ACLU argues that

> mandatory testing of pregnant women and newborns would have detrimental public health consequences, most significantly by deterring women, especially low income women, from seeking prenatal care. . . . Without trust there is rarely compliance, especially when a woman is confronting not only the possibility that her child has an incurable disease, but the certainty that she does as well.[50]

The Gay Men's Health Crisis concurs: "Mandatory or coercive proposals, which offer no guarantee of services and which ignore the need to involve the mother in the care of her child, neither reduce the possibility of HIV transmission nor increase the likelihood that infants or their mothers will receive the care they need."[51]

These claims have been countered by the Association to Benefit Children (ABC), a foster care provider in New York City. After years of work in this field, this agency observes that "an HIV-positive result typically meant that a mother took strengthened interest in managing her health and that of her child."[52] Observations by both sides on this point are anecdotal, however; until systematic data are generated, this argument cannot be employed to oppose unblinded testing any more than it can be used to support it.

Some opponents claim that there is little or no support in the medical community for unblinded newborn testing. Elizabeth Cooper, an associate professor at the Fordham School of Law, writes that "it is alarming when any arm of the government . . . chooses to pursue a path of policy development that not only has not been endorsed by, but in fact has been rejected outright by virtually every well-respected medical, scientific, and public health organization."[53] Although it is true that several health groups, already cited, have opposed unblinding the newborn test, support has arisen from several others, including the New York State Association of County Health Officials, the Council of Family and Child Caring Agencies, the New York chapter of the American College of Emergency Physicians, and the AIDS Institute Committee for the Care of Children and Adolescents with HIV Infection. Additionally, former Surgeon General C. Everett Koop has supported the measure.[54] Although the American Academy of Pediatrics opposes unblinding, the American Medical Association has endorsed it.[55] Clearly unblinding is not a measure without significant professional support.

THE CDC'S CONCERNS

The CDC suspended its testing of infants in 1995 as unblinded testing began to gain support. The CDC states that it suspended the testing to "re-evaluate how best to combine prevention and surveillance strategies" in light of new findings on the effectiveness of prenatal intervention.[56] However, the CDC has made no secret of its opposition to unblinded tests. A CDC spokeswoman, Terry Hammond, has commented that "testing newborns is too little, too late. The CDC feels very strongly that voluntary testing is the most effective way to reach women and children who need care."[57] Dr. Helene Gayle of the CDC testified before a congressional hearing that the CDC suspended the program because it intended to call for voluntary testing of all pregnant women.[58] Dr. James Curran, head of the CDC's Division of HIV/AIDS Prevention Surveillance and Epidemiology, commented that through voluntary testing, "every pediatrician will know every baby who's exposed [to HIV]," obviating the need for newborn testing.[59]

Others contend that the CDC feared that unblinding the results could jeopardize the quality of its demographic and statistical work.[60] This point was stressed repeatedly in a long letter to the author from Dr. Robert Janssen, deputy director of the CDC's AIDS division. He states that the CDC is mandated "to examine, evaluate and monitor the extent of the HIV epidemic in this country." The agency's mission is not to find cures or prevent the spread of the dreaded disease. Indeed, the role of the CDC is often to collect information that will assist policymakers and researchers, an effort that does not necessarily entail actual medical research directly seeking to find a cure, let alone administer it to the ill.

Discussing the ethical concerns surrounding the surveillance studies, Dr. Janssen writes:

> In response to questions regarding the ethics of these studies, we suspect that this question arises now because of the extensive publicity of the importance of newly available therapies for HIV. Important therapy for HIV . . . ha[s] been available for a decade or more. . . . The recent identification (since 1995) of the class of protease inhibitor drugs has been important for certain individuals with HIV infection; however, these drugs do not cure the infection and its ultimate disease course. Problems with the existing limits on the access to, availability of, and adherence to these drugs also limit their ultimate effectiveness in the population of HIV-infected persons. These comments are not to belittle the advances in therapy, but to simply balance these advances with the ongoing needs to monitor the epidemic, particularly with tools that can evaluate populations where new HIV infections are emerging.

Dr. Janssen crowns his observations with the following comment:

> In fact the question is really about whether public health officials need to know the extent and the movement of the HIV epidemic in the United States. Based on the assumption that public health programs and public health leaders need accurate and representative information on important diseases, the survey methodology (unlinked anonymous) is critically necessary.[61]

In effect Dr. Janssen is saying that keeping the data straight is more important than ameliorating the effects of the disease, as far as the work of his agency is concerned. (Note that the data do not evaluate various treatments but merely provide a picture of the level of the epidemic). Sadly he does not consider that, without continued and unblinded tests, infants whose lives could be saved if they were given AZT and/or if they were not breast-fed will die.[62]

Even from a purely social science perspective it is difficult to find fully compelling the CDC's arguments against unblinding. To begin with, testing an entire population rather than smaller samples is usually not a favored procedure. Most important, it does not automatically follow that such a loss to the cause of epidemiology would outweigh either the medical benefits to newborns or the additional normative concerns I explore next.

It should also be noted that in many medical research studies the test results have often been unblinded once it became clear that doing so would enable health authorities to provide better care to those involved—and certainly when lives could be saved. As I noted earlier, infants are already tested for a variety of illnesses, and the results of all but the HIV test are readily disclosed to the mother. These include routine tests for hepatitis and syphilis, the results of which are released to the mother owing to the overriding health benefits of disclosure.[63]

Once one recognizes that such testing has become routine, the course of action seems self-evident. In fact, when health officials implemented mandatory testing of infants for sickle-cell disease, many of the same objections facing unblinded HIV testing were raised. However, it became clear that the medical benefits of the tests outweighed other concerns.

The epidemiological studies in question are not tests of medication that would allow HIV to be cured, in which case one could argue that it might be proper to endanger some lives now to save many more later. At issue here are studies that have much more indirect and limited health benefits than those associated with a vaccine or cure. And, to reiterate, these purposes can be served even if the test is unblinded.

CONSENT TO DISCLOSURE?

The public policy debate has focused on whether test results should be unblinded and mothers informed, but another option comes to mind, one that has in effect already been tried: seeking the mother's consent to be informed about the test's results (or, if the infant's blood is not tested for HIV, to allow it to be tested and the results disclosed). At first blush, this approach would seem to combine the best of both worlds: Practically all the mothers could be reached because even though only some pregnant women present themselves for prenatal care, almost all deliveries take place in hospitals or other health care facilities; in addition, consensual disclosure is assumed not to violate privacy.

One disadvantage of this approach is that the costs would be substantially higher than those entailed in unblinding the test, because all mothers would have to be counseled (before they could be asked to consent), not just the much smaller number whose infants' test results are positive (if no a priori consent is required).

Even more important, the consent given under these conditions is far from compelling and would likely be considered unsatisfactory by a typical bioethical committee. First of all, it has been observed that many of the treating professionals are of a much higher socioeconomic status than the mothers and thus are perceived as strong authority figures. Marcia Angell, the executive editor of the *New England Journal of Medicine*, notes that "many people can be coerced into submitting to harmful experiments, especially if they are poor and uneducated."[64] Although this statement was made in reference to overseas AZT experiments involving pregnant women, the same principle applies in this country. Even many white middle-class mothers find it difficult to object to suggestions by their physicians.

Most important, the consent must generally be sought as the pregnant woman is in labor, a point at which it would be unethical to ask her to consider agreeing to a test that might establish that she has a horrible, fatal illness, one she might already have transmitted to her about-to-be-born child. Counseling under these conditions would, at the very least, be ethically suspect and difficult to carry out.

Although requests for consent to disclose might be delayed until after delivery, they must still be made very shortly thereafter to prevent breast-feeding and to start whatever medications are necessary; moreover, mothers usually remain in the hospital for only a short time. Hospitals would also have to ask all mothers for consent, because a practice of asking only those whose infants test positive would soon become known and would be tantamount to disclosure without consent.

Last but not least, some mothers will refuse to consent. The fact that their numbers might be small (which is far from well established) does not answer the ethical questions involved. Should a mother who does not consent to be tested be informed that she will gravely endanger the life and health of her child if she breast-feeds and does not provide that child with AZT?

When all is said and done, consensual disclosure (if issues of costs are not allowed to prevail) has some advantages over nonconsensual disclosure, but these are offset by the difficulty of obtaining consent under the typical conditions. In either case, the ethical issues that arise when mothers prefer not to be informed cannot be avoided.

ETHICAL-LEGAL ISSUES

Many oppose testing infants for HIV and unblinding the results on the grounds that doing so violates the mother's right to privacy.[65] The right to privacy includes "the right to bodily integrity, including the right to make personal decisions regarding medical tests and treatments,"[66] and the right to make medical decisions on behalf of one's children. These rights are protected by civil tort law, by state statutes, and by the Constitution.[67] In addition, there are specific laws requiring that individuals be given the opportunity to grant written, informed consent before submitting to an HIV test[68] and providing for the strict confidentiality of HIV test results.[69] A law that requires mandatory, unblinded testing of newborns would override a woman's right to informed consent and confidentiality.

Opponents argue that violations of rights besides privacy, as well as other injuries, are likely to follow. The harms they claim include discrimination, stigma, loss of jobs, health and life insurance, and housing, and even domestic abuse or loss of family, all supposedly stemming from the violation of privacy. The ACLU argues that "these woman are susceptible to the same kinds of discrimination faced by others if it becomes known that they are infected with HIV."[70] AIDS Project Los Angeles and the San Francisco AIDS Foundation point out that "there have been numerous court cases involving HIV-positive individuals who have lost their health insurance, their job, or both. The reality is that we cannot legislate away the stigmatization that people with HIV experience."[71] According to data provided by the Equal Employment Opportunity Commission (EEOC), 2,327 HIV-related cases have been filed with the EEOC since 1992. Of these, about 60 percent have centered on wrongful firings.[72]

Karen Rothenberg and Stephen Paskey, writing for the *American Journal of Public Health*, have opined, "We believe that HIV-infected women are particularly vulnerable to the risk of domestic violence."[73] Although no studies have documented this observation on a large scale, one study conducted in Baltimore found that the fear of violence or abandonment is prevalent among HIV-positive women: "Forty-five percent of all providers surveyed had at least one female patient who expressed fear of physical violence resulting from disclosure of her diagnosis to a partner, while 56% of providers had patients who expressed fear of emotional abuse and 66% had patients who expressed fear of abandonment."[74] If infant HIV testing remains blinded, the reasoning goes, such violent outcomes are far less likely because nobody can identify the subjects who have tested positive. They are merely nameless numbers in statistical tables.

Opponents also argue that unblinded testing raises questions as to whether such a procedure might violate a mother's right to freedom from unreasonable search and seizure. Taking a blood sample has been shown many times in court to be a search within the context of the Fourth Amendment.[75] However, the Fourth Amendment permits searches under certain circumstances, such as when the search is intended to protect the health of an individual. Because the search is intended for precisely such a purpose in this case, some legal scholars argue that a mother's civil rights would not be violated.[76]

As in many ethical deliberations, the conflict here is not between a wrong and a right but between two or more rights. Several questions are at issue: Which rights should take precedence? Should the intervention be modified to minimize the damage to the right, or do the rights need to yield? What are the implications of the new balance struck among the different rights for the common good (a particular concern for communitarians)?

LOSS OF LIFE

In ranking the rights and values involved in the question of whether HIV testing of newborns should be mandatory, one can rely on abstract ethical considerations, such as weighing autonomy against beneficence. I draw mainly, however, on the core values of the democratic society in which these issues must be worked out.[77] As I see it, these values provide clear guidance in the case at hand. Our core values and the legal code that expresses them generally rank the loss of life over loss of limb, and both higher than the loss of property. Other concerns are less clearly prioritized but usually do not take precedence over threatened loss of life, including the knowing infliction of a major illness or the failure to treat it when it can be cured.

The Tuskegee Experiment is a case in point: Not informing the syphilis patients who were participating about their condition, and not providing them with the available treatment, is considered one of the great ethical failures of American public health policy. The parallelisms between HIV testing and withholding information and the Tuskegee Experiment have been very well drawn by Marcia Angell.[78]

Laws reflect this type of value "ranking" in court cases where the well-being of children is involved. Although parents have the right to give informed consent for treatment on behalf of their children,[79] the "parents' right to determine the course of treatment for children is limited." Renna explains that "a parent may not deprive a child of life-saving treatment," and adds that "courts have consistently allowed the state to intervene when a child's health is in danger."[80]

From this standpoint, one set of facts stands out: Given that keeping infant tests blind, or not conducting them at all, will directly contribute to the deaths of a significant proportion of infants born to mothers who have HIV, this is in line with our values and legal tradition.

A Devastating, Prolonged Illness

Untreated infants are condemned not only to early death but also to severe illness. AIDS, of course, differs from most other illnesses in that it entails a very debilitating and extended period of suffering for both infants and their families. As noted earlier, a newborn with AIDS is subject to many devastating, opportunistic infections that will kill him or her painfully over the course of many months or years. Infants with HIV also suffer from "recurrent severe bacterial infections, cancers, specific encephalopathy, and wasting syndrome."[81] Even if keeping the information from the mothers did not cause the deaths of a significant number of infants, the severity of the illness to which they would be exposed is itself a major concern.

MOTHERS' SUFFERING

Opponents are correct in pointing out the psychological and sociological effects of having one's privacy violated. We must also consider, however, the suffering inflicted on the infants' mothers if they are not informed about positive test results. Here is one far from atypical account.

A baby girl was born to a mother at Mount Sinai Hospital in New York City on the morning of 31 January 1991. The doctor assured the mother that her baby was normal and healthy. Nine months later the mother rushed her child to the same hospital. Her child was having seizures and had stopped breathing. To the mother's astonishment, she learned that her child was HIV-positive and suffering from meningitis, a pneumococcal infection brought on by an HIV-weakened immune system; the infection eventually left her child blind, deaf, brain-damaged, and paralyzed. The mother was incredulous when she discovered two agonizing facts: first, that this debilitating infection could have been prevented if her child had been diagnosed and treated soon after birth; and second, that her child had actually been tested for HIV as a newborn in the hospital but the results were withheld from her "to protect her own privacy."[82]

Similar scenarios have occurred many times across the country for more than ten years.[83] Mothers who take their infants home without being informed of the latter's HIV status may have children who will gradually develop a variety of undiagnosed illnesses that may seem like a severe flu, pneumonia, diarrhea, and so on. After continued treatment for these various illnesses, however, the mothers soon discover the true nature of their child's problem, and its prospects. The guilt these mothers may feel about having inadvertently contributed to the illness and death of their child is a very serious concern, as is their anger at the medical community for denying them information that could have prevented their child's death and suffering. Indeed, one may ask whether these mothers have a legal, or at least an ethical, claim against those who failed to inform them of their child's severe but treatable condition.

Other benefits for mothers may result from unblinded tests, aside from being spared considerable agony. As explained earlier, a positive newborn test result indicates the mother's HIV status. If the tests are unblinded, the mother may obtain medical treatment for herself. Given the favorable results obtained through "drug cocktails" that include protease inhibitors, the medical benefit of knowing one's HIV status is undisputed, provided that care is available.

Not only does the mother's treatment indirectly benefit the infant, who depends on her for care, but "identification of a mother's seropositive status helps her make informed decisions about her future family plans."[84] She can make informed choices regarding future pregnancies and appropriate care if she does plan to have additional children. She can also make early arrangements for the care of her children who may survive her. Finally, the knowledge of her HIV status gives the mother an opportunity to take precautions against further transmission of HIV to sexual partners, certainly no small consideration.

VIOLATION OF PRIVACY

There is no denying that unblinded tests entail a diminution of the mother's privacy. It should be noted, though, that privacy is not an absolute value and does not trump all other rights or concerns for the common good. As Alan Westin has observed, "An individual's desire for privacy can never be absolute, 'since participation in society is an equally powerful desire.'"[85] Even civil libertarians recognize that the police have a right to search a person's home if there is specific evidence that, say, a criminal or a murder weapon is hidden therein. It is therefore insufficient simply to argue that unblinding violates privacy and then rest one's case. One must weigh the harm inflicted on the mother, infant, and community when there is no disclosure compared to the harm inflicted by violating privacy.

Moreover, even if newborn test results remain blind, privacy will not be preserved for long. As Renna observes:

> The reality is that she [an HIV-positive mother] is likely to learn of her newborn's HIV status in short order. . . . Without treatment, the probability that an HIV-infected infant will develop an opportunistic infection within the first year is great. . . . She not only will be forced to deal with

> the sudden revelation of her and her infant's status, but will be forced to deal with her infant's serious HIV related illness (and possibly her own), as well as the realization that this illness might have been preventable.[86]

In short, the HIV status of both the baby and the mother will eventually be revealed whether the newborn is tested or not; the issue of discrimination and other ill effects of disclosure will have to be faced when either the infant or the mother develops more visible symptoms over time.

All this means not only that the claim of privacy is trumped by concern for saving lives, avoiding severe illness and suffering, and directly improving the well-being of others, but also that the privacy claim is itself rather limited.

VIOLATION OF AUTONOMY

The argument has been made that not only the privacy but also the autonomy of mothers is violated when they are informed about the results of a test that they did not seek and provided with information they do not wish to have. This argument calls attention to the complex and often confused relationship between privacy and autonomy.

Violations of autonomy may occur even when mothers are merely asked to consider whether they wish to know, because the mothers may be perturbed by having to face such considerations.

One could enter here into an extensive discussion of what autonomy encompasses, the difference between a right to know and a right not to know, and related issues. The main question that must be faced at this point, however, is not whether and to what extent autonomy is infringed by unblinded HIV testing in newborns, but whether there is another consideration that justifies a diminution of autonomy. The moral equation is similar to the one invoked by privacy considerations: Given that fully honoring autonomy significantly increases the chance of loss of life, and that a serious illness will fester untreated, and given that the intrusion is limited to sharing information, it seems that the other considerations should take precedence. Indeed, a case can be made that health care personnel have a moral obligation to share such information with mothers and those who treat their children.

An analogy might illuminate the point. Assume that a patient asks her physician for a battery of tests but informs the physician that she would like to know all the results but one: If she is found to have cancer, she would rather not be told. Assume also that a cancer is indeed caught early by these tests, and it is of the highly treatable kind. The physician in this case is able *directly* to save a life. (Very often the connection between the physician's action and the saving of a life is indirect and comparatively weak—for example, when a physician counsels the patient to exercise and maintain a proper diet.) Assume also that the patient has a very high probability of dying relatively soon if not treated. As I have suggested already, to not offer a warning in such a situation is like not pulling someone away on spotting the approach of a speeding truck. Under these conditions, the physician would seem obligated to do all she can to gain the patient's consent to be informed. (This consent must, of course, be obtained before the test is undertaken because seeking it after the fact might be seen as a communication that the test results were positive.) If the patient still refuses to be informed, the physician seems obligated to at least instruct the patient in the care she needs.

The same argument is even more valid when the patient is a mother who, even if one could completely respect her autonomy, is likely to cause irreparable harm to a defenseless infant if she is not informed. Even strong libertarians concede that our various rights do not include a right to cause serious damage to others, let alone endanger their lives. Indeed, our laws and ethics fully support taking the much more drastic step of removing children from abusive or neglectful parents. Informing mothers about actions that must be undertaken—such as not breast-feeding their infants and giving them antiviral medications—without spelling out the reasons may be a poor but justified compromise, given that lives might well be saved. Such limited disclosure would allow mothers to stay in denial, if they cannot face the truth, and still do right by their children.

DISCRIMINATION

It is certainly of grave concern that HIV-positive mothers may be subject to discrimination. Many of these mothers are members of social groups that are already subject to discrimination even when not infected with HIV. Of all children reported with AIDS between 1982 and 1996, 23 percent were Hispanic and 58 percent were black. An estimated two-thirds of mothers whose newborns tested positive were poor and members of minorities. Further, the greatest percentage of the children's mothers contracted HIV through intravenous drug use (41 percent).[87] By the same token, it should be noted that laws against discrimination based on a person's HIV status have already been strengthened in many states. Additional penalties for unauthorized disclosure of HIV status might well be called for and are currently being contemplated for personal medical information in general.

One must not forget, however, that unblinding the HIV tests entails informing only the mother and possibly the health care personnel who directly treat her and her child. It does not require that the information be reported to public health authorities, included in public records (as when a crime is alleged to have taken place, long before conviction), or revealed to employers and neighbors (as in Megan's Laws). If the mother and the health care professionals involved keep the information confidential, as they are required to do by law, professional code, and elementary ethics, there are no obvious ways in which she or the child will suffer discrimination.

As a further objection to newborn testing, Elizabeth Cooper suggests that mothers with HIV fear that their children will be taken from them.[88] To the extent that this fear is warranted, it should be alleviated as much as possible. It does not, however, seem to constitute a compelling reason not to treat the mothers or their children. Children are indeed sometimes removed from their homes, a fact that raises a whole host of new questions that run in two directions. First, are children removed solely because their mothers are HIV-infected or also because their mothers have been found to neglect their children (as a result of severe drug addiction, for instance)? Second, what conditions justify removing children from their mothers (or fathers)? These questions cannot be answered within the confines of this study but must be addressed if evidence arises that infants are being removed primarily because of their mother's HIV status.

Above all, one must avoid the simplistic argument that unblinded testing will lead automatically to additional discrimination. Fourth-criterion considerations are relevant here: When testing is unblinded, additional safeguards can always be introduced so that the information will not travel beyond the mother and those directly involved in treating her and her child. Such protective measures might include unique identifier numbers and audit trails (see Chapter 5).

A Communitarian Note

The communitarian perspective is critical to this discussion in several ways. First, it underscores the important reality that we are not merely rights-bearing individuals but also community members who are responsible for each other. None of our communal bonds and responsibilities is more important than the mother-child bond and the mother's responsibility to attend to her children's well-being. One may argue about what a child's rights encompass and whether these take precedence over the mother's rights; I have already suggested that the child's right to life and health takes precedence over the mother's right to privacy. But even if one were to reject this conclusion, it would still hold that being a parent entails a series of responsibilities, even if these exact various "costs" from the parents.

The communitarian perspective also enters this analysis by reminding us that a given individual right cannot be used to trump all other considerations, including the common good. Obviously, limiting privacy in the case at hand benefits not merely the child but also the community. Allowing children to develop severe illness or to die, when these outcomes can be avoided, is demeaning to the community. That we allow this to happen on other fronts does not mitigate the moral defect here. Unblinding also benefits the community by curbing public costs: Testing and counseling are much less costly than the treatment of infants infected with HIV.

Finally, the communitarian perspective points to the need to respect shared formulations of the good, those societal values that tend to give precedence to life over privacy, especially when the correlation between the privacy-violating act and the saving of a life is direct and strong.

2

Sex Offenders' Privacy Versus Children's Safety

Megan's Laws and the Alternatives

"Megan's Laws" pop in and out of the headlines and evening news every few months. The debate about their appropriateness is rekindled whenever a sex offender abuses a child in a particularly gruesome manner, or a sex offender is harassed or roughed up, or worse, by his neighbors. Few crimes horrify parents more than sexual abuse of their children. In many cases, children are also kidnapped and even murdered by their abusers. Many believe that once a person is a sex offender, he is very likely to continue to abuse, regardless of the prison terms he has served or psychological treatments he has undergone. This has led states and communities to seek more effective ways to protect children from sex offenders. At the same time, civil libertarians defend the rights of sex offenders on numerous grounds: They have paid their dues to society when they complete their jail sentence; they need help rather than additional punishment; and they have the same inalienable rights to privacy and autonomy as the rest of us. As we shall see, Megan's Laws are important attempts to deal with this difficult public safety issue, but they also provide a powerful object lesson in how *not* to deal with the tension between privacy and the common good.

In the early 1990s, as a result of the furor over what happened to Megan Kanka of New Jersey and other young victims of sex offenders, many states sought to improve the protection of children by enacting laws that require sex offenders at large to register with local authorities. In 1994 Congress enacted guidelines encouraging the remaining states to follow suit. All states have by now passed laws that require released sex offenders to register with their local law enforcement agencies. The states differ in the requirements they impose beyond registration: Some allow law enforcement officers to notify the community that a sex offender has moved into the neighborhood; others actually publicize the address of the offender. Still others require such offenders to provide blood, hair, or saliva samples to a DNA database to be used as evidence if future charges are brought against them.[1]

Civil libertarians and legal scholars have raised numerous objections to these laws, arguing that they are unfair and punitive to the sex offenders because the notification requirement subjects them to various abuses. Being a sex offender, the critics argue further, is an indication of a major psychological illness (indeed, many offenders are said to have been abused themselves as children), and thus offenders should be treated rather than punished. Critics also believe that the shaming involved is itself shameful and damages the person subjected to such "scarlet letters."[2] Moreover, these laws are said to violate various constitutionally guaranteed rights of the offenders. Finally, Megan's Laws have been attacked as worse than useless on the grounds that most offenders are relatives of the victims, the penalties for not registering are minuscule, these laws provide a false sense of security to parents and those concerned about children's welfare, and they lead to vigilantism against the offenders.

The issue at hand is *not* a conflict between the rights of the victims and those of perpetrators; that issue arises when the sex offenders are charged and tried. Rather, the issue is the weight of the offenders' rights after they serve their term as compared to the community's perceived need to ensure children's safety and attain peace of mind, especially, but not limited to, that of the children's families. Although Megan's Laws serve as the springboard for the discussion that follows, both the evidence and the arguments presented are fully relevant to other approaches to the same dilemma. Indeed, both the evidence and ethical and legal considerations seem to me to point to a third response beyond Megan's Laws, on the one hand, and mere treatment on the other. But this alternative cannot be entertained until Megan's Laws and the issues they raise are introduced.

The Scope and Nature of the Threat

One can only imagine the despair of those who were assigned to search for seven-year-old Megan Kanka when they found her body lying in the tall grass next to her house, the victim of brutal rape and strangulation. Jesse Timmendequas, who lived across the street from Megan's family, had been described by his neighbors as a mild-mannered, blue-collar man. Prior to moving into a suburban neighborhood in Hamilton Township, New Jersey, however, he had been convicted of two sexual assaults against young girls and spent six years in the prison and treatment facility for New Jersey's most violent and compulsive sexual offenders. None of this information was known to Megan's parents or other residents of their community. After their daughter's body was discovered, Timmendequas was accused of, and then confessed to, her rape and murder. As one would expect, Megan's parents were not only grief-stricken but also outraged to discover that they had not been told of Timmendequas's past criminal history of assaults against minors.

If Megan Kanka's death fails to evoke concern for community safety, consider the case of Larry Don McQuay, a Texas child molester whose 240 victims included a child whose penis McQuay cut off before leaving him alone to wander, bleeding, in the street.[3] Westley Dodd, a man with a fifteen-year record as a sexual offender, was put to death by the state of California for raping and murdering a four-year-old boy. Dodd was quoted in one of his court briefs as saying, "If I do escape, I promise you I will kill and rape again, and I will enjoy every minute of it."[4] McQuay wrote from prison: "I do not want to return to prison; I would like to be a law-abiding citizen. But the threat of being incarcerated for the rest of my life . . . will not stop me from reoffending when I am released."[5] During a Supreme Court hearing, Tom Weilert, attorney for the pedophile Leroy Hendricks, said that "certainly there is no doubt that Mr. Hendricks presents a risk of committing further crimes if released."[6] During the 1994 state trial to determine whether he would be set free, Hendricks was asked whether he could guarantee that he would not molest other innocent children. He replied, "The only way to guarantee that is to die."[7]

Although these and other horror stories have caught the attention of the media and the voters, they are merely anecdotal. Let us turn now to the statistics in determining the scope of the problem.

BROAD VERSUS NARROW DEFINITIONS

How serious is the problem of sexual offenses against children? The answer depends in part on the way we define such offenses. Some definitions are broadly inclusive. For instance, according to one definition by the legal scholar Michele Earl-Hubbard, "sexual abuse is not restricted to physical sexual contact, but may include visual or verbal exposure to sexually explicit materials or attempted solicitation of sexual behavior with a child."[8] Under this definition, "one out of every three girls and one of every seven boys"—that is, millions of children—"will be sexually abused before they reach the age of eighteen."[9] Broad definitions also tend to include offenses committed against those between ages thirteen and eighteen, which would include, for instance, a consensual relationship between a nineteen-year-old and a seventeen-year-old.

Other definitions are much narrower, including the one I draw on, a definition provided by the Washington State Institute for Public Policy (WSIPP). According to the institute, sex offenders include rapists; pedophiles, including offenders who rape children who are not members of their own family; incest offenders, who have physical sexual contact with children who are members of their own family; and "hands-off" sex offenders—exhibitionists, voyeurs, and obscene phone callers.

In the following analysis, I exclude the last type to the extent that the data allow me to do so, because of the less serious nature of the acts. I do include offenders who have abused adults provided they also have abused children. Many offenders convicted for raping an adult also admit to having raped children; 34 percent of child molesters officially known to have committed offenses outside the home revealed that they had also engaged in incest, and 50 percent of incest offenders admitted to undetected abuse outside the home.[10]

Number of Sex Offenders in the Community

In 1995 there were, according to one reliable source, a total of 234,000 sex offenders in the criminal justice system, including offenders who had been convicted of sex crimes against both children and adults. In a survey of incarcerated sex offenders, approximately 15 percent of rapists had targeted children under the age of thirteen. Another 22 percent targeted children age thirteen to seventeen.[11] In fact, of all state prisoners, one in five had committed a crime against a minor, and 71.4 percent of these offenses were of a sexual nature.[12] Among those incarcerated for sexual assault (i.e., non-rape sex offense), 45 percent had targeted children under thirteen, and another 33 percent targeted children age thirteen to seventeen. Of the 234,000 sex offenders in the correctional system (meaning in prison or on parole or probation), 60 percent reside in the community—106,700 on probation and 27,600 on parole in 1995.[13] The number of offenders is clearly substantial. If one uses the most conservative estimate of 37 percent, then 49,691 known sex offenders "specialize" in children. Given, however, that it is impossible for a professional, let alone an ordinary citizen or parent, to distinguish between one kind of sex offender and another, Megan's Laws encompass both those who are known to target children and those for whom children are only a past or potential target of abuse.

Sex Offender Recidivism

The data briefly reviewed so far point to such large numbers of offenders, of which a large number have targeted children, that we can conclude with considerable assurance that sexual offenses against children are a major societal problem. However, the main controversy over Megan's Laws hinges on a different, though clearly related, issue: Are sex offenders particularly likely to reoffend, so much so that they pose an especially high danger to the community in comparison to other criminal offenders? Proponents of Megan's Laws try to demonstrate that the offenders pose a particularly high risk, one that justifies the special way they are handled. Critics counter that sex offenders are unfairly singled out, that they pose no greater risk to the community than other convicted criminals, and hence that Megan's Laws are discriminatory. Louise van der Does, an advocate of Megan's Laws, argues, "Sexual offense is like alcoholism. It is a chronic, progressive condition that can never really be cured."[14] Some studies have indeed found rates of recidivism that run as high as 52 percent.[15] For example, a Massachusetts treatment center followed a cadre of released offenders and found a 55.6 percent recidivism rate[16]; a 1973 Swiss study found rates of 76.9 percent in its untreated group.[17]

Critics, however, point to data that suggest the recidivism rate is low, perhaps lower than 5 percent. W. L. Jacks conducted a study that found recidivism rates of only 3.7 percent,[18] and T.C.N. Gibbens, K. L. Soothill, and C. K. Way found rates of 4 percent.[19] Some even report that among untreated offenders the rate is only 18.5 percent.[20] Megan's Laws are therefore, according to the ACLU, basically unfair: "Unlike people who commit other types of crime, former sex offenders must endure continuing punishment for their crime."[21]

Studies find very different recidivism rates for several reasons. They focus on different types of sex offenders, each type varying in its risk for recidivism.[22] Some studies define recidivism as reoffense of any kind (e.g., drunk driving), while others consider only sexual reoffense[23]; some studies focus on first-time offenders, while others include offenders with prior records[24]; some studies have short follow-up periods (e.g., six months to a year), providing offenders less opportunity to reoffend than do other studies with significantly longer follow-up periods (five years or even several decades)[25]; some studies define recidivism in terms of re-arrests, capturing a larger pool than studies that define recidivism as reconvictions or reincarceration.[26] Study results are also difficult to compare because of differences in the populations studied: Subjects may be incarcerated or on probation[27];

treated or untreated[28]; undergoing different types of treatment[29]; or treated in different settings, such as correctional facilities, psychiatric hospitals, or outpatient programs.[30] Finally, many studies fail to establish adequate experimental designs such as sufficient sample sizes or control groups.[31] For all of these reasons, it is impossible to rely on the results of any one of these numerous studies to estimate the recidivism rate for sex offenders, and it is difficult to aggregate results across studies owing to their incomparability.

Recently it has become fashionable to draw on meta-analyses that take numerous studies and try to tease out conclusions from the combined data. One widely cited meta-analysis, by Lita Furby, Mark Weinrott, and Lyn Blackshaw, cautiously concludes that treatment is to no avail, at least so far as can be determined: "There is as yet no evidence that clinical treatment reduces rates of sex reoffenses in general and no appropriate data for assessing whether it may be differentially effective for different types of offenders."[32] This conclusion is supported more recently by V. L. Quinsey, G. T. Harris, M. E. Rice, and M. L. Lalumiere, who conclude that the "effectiveness of treatment in reducing sex offender recidivism has not yet been scientifically demonstrated."[33]

However, a meta-analysis by Gordon Hall finds relatively low recidivism rates: Untreated offenders had an average rate of 27 percent, and treated offenders had an average rate of 19 percent.[34] His finding suggests that treatment may have some beneficial results. Particularly noteworthy is the inclusion in his analysis of only recent studies that best represent state-of-the-art treatments; the Furby analysis was limited to studies from the 1950s through the 1980s.

The most recent meta-analysis is more optimistic. Margaret Alexander reviewed 81 studies with a total of 11,350 subjects.[35] She found a recidivism rate of 25.8 percent for untreated pedophiles and 14.4 percent for treated pedophiles. She also found that treatment intervention outcomes of the 1990s show improvement over treatment intervention outcomes of the 1980s. Once again, however, the differences are neither dramatic nor universal; the impact of these "improvements" on the recidivism of today's sex offenders is unclear.

We can draw several main points from these various studies and meta-analyses: (1) we do not know enough to draw firm conclusions;

(2) recidivism rates, although varied, are substantial; and (3) treatments seem to have some beneficial effects but by no means solve the problem. Thousands who are treated, even if they are fewer in number than the total of those who are untreated, violate children again and again. But are they worse than criminals who commit other offenses, such as murder or peddling drugs?

RECIDIVISM COMPARED

The debate over Megan's Laws hinges on the question not of whether sex offenders are likely to reoffend, but of whether their recidivism rate stands out in comparison to that of other kinds of criminal offenders. This question arises because Megan's Laws impose special requirements on sex offenders that are not imposed on others. I am aware of only one study that provides data directly applicable to this question, and this study does not specifically distinguish sex offenders who target children from other sex offenders. Allen J. Beck and Bernard E. Shipley analyzed the recidivism of more than 100,000 persons released from prisons in 1983.[36] They found that after three years 8 percent of released rapists were re-arrested for another rape; 7 percent of released murderers were re-arrested for another homicide; 20 percent of released robbers were re-arrested for another robbery; and 22 percent of released assaulters were re-arrested for another assault. In short, if the Beck and Shipley findings are valid, they suggest that sex offender recidivism is no higher than the recidivism of other offenders, and actually lower than some. Furthermore, the National Center on Institutions and Alternatives calculated a recidivism rate among treated sex offenders that is lower than that of other offenses: 8.4 percent as compared to 25 percent for drug offenses and 30 percent for violent offenses.[37] It follows that Megan's Laws cannot be justified on the basis of a greater propensity of sex offenders to reoffend—if one relies on recidivism rates to determine that tendency.

REOFFENSE RATES

Additional data drastically change the picture. The recidivism rates used so far are based on those who have been re-arrested, reconvicted, or reincarcerated. It is clear, however, that even though few murders go unreported (and relatively few other violent crimes), *many, perhaps most, sex offenses go unreported.* It is also clear that the reoffense rate is much higher than the recidivism rates. These two concepts are often confused. Recidivism measures the number of those who have been arrested (or arrested and convicted), and people often assume that this figure is similar or at least close to reoffense rates. But the reality is that it never is, particularly when dealing with sex offenders.

The reported numbers of sex offenders significantly underestimate the problem because many acts go unreported and many offenders are never apprehended. Indeed, child sexual victimization is particularly unlikely to be detected.[38] The Department of Justice's 1994 National Crime Victimization Survey found that almost two-thirds (64.3 percent) of rape/sexual assault incidents perpetrated against victims age twelve to nineteen are not reported to police; this statistic only hints at the scope of undetected sex offenses.[39] This underreporting is due to numerous factors, including the psychological trauma experienced by young victims, the credibility of child witnesses, and intimidation of the victims by the offenders.[40] Official statistics, such as those for correctional control and conviction, also underestimate the problem because many felony charges are reduced through the plea bargaining process. In other words, the nature of the crime may well differ from the nature of the conviction.[41]

Supplementing official estimates with victimization surveys, in which people are asked about offenses that have been committed against them, one can include in an assessment of the number of crimes those cases where the perpetrators were not apprehended or, if they were apprehended, were not convicted. Unfortunately, the most comprehensive victimization survey, the Justice Department's annual National Crime Victimization Survey, studies only those who are age twelve or older; these data are thus of little use for the purposes at hand. One can gain a sense of the magnitude of the issue from a 1994 study based on a random sample of 2,000 children between the ages of ten and sixteen: 3.2 percent of girls responding and 0.6 percent of boys had experienced some form of sexual abuse that involved physical contact.[42] Extrapolating from these findings using census figures, approximately 1.9 million children in this age group had been abused in their lifetimes.

Additional data come from another important source: the offenders themselves. Three important studies ask offenders about crimes they committed other than the ones for which they were caught.

One study reports the results of a survey of 83 rapists and 54 child molesters.[43] The rapists admitted to a mean of 5.2 rapes per man as compared with only 2.8 that were officially documented. Child molesters admitted to an average of 4.7 sex assaults, while the official documentation reported an average of one assault per offender. That is, offenses were between *two and five times* more common than reported.

Although not a random sample of offenders, a significantly more intensive study by Gene Abel and his colleagues found that 561 offenders reported a total of 291,737 "paraphilic acts" (which included deviant sexual fantasies as well as illegal actions) committed against 195,407 victims under the age of 18.[44] These paraphilic acts covered a wide range; not all of them were prohibited by criminal law. However, many of the acts surveyed included serious sex crimes: 126 rapists reported an average of 7.2 rapes per offender; 224 child molesters (non-incest) reported an average of 23.2 assaults against female victims; 153 child molesters (non-incest) reported an average of 281.7 assaults against male victims; 159 incest offenders reported an average of 81.3 assaults against female victims; and 44 incest offenders reported an average of 62.3 assaults against male victims. These figures resulted from structured clinical interviews with nonincarcerated offenders voluntarily participating in a sex offender treatment program.

A third study also found a large discrepancy between official estimates of sex offenders' repeated acts and offenders' self-reports. Mark Weinrott and Maureen Saylor interviewed 99 sex offenders committed to a psychiatric hospital. The 37 rapists reported a total of 433 rapes, and the 67 child molesters admitted to more than 8,000 inappropriate contacts with over 959 different children.[45]

In short, *there are strong reasons to assume that the reoffense rate among sex offenders is much higher than recidivism rates*. To the extent that justification of Megan's Laws rests on the notion that the community must assume that those released from prison are very likely to reoffend, these figures provide such justification.[46] At the same time, there is no compelling evidence that other offenders, say drug dealers or thieves, are not as likely to reoffend. But this does not necessarily mean that hard-core sex offenders do not need special treatment when released into the community. Indeed, by the logic advanced here, such a comparison suggests that residents should also be notified when hard-core drug dealers are released into their community, especially if many of them have been targeting children by, for example, hawking their illicit wares around schools and playgrounds. Last but not least: We hold children especially dear, and hence those who violate them are regarded as deserving harsher penalties than those who prey on most others. (I return to this later.)

Are Megan's Laws Excessively Intrusive?

We have established that sex offenses against children are a very serious problem, and that second-criterion approaches—various forms of psychotherapy and other modes of treatment—are clearly insufficient, considering the tendency of offenders, even if treated, to reoffend. Passing Megan's Laws constitutes a third-criterion approach, and the first question we must answer about that approach is whether such laws violate the Constitution.

Civil libertarians and some legal scholars argue that Megan's Laws violate the Fifth Amendment's injunction against being punished twice for the same crime ("double jeopardy"); the offender's right to due process (because offenders have not been made aware [that they may be subject to public notification] at the time of sentencing); the Eighth Amendment's ban on cruel and unusual punishment; and the Constitution's ex post facto provision when the law is applied retroactively (i.e., to offenders released from prison before its passage).[47]

The discussion here focuses on the offender's privacy, because the violation of this privacy is what drives all the other issues. If offenders were allowed to move into a community without it being known to the local authorities and the public that they have been convicted of sexual offenses, the constitutional issues would not arise. Hence, the first question to address is whether such a violation of privacy is justified in view of the contribution (if any) it provides to the safety of the community. I return to the question of the constitutionality of Megan's Laws in a later section.

In addressing this question, two major issues must be faced: the use of shaming as a measure of community justice, and the alternative approaches that could be applied to the same offenses if one rejects Megan's Laws and the concepts on which they are based.

A Net Cast Too Widely

Critics have charged that Megan's Laws cast a net much too widely.[48] Note that they criticize not decisions about who is jailed, or the level of punishment meted out, but rather the determination of who is required to register with public authorities upon being released from jail, and who might be flagged to public attention. Although Megan's Laws differ on these points, several are indeed overly broad. Some of these laws rely on legal definitions of sex offenders that include people who are not dangerous but whose acts technically qualify as criminal[49]—for example, the eighteen-year-old Wisconsin boy who attempted to marry his pregnant fifteen-year-old high school sweetheart.[50] Some of these laws require any convicted sex offender who is out of jail to register, even if the offense took place many years before, under different laws and mores. Still on the books, for example, is the case of a ninety-year-old California man who had been convicted of lewd conduct for touching another man's knee in a parked car in 1944. Also, many gay men who were arrested under sodomy laws during less tolerant times (consensual gay sex was not decriminalized until the mid-1970s) remain on California's database of sex offenders.[51]

Such overbroad definitions, aside from being unduly punitive and unfair on the face of it, squander the moral voice of the community rather than shoring up its moral order. Communities, even well-formed ones, have a limited store of moral concerns. If these are exercised on small matters, or are brought to bear with equal fervor on both minor and major offenses, they are soon exhausted. Indeed, most religions, laws, and ethical systems distinguish between cardinal sins and less weighty ones for this very reason. As American society was trying to strengthen its moral foundations in the early and mid-1990s, it often ignored this piece of age-old sociological wisdom.[52] For instance, the improper use of language (for example, telling off-color jokes) and the display of *Playboy* pinups were defined along with pressuring an employee or student to have sex as "sexual harassment." Similarly, some individual states' Megan's Laws defined sex offenses rather loosely.

Although some Megan's Laws are overly broad, it does not follow that all of them should be overturned, as groups like the ACLU imply.[53] Megan's Laws can be narrowed, and indeed, several already have been.

The public notification provisions of Washington State's Megan's Law apply only to those individuals who the state determines have engaged in a repeated pattern of sexually deviant behavior and who are believed to be very likely to continue their pattern of predatory behavior.[54] Moreover, some carefully crafted statutes, such as those of Washington and New Jersey, operate under a tier system, imposing higher community notification requirements when there is an increased likelihood that the person will reoffend.[55]

When narrowly crafted, public notification is required only when offenders are deemed dangerous; otherwise, they are required only to register with their local police departments. Washington was the first state in the nation to enact a public notification law. Since the law's implementation in 1990, only 11 percent of released sex offenders have been subject to some form of community notification.[56]

New Jersey's law calls for released sex offenders to register with their town's chief law enforcement officer if the court that sentenced them determined that their crime fit a pattern of repetitive and compulsive behavior. If the court feels that reoffense is a strong possibility, prosecutors can then require the relevant police department to reveal the sex offender's record to those who are likely to come into contact with him, especially those residing in the same neighborhood. Otherwise, nothing more is done besides forwarding the offender's file to other state police departments and organizations that deal specifically with children.

Indeed, New Jersey has recently attracted national attention for the painstaking specificity of its statute. After its Megan's Law was rushed through the state legislature late in 1994, episodes of harassment of sex offenders led to several legal battles and a federal court ban that suspended the implementation of the law until December 1997. The three years of statutory limbo resulted in a law that acts both to temper community reaction and to avoid unnecessary notification. The spread of information about released offenders is now strenuously restricted in New Jersey; the notification requirements for both moderate and high-risk offenders allow only those authorized by the law to be privy to the information. For example, school principals or daycare operators may be notified of a moderate-risk parolee's whereabouts, but they are prohibited (under threat of contempt-of-court citation) from telling either their charges or the children's parents.[57] Under the present New Jersey law, only about 600 parolees are subject to notification and registration—about one-third of all offenders. (Two-thirds of the state's 1,939 sex offenders have been deemed low-risk.)

VIOLATION OF BASIC RIGHTS?

Critics argue that even narrowly defined Megan's Laws are unconstitutional because their registration and notification requirements violate various rights. Fully evaluating these challenges would require a major tome and a great deal of legal scholarship. The matter is further complicated because different states have different constitutions, Megan's Laws differ significantly from state to state, and different state supreme courts have ruled differently about the standing of these laws. (And even when ruling the same way, they have relied on different rationales.) Such an extensive evaluation, though, is unnecessary for this discussion: So far, after all the arguments have been aired, virtually all courts, including state supreme courts, have upheld the constitutionality of Megan's Laws.[58] Indeed, in 1997 the U.S. Supreme Court refused a stay of law for the New Jersey community notification statute, allowing the Third Circuit U.S. Court of Appeals' August 1996 decision to stand, and New Jersey to implement the law.[59]

Nevertheless, the ACLU, a leading critic, maintains that Megan's Laws are a violation of the Constitution's prohibition on double jeopardy. The ACLU's legislative counsel states: "The fact is that you

MORE PRINCIPLED OBJECTIONS: VIOLATIONS OF THE CONSTITUTION?

Individualists often assert that the suggested measures to enhance public safety in this area violate Americans' right to privacy, chill free speech, undermine liberty, endanger the freedom of association, and are otherwise highly intrusive. Because some of these assertions are so general and sweeping in scope, they provide no specifics one could examine and thus should be treated as expressions of concern rather than as fully developed arguments. There are, however, some carefully laid out arguments that can be closely evaluated. Many of these have been made by Michael Froomkin, a highly regarded and frequently cited legal scholar who has written two important articles on the subject.[32]

Froomkin assesses the effects of a prohibition on the use of strong cryptography (i.e., with no key recovery features) in terms of privacy rights and First, Fourth, and Fifth Amendment rights. I will briefly summarize and respond to these arguments without examining Froomkin's numerous subpoints and asides.

Froomkin argues that privacy, the right to be let alone, is violated when individuals are required to disclose information about themselves, something that he claims occurs when public key recovery is introduced.[33] He argues that such keys also violate another privacy right, "the right to autonomous choices regarding intimate matters," because people exchanging escrowed messages in intimate matters would no longer be able to do so in reliable privacy.

Froomkin further maintains that law enforcement key recovery violates the First Amendment because by disclosing matters people prefer to keep secret, the possibility of recovery compels speech. Such keys also chill speech because people may fear that others might be listening in. Additionally, he believes these keys diminish freedom of association because some people are willing to band together only under conditions of anonymity.

Froomkin also suggests that the very existence of law enforcement key recovery constitutes a warrantless search—a violation of the Fourth Amendment. And he believes that the Fifth Amendment restricts the introduction of key recovery by public authorities because decryption entails self-incrimination.[34]

The ACLU has embraced a similar position, although Froomkin focuses on mandatory systems while the ACLU strongly opposes voluntary systems as well.[35] The rights organization's reasons are laid out in a page on its Web site:

> Free speech: In one recent case, a computer scholar wrote a new encryption program but when he submitted it for export approval, he was told that not only was his code a "munition," but even a paper he wrote about it could not be sent abroad. A federal court disagreed, ruling that encryption is a form of speech protected by the First Amendment.
>
> Compelled speech: If encryption is speech, then being required to give your key code to the government is a form of forced, or compelled speech—also prohibited by the First Amendment.
>
> Academic freedom: Classifying encryption technology as a form of munitions compromises academic freedom, since academics must refrain from discussing their work with foreigners (considered exportation), and American instructors are afraid to teach encryption technology to foreign students—even in their stateside classrooms.
>
> Search and seizure: The Fourth Amendment protects people from unreasonable searches and seizures. A blanket requirement that all individuals, whether or not they are suspected of criminal activities, turn over their encryption keys to the government, or its licensed agents, is an unconstitutional seizure. The government should foster privacy protection through encryption technology—not demand the keys to our telephone, computer and online privacy.[36]

On 23 September 1997 a group of law professors wrote an open letter to the House Commerce Committee, opposing key recovery.[37] The letter is particularly important because it conveys the opinions, not of extremists, but of thirty legal scholars, including some at well-known law schools such as Harvard, UCLA, and Stanford. *The letter addresses only the professors' concern that various rights might be violated; it does not even mention, let alone seek to address, any public safety concerns.*

The letter opens with the statement: "We write to express alarm about an unprecedented proposal that has been advanced to impose criminal penalties on the manufacturing or distribution of domestic encryption products that do not contain a government mandated 'backdoor.'" The proposal was "in large part drafted by the FBI"—apparently prima facie evidence against the proposal. The professors argue: "Never in peacetime has our government attempted so completely to monopolize a single form of communication; never has it required, in effect, a license to exercise the right to speak." The analysis of the alleged violations of rights mirrors closely the arguments made by Froomkin, one of the signatories.

THE DIFFERENCE BETWEEN LAW-ABIDING CITIZENS AND "CRIMINAL SUSPECTS"

The various objections raised by the ACLU, Froomkin, and other constitutional scholars—their concerns that privacy and First, Fourth, and Fifth Amendment rights, among others, will be violated by public key recovery—all assume that the government could and would use at will this power to listen in arbitrarily on the conversations and search the documents of "all individuals," "Americans," or "all free people."[38]

Interceptions of this sort would indeed be the equivalent of the government arbitrarily listening in on telephone conversations, opening mail at will, or placing microphones in people's homes. One can readily concede that such wanton and large-scale intrusions on privacy might well cause the assorted unconstitutional and antidemocratic effects that individualists fear. However, the arrangement the government proposes, and which various individualist groups and their business allies continue to reject and effectively block, is not at all addressed by these critics. To demonstrate this point, it is necessary to reexamine precisely what the government wants to be able to do, as well as the constitutional principle this capability is based on.

The government seeks the capability to decipher messages, but this capability would be activated only after independent judicial approval.

The government would have to make a specific case that there was sufficient reason to suspect that criminal activities had taken place, and that evidence was likely to be found in encrypted communications. Once a judge was convinced of the validity of these claims, he or she would authorize the issuance of a warrant to decipher a specific set or flow of communications. In short, decryption would be governed by the same procedural safeguards as wiretaps. (There are some exceptional conditions—for instance, a national emergency—under which warrants are not required and other judicial procedures are used for the tapping of telephones. These exceptions might apply to decryption as well, but because they are just that—very exceptional—they are not discussed here.)

In addition, although the government initially suggested that it should be responsible for holding the keys (split between two agencies, to minimize further the possibilities of unauthorized use), it has since offered a compromise to allay fears of abuse by the government: The keys would be deposited with third parties (trustees or even private corporations).

Let us assume that the government has specific and credible evidence that someone is holding a kidnap victim, but the FBI is not sure where. Evidence to this effect is presented to a court, which then grants (as other courts have under similar circumstances) the government the right to tap the suspected kidnapper's phone. The suspect, fearing such tapping, pushes a button on his phone and thus encrypts some of his calls. It seems illogical to allow tapping and "reading" of the calls if they are transmitted in one form, but not to allow the use of the technical measures needed to "read" the same calls transmitted on the same lines but in some other form. In other words, despite some technical differences, *key recovery is basically an updated tap.* To argue that the government is permitted to tap regular phone calls, even if the callers are using some kind of coded language (many criminals use code words or dialects they believe few know), but not to eavesdrop on encrypted messages, is no more logical than to suggest that the government may search and seize old-fashioned paper files (if granted a warrant) but not computerized ones.

One may argue that phone taps are legally introduced only *after* court approval, but that the *capacity* to decrypt messages must be in place *before* such action. This, however, is a distinction without a difference. The capacity cannot be legally *activated* without a court order. Indeed, the proposed law enforcement key recovery provides additional protection in the form of third parties or trustees and split keys, safeguards that phone taps do not have.

To put it differently, our system of justice assumes that there are three kinds of people: most citizens, whose rights are fully intact; criminals who have been convicted and thus have many of their rights suspended while they are incarcerated; and those "criminal suspects" who are *legally* suspected of having committed a crime and whose status is thus in between ordinary citizen and convicted criminal—some of their rights have been suspended, but not as many as those of convicted criminals. (I stress "legally" because it is not sufficient for a police officer to claim someone is a suspect and then treat him or her as such; as already indicated, evidence must be presented, and so forth, before anyone becomes a criminal suspect.) For instance, under certain conditions the government can restrict people's movements (for instance, by asking them to surrender their passports) and detain them for short periods of time even though they have not yet been indicted, let alone convicted, of any crime.

Even the ACLU, although it is always seeking to raise the bar that determines whether reasonable suspicion has been legally demonstrated, accepts that if the government has made its case, its claims have been subject to sufficient scrutiny, and a warrant has been issued—effectively transforming an ordinary citizen into a legal suspect—public authorities may search such a suspect's home, read his mail, and tap his phone. Under key recovery, it is these kinds of individuals, not "all individuals," and not "all Americans," who would have his messages decrypted by public authorities. To imply that the mere existence of a capacity for law enforcement key recovery turns all Americans into suspects is like arguing that because phone lines run outside homes, and hence are accessible to public authorities without the active knowledge of those who are tapped, the privacy and freedom of all Americans is violated.

Because much rides on the question of whether key recovery constitutes a greater violation of privacy than phone taps, I compare next the steps involved in each process.

When public authorities have specific and credible evidence that a person has committed a crime, they present that information to a court, and if the court finds the evidence sufficient, it allows the police, in accordance with the Fourth Amendment, to conduct a "search"—in this case, to tap a phone. The police then implement the tap, typically placing it at some juncture of the phone lines outside the home, unbeknownst to the suspect inside.

Decryption entails more steps, and a greater number and variety of privacy safeguards than phone-tapping. Under the suggested system, when public authorities have specific evidence that a person is suspected of having committed a crime, they would present this information to a court, and if the court found the evidence sufficient, it would issue a warrant allowing the authority to retrieve the private key from the places where it is escrowed. The various escrow agents would verify that the authority has a proper warrant. They each would then provide the authority with a part of the needed key. That is, the authority would have to demonstrate to at least two independent (nongovernmental) agents that a valid warrant has been issued. The retrieved key components could then be reassembled and used to decrypt the particular messages.[39] It seems reasonable to conclude that, if anything, privacy is better protected when public authorities seek to decrypt messages rather than when they are tapping phones.

The main flaw in the individualists' analysis of key recovery is that it presumes that everyone will be treated as if they were criminal suspects. There is neither reason nor evidence to support this assumption. Listening in on suspected criminals—not on those the police declare are criminals, but those the courts have decreed as such—is not the same as eavesdropping on "all free citizens." And it is already routinely and legally carried out. Indeed, if limiting the freedoms of suspected criminals had the debilitating effects that the individualists fear, American liberty and democracy would have been lost long ago.

One might object to the very concept of criminal suspects and argue that unless a person is convicted he or she should be treated the same way as those who are not suspected of wrongdoing. But this is an argument not against key recovery but against a major foundation of our system of justice. Anyone holding this position would also have to object to all the various measures involved in gathering evidence of criminal wrongdoing, not merely to key recovery. But none of the individualists cited embrace this position—and for good reason. If we were to abolish the category of criminal suspect, we would cripple our capacity to maintain public safety when we ended up either treating all citizens as suspects or treating all suspects like criminals, as totalitarian regimes do. Assume there is credible evidence that John Doe may have committed a crime, but insufficient evidence for arrest and conviction. The public authorities have only three choices: ignore the evidence (let a man who might well have committed a crime run free); act as if the evidence is sufficient (jail a man who may not have committed a crime); or take additional steps to clear up or verify the suspicion.

Democracies have made a special point, from the Magna Carta on, of treating suspects as a special category. To attack key recovery is to oppose, however unwittingly, this critically important principle.

OVERBLOWN ANALOGIES

The debate about the legitimacy of key recovery is not confined to courts of law and law professors. To make their case in other arenas, individualists have employed powerful, evocative analogies. Most of these are similar to the one explored here.

In 1994 Ron Rivest wrote to Dorothy Denning, a supporter of the Clipper chip: "You seem to believe that anything that will 'block crime' must therefore be a 'good thing' and should therefore be adopted. This is not true, even if it is not subject to government abuse."[40] No such belief is in evidence. The argument advanced by Denning and others is not that "anything goes," but that such a measure is justified in light of the scope of the danger posed by terrorists and other criminals, and given the minimal, if any, intrusiveness (compared to phones) introduced by public key recovery.

Rivest continued:

> For example, a system that could turn any telephone (even when on-hook) into an authorized listening microphone might help law enforcement, but would be unacceptable to almost all Americans. As another example, tattooing a person's social security number on his or her but-

> tocks might help law enforcement, but would also be objectionable. Or, you could require all citizens to wear a bracelet that could be remotely queried (electronically, and only when authorized) to return the location of that citizen. There are all kinds of wonderfully stupid things one could do with modern technology that could "help" law enforcement. But merely being of assistance to law enforcement doesn't make a proposal a good thing; many such ideas are objectionable and unacceptable because of the unreasonably large cost/benefit ratio (real or psychological cost). The Clipper proposal, in my opinion, is of exactly this nature.[41]

Analogies of the kind that Rivest employs are indeed powerful. One cannot but at first be horrified contemplating such an intrusion by Big Brother into every home. Upon closer examination, however, none of these analogies hold. Tattooing people, aside from being reminiscent of Nazi atrocities, entails a much higher level of intrusiveness than simply reading messages.

Most important, Rivest—like Froomkin—presumes that the government would in fact listen in randomly on all or millions of Americans' phones, or turn television sets into microphones, rather than merely eavesdrop on those who are criminal suspects. For the latter, the differences between turning an on-the-hook phone into a listening device (a relatively new capability) and surreptitiously driving spike microphones into the walls of the homes of suspected criminals, an act long considered legal by the highest court in the land, are technical and limited in import. The Supreme Court ruled in *Dalia v. United States* (1979) that police, provided they have a warrant, can even break covertly into a suspect's home "for the purpose of installing otherwise legal electronic bugging equipment." The latter category includes not only phone taps but also microphones, tape recorders, and other electronic eavesdropping devices. And these may legitimately be placed in all manner of locations—in lamps, closets, and elsewhere. In short, on closer examination, the far-fetched analogies simply do not hold.

CYBERSPACE ANARCHISTS

In most, if not all, ideological camps there are moderates and there are more extreme advocates. The same holds for various groups of civil rights advocates, libertarians, and other individualists. According to several accounts, however, the camps of strong cyber-libertarians (sometimes referred to as cypherpunks) are particularly large and dedicated. Cyberspace seems to be the new territory where hyper-libertarians congregate, and the medium on which they pin their hopes for a world free of any government.

Steven Levy described cypherpunks in the pages of the *New York Times:*

> Cypherpunks share a few common premises. They assume that cryptography is a liberating tool, one that empowers individuals. They think that one of the most important uses of cryptography is to protect communications from The Government. . . . The Cypherpunks consider the Clipper the lever that Big Brother is using to pry into the conversations, messages and transactions of the computer age. These high-tech Paul Reveres are trying to mobilize America against the evil portent of a "cyberspace police state," as one of their Internet jeremiads put it. Joining them in the battle is a formidable force, including almost all of the communications and computer industries, many members of Congress and political columnists of all stripes. The anti-Clipper aggregation is an equal-opportunity country club, uniting the American Civil Liberties Union and Rush Limbaugh.[42]

Many cyber-libertarians believe that cyberspace could—and should—be a world free from all government intervention and regulation. Moreover, as the proportion of all communications that are carried out electronically eclipses the older forms of face-to-face communication, so too will we see an increase in the importance of cyberspace.[43] In short, the old dream of the withering away of the state has found a new life on the Internet. In such a world the government would not decrypt messages; it would either not be allowed in or be rendered irrelevant and gradually cease to exist.

Sameer Parekh, addressing a conference sponsored by the libertarian Cato Institute, contended that "the rapid development of strong cryptography is the antidote to the disease of government."[44] And Tim May, a leading crypto-anarchist, writes: "Many of us see strong crypto[graphy] as the key enabling technology for a new economic and social system, a system which will develop as cyberspace becomes more important. At issue is the end of governments as we know them today."[45]

Phil Zimmermann is a leading figure among the strong cyber-libertarians. He defied public authorities by putting his powerful encryption program on the Internet, making it freely available worldwide to all comers, including, of course, criminals and terrorists. Like other cyber-libertarians, Zimmermann views the government as the problem because it is, or may turn into, a tyranny. Zimmermann declares: "When making public policy decisions about new technologies for the government, I think one should ask oneself which technologies would best strengthen the hand of a police state. Then, do not allow the government to deploy those technologies. This is simply a matter of good civic hygiene." Zimmermann acknowledges that blocking the government's endeavors will help criminals, but he argues that this is a cost we must bear—much like the pollution caused by cars—for the liberty such efforts will ensure.[46]

John Perry Barlow, founder of the Electronic Frontier Foundation and a prominent cyber-libertarian, issued the "Cyberspace Independence Declaration," which decries external control of digital communications:

> I declare the global social space we are building to be naturally independent of the tyrannies [that governments] seek to impose on us. [Governments] have no moral right to rule us nor do [they] possess any methods of enforcement we have true reason to fear.
>
> . . . Increasingly hostile and colonial measures place us in the same position as those previous lovers of freedom and self-determination who had to reject the authorities of distant, uninformed powers. We must declare our virtual selves immune to [governmental] sovereignty.[47]

Cyber-libertarians tend to be more than just strong advocates of privacy and freedom; they are often highly suspicious of the government. They believe that the whole institution, not merely some of its acts, is illegitimate and inherently untrustworthy. A rather moderate advocate, Marc Rotenberg, director of the Electronic Privacy Information Center (EPIC), points out that efforts to prevent strong encryption programs from reaching the wrong hands are "naturally viewed with suspicion" by his followers.[48] "You don't want to buy a set of car keys from a guy who specializes in stealing cars," he says. "The NSA [National Security Agency]'s specialty is the ability to break codes, and they are saying, 'Here, take our keys, we promise you they'll work.'"[49] John Perry Barlow, in his 1992 essay "Decrypting the Puzzle Palace," claimed that "relying on government to protect your privacy is like asking a peeping tom to install your window blinds."[50]

The cypherpunk position is viewed as verging on the "paranoiac." "Because Skipjack [included in the strong encryption provided by the U.S. government] is not open to public review, some people have questioned whether NSA might have intentionally sabotaged the algorithm with a trap door that would allow the government to decode encrypted communications while bypassing the escrow agents."[51] When researchers at the University of California at Berkeley cracked the encryption code used to scramble cellular phones, they believed the government had intentionally weakened the code for surveillance purposes. However, they presented no evidence in support of this claim. In addition, rumors abound in the computer software industry that NSA agents posing as encryption engineers have written elaborate encryption programs to which they secretly have the keys.[52]

Froomkin suggests that the fundamental issues raised by encryption

> revolve around trust: whether citizens should be asked to trust the state with the means of acquiring the citizens' secrets, and whether the community and the state feel they can afford to allow citizens, as well as foreign citizens and foreign states, access to technologies that enhance secret-keeping to the point that police or intelligence agencies might find it impossible to monitor communications or search a computer's hard drive.[53]

My concern is with both forms of trust, and with finding a judicious balance between them. Cyberspace is not extraterritorial. It is subject to the same basic balances of liberty and social order, privacy and the common good, as other areas of social life.

A SERIES OF CONCESSIONS THAT FAILED

Encryption has been around for 4,000 years,[54] but the issues under discussion only recently came into public focus, in 1993, when the government first floated the idea of so-called public (or law enforcement) key recovery. The idea has been to give private parties that wish to use encryption two choices: (1) use hyper-encryption but provide public authorities with the key (public keys are deposited in a safe place, or "recovered," in contrast to a private key depository utilized by private parties to store spare keys in case they lose a key and are unable to access their encrypted data); or (2) use weaker encryption, without giving public authorities any keys, presumably on the grounds that the government could crack these messages on its own. Basically the choice was either to grant police a peephole for your new steel door or to make it out of glass.

Since 1993 the U.S. government has tried to promote its approach voluntarily, drawing on an odd measure that did not require legislation, namely export controls. The U.S. government decreed that export of encryption must be limited to weak systems and to hyper-encryption that contains a key the government can use.

Although theoretically private parties *in* the United States could build and sell any encryption system, the government hoped at the time that the exportable model would become the standard, because it makes little economic sense to produce different models for export and domestic use. Law enforcement officials would thus be able to decipher messages when appropriate, one way or the other. The government also assumed that the encryption model it provided, equipped with a chip that had a public key in it (known as the Clipper chip),[55] had a stronger encryption program than was otherwise available.

The government approach was widely criticized for curbing American ability to export ("Who would buy such programs?"), for giving itself ready access to encrypted messages, and for other weighty reasons spelled out later in this chapter. The opposition, by American corporations seeking unfettered exports of their encryption products and privacy advocates fearing government eavesdropping, was so intense that the government soon modified its position.

In mid-1994 Vice President Gore wrote to Representative Maria Cantwell (D-Wash.) that the Clinton administration was "willing to engage in serious negotiations leading to a comprehensive new policy on digital privacy and security."[56] However, civil libertarians felt that Gore's letter marked the administration's continuing desire to increase electronic surveillance.

In 1996 software companies were allowed to export somewhat more robust systems, and soon thereafter even more robust ones. Export control was moved from the somewhat strict State Department to the more accommodating Department of Commerce. Suggestions were made that the keys needed to crack messages be moved from a government depository to escrows to be maintained by select private parties, organizations, or trustees to assure users that the keys could not be employed in an inappropriate manner. These suggestions were also rejected by the opposition.

In 1997 a bill was drafted by the Clinton administration that further clarified the limited conditions under which the keys would be released for use by the government and added criminal penalties for those who abused them. The administration also suggested that keys be split among two or more depositories so that no single party could activate them. The bill, like many others, has not been enacted because of strong opposition from libertarians, civil libertarians, and commercial groups.

In July 1998 the Clinton administration announced that it would allow virtually unbreakable encryption packages to be exported *without* the option of key recovery or "backdoor" access, for banks and financial institutions in forty-five countries. According to the new policy, encryption software can be exported to member countries of an international anti-money-laundering accord or to those that have enacted approved anti-money-laundering laws. The software is subject to a onetime review before it can be exported. Nonetheless, a group of software companies, privacy advocates, and libertarians expressed dissatisfaction, calling the government's concession "insignificant."[57]

IN CONCLUSION

"Compromise" is a term that appears often in news reports about encryption.[58] The term is somewhat inaccurate because practically all concessions so far have been made by the government, and yet the opposition still opposes the government proposals. No compromise has been reached with those who campaigned against the revised and diluted law enforcement key recovery systems and have so far succeeded in blocking them. It is testament to the scope of the opposition that when one of the earlier plans—the introduction of the Clipper chip and export controls—was submitted by the Clinton administration for public commentary, the opposing comments ran 318–2 against it.[59] In none of the cases studied in this volume do we see more forces, or stronger ones, so intensely focused on the real and imagined dangers of overbearing public authorities or so unmindful of the dangers to public safety.

One can readily grant that public authorities in a democracy can abuse their powers, and that a free society requires constant vigilance against such abuses. But our detailed examination suggests that the dangers encryption poses to a free society (not to be confused with an anarchist dream of an ungoverned cyberspace) are particularly limited—compared to phone taps, for instance. Moreover, the dangers to public safety and national security of allowing criminals and terrorists free access to uncrackable encryption are particularly high. It is quite possible that some new technological development may eventually render the whole issue obsolete. The NSA might, for instance, come up with a way to crack encryption without being granted keys. Nevertheless, this examination still stands as a grand illustration of the nature of the arguments advanced by cyber-individualists, and as an indication of their pervasive influence on public policies.

4

Big Brother or Big Benefits?

ID Cards and Biometric Identifiers

"ID cards" are domestic passportlike documents that citizens of many countries, including democracies, are required by law to have with them at all times. They are cards or documents that provide identifying data about the bearer, such as name, age, and address. ID cards are viewed by Americans as a major tool of oppressive governments; indeed, these cards are so alien to Americans that ID cards are not considered fit for discussion. As a rule, think tanks do not study them, nor are they a subject of public policy debates. A few advocates of ID cards have faced such strong criticism that they stopped speaking and writing about their merits.[1] Nevertheless, the issue frequently arises—although in an indirect, fragmented, piecemeal manner—in discussions of how to combat welfare fraud, cheating on SATs, and phony green cards. American society incurs high costs—social, economic, and other kinds—because of its inability to identify many hundreds of thousands of violent criminals, white-collar criminals, welfare and credit card cheats, parents who do not pay child support, and illegal immigrants. If individuals could be properly identified, public safety would be significantly enhanced and social and economic costs would be reduced significantly.

In the past such identification has been facilitated in many other countries by actual ID cards; now radically new technologies, known collectively as "biometric identifiers," make identification much easier and much more reliable. We must hence ask: Do the benefits to public safety and other public goals of ID cards or biometrics outweigh the cost to privacy?

Significant segments of the American public, libertarians, many civil libertarians, and others have objected to the introduction of ID cards and biometric identifiers in the United States, principally because they consider such identifiers a gross violation of privacy and a major opening to Big Brother government. In trying to assess whether the diminution of privacy and autonomy involved in the introduction of ID cards or biometrics is justified, I consider the following questions in light of the four criteria that guide the analyses throughout this volume: How high are the costs to society and its members when identifiers are not utilized? Can these costs be reduced significantly without introducing identifiers? If ID cards or some other means of identification are to be introduced, can their intrusiveness be minimized? What are my responses to civil libertarian concerns? Finally, what is to be done to minimize any undesirable, unintended consequences of or side effects caused by the introduction of a universal (covering one and all) identification system?

THE HIGH COSTS OF NOT HAVING ID CARDS

What are the social costs that could be reduced if universal, tamper-proof identifiers were available?

CRIMINAL FUGITIVES

Each year at least half a million criminals become fugitives, avoiding trial, incarceration, or service of their full sentence. Often they commit additional crimes while on the lam.[2] In 1976 the Federal Advisory Committee on False Identification reported that between 1973 and 1975 an average of "160,000 'criminal wanted' records . . . were entered into the National Crime Information Center (NCIC), but not all persons sought under fugitive warrants are entered into the NCIC."[3] That is, the actual number of fugitives was almost certainly higher. In 1988, according to the director of the U.S. Marshals Service, more than a third of a million escaped or suspected criminals were at large.[4] In 1995 nearly 29,000 individual *federal* fugitive entries appeared in the NCIC, and again, the actual number is most likely higher.[5] Fugitive criminals also contribute to Americans' fears about crime and to "the loss of public confidence in law enforcement caused by the success of notorious fugitives in maintaining their covert status."[6]

CHILD ABUSE AND SEX OFFENSES

People who are hired to work in child-care centers, kindergartens, and schools cannot be effectively screened to keep out child abusers and sex offenders.[7] One major reason is that when background checks are conducted, convicted criminals escape detection by using false identification and aliases. In 1990 six states identified "more than 6,200 individuals convicted of serious criminal offenses, such as sex offenses, child abuse, violent crimes, and felony drug charges . . . who were seeking jobs as child care providers."[8] In one case, a convicted child murderer coached children part-time at a YMCA in New Jersey for four months before the organization learned of his crime and fired him.[9] A report by the state of California to a U.S. Senate hearing concerning the National Child Protection Act revealed that in a single day in 1991 a convicted murderer, a convicted rapist out of jail for fifteen months, and a convicted drug dealer all applied for jobs caring for children.[10] Although these criminals were identified, many more using fraudulent identification tactics continue to escape notice.

INCOME TAX FRAUD

People who fraudulently file for multiple refunds using fake identities and multiple Social Security numbers cost the nation between $1 billion and $5 billion per year.[11] In the 1970s the Federal Advisory Committee on False Identification reported that taxpayer losses through identity crimes exceeded $16 billion (in 1976 dollars).[12] Between 1993 and 1997 the IRS's Questionable Refund Program, just one of the agency's many criminal investigation programs, detected thousands of questionable returns claiming between $82 million and $161 million in refunds each year.[13]

NONPAYMENT OF CHILD SUPPORT

Many divorced parents escape their financial obligations to their children by avoiding detection when they move or change jobs. The Census Bureau estimates that, in 1989, $5 billion of a total of $16 billion owed in child support payments was not paid.[14] In 1992 Senator Joseph Biden testified before a Senate subcommittee that "16 million children in America today are owed $18 billion in back child support payments."[15] In 1994 the national Child Support Enforcement Program, which locates absent parents and attempts to establish and enforce child support orders for all families needing such services, handled more than 18.6 million cases. Nearly 10.5 million of those cases involved families receiving Aid to Families with Dependent Children (AFDC).[16] Indeed, the public costs of welfare could be significantly reduced if most of the parents who owe child support could be located and would pay what they owe.

ILLEGAL GUN SALES

Various gun control laws are under consideration, and some have already been enacted. Most, if not all, rely on identification of the person purchasing the gun. Even the National Rifle Association (NRA) agrees that convicted felons should not be able to purchase firearms, and in some states the NRA has also agreed that minors should be excluded from gun ownership. Both limitations, and others currently under consideration, have limited value until reliable ID cards or their equivalent are widely introduced. As a former Senate staff member, Richard Velde, put it in testimony before Congress on the security of ID documents, "Without a physical or biometric verification of identity . . . the Brady check is only as good as the paper that is presented to the dealer."[17] As things stand now, guns can be purchased in many states with inexpensive forged driver's licenses or other such counterfeit forms of identification.

A study in Colorado Springs identified sixty-one handguns (mostly semiautomatic pistols) purchased illegally during a three-month period. The Bureau of Alcohol, Tobacco, and Firearms (ATF) determined that Colorado identification cards and driver's licenses, many with false names or addresses, were used in several instances. In a typical case, a twenty-three-year-old man was rejected by a gun store for having an expired driver's license when he tried to purchase two semiautomatic weapons for two juveniles; he left the store, bought a fake Colorado ID card for $3.50, returned two hours later, and bought the guns. A week later one of the weapons was used to murder an out-of-state tourist during a robbery attempt.[18] As of November 30, 1998 states and the FBI will rely on an "instant" check system, to ferret out those not entitled to purchase guns. The system relies heavily on the ability to identify potential buyers of arms.

ILLEGAL IMMIGRATION

It is estimated that there are between 4 million and 8 million illegal immigrants in the United States, accounting for between 9 and 12 percent of the country's population growth. Each year hundreds of thousands of tourists and foreign students whose visas expire simply disappear in the country; the Immigration and Naturalization Service (INS) estimates that 4 million people nationwide are here on expired tourist visas.[19] Numerous illegal immigrants who commit crimes vanish while they await deportation hearings.[20]

The United States loses an estimated $18 billion a year to benefit fraud committed by illegal aliens using false IDs.[21] Illegal immigrants who commit other crimes are difficult to track as well. For instance, one career criminal, "a thief, burglar and heroin addict," was deported from the United States to Mexico six times between 1974 and 1994; each time he returned, walking across the border bearing a California driver's license.[22]

Although sociologists, economists, and politicians disagree as to whether illegal immigrants ultimately pose an economic net gain or net loss to the American economy,[23] it is clear that millions live in the

United States in direct violation of the law. As Robert Kuttner puts it, illegal immigration "has the corrosive side effect of eroding the rule of law."[24] In addition, "hard-won benefits to American workers—minimum wage, the eight-hour day, pensions—are undermined by the enormous underground economy" created by employed illegal immigrants, who often work longer hours for lower pay than most legal American residents and citizens will tolerate.[25] Also, many illegal workers collect their salaries virtually tax-free by claiming a large number of dependents so that no tax is withheld from their checks.[26]

WELFARE FRAUD

From 1987 to 1993 one woman alone collected $450,000 in public assistance from New York State's welfare bureau by using false IDs to collect benefits under fifteen names, for seventy-three fictitious children. In 1994 a man was arrested and charged with welfare fraud for fraudulently collecting benefits while living in luxury at Trump Tower in Manhattan. In July 1997 a Tennessee woman was charged with defrauding the welfare system of $14,858. She had been convicted of similar charges twice before.[27] Estimates as to the extent of welfare fraud vary, but many assess the nationwide costs to be between $2.5 billion and $10 billion; additional state-level costs are estimated in the many millions.[28] A 1998 General Accounting Office (GAO) report estimates that identity fraud costs $10 billion annually in entitlement programs alone.[29] One report indicates that in 1995, 10 percent of all welfare claims—hundreds of thousands of claims—were false. In 1996, 3,906,000 families received public assistance. Thus, if 10 percent of these claims were false, the government would wrongly have paid 390,600 families.[30] Although not all such fraud would be eliminated if welfare clients could be properly identified, its scope would be reduced significantly.

IDENTITY THEFT

Identity theft (or identity fraud) includes a range of crimes perpetrated against individuals, defined broadly as "the misuse of personal identifying information to commit various types of financial fraud."[31] Identity thieves steal an individual's personal data, such as Social Security number, name, and address, and often obtain personally identifying documents, such as a driver's license and credit cards. These thieves then rent apartments, take out loans, and run up expensive credit card charges in the victim's name. Some identity thieves commit violent crimes and when arrested give their stolen identity. These thieves obtain the information they need by stealing wallets, purses, and mail, by taking preapproved credit card applications or loan applications from the trash—all old-fashioned, paper-based means—and by accessing databases of personally identifiable information, whether at their own place of employment (credit bureau, doctor's office, state motor vehicle department, bank, etc.), on the Internet, or through data brokers' services.[32]

The costs to victims are high. One identity thief obtained the Social Security number and other personal data of a physician and was able to use this information to access his bank account and obtain a credit card in his name. The identity thief had run up $30,000 in fraudulent charges by the time the case was reported.[33] In another case, a woman used a name similar to that of Sandra Montgomery of St. Louis, obtained money from Montgomery's accounts, and engaged in a "year-long spending spree under the assumed identity." Using Montgomery's Social Security number and her mother's maiden name, she re-routed some of Montgomery's mail, obtaining credit cards in this manner. Eventually, the identity thief had spent almost $150,000 on a car, jewelry, and other items. In addition, "Montgomery's credit record remains in tatters. Her attorneys have had to sue credit bureaus, retailers and collection agencies to force them to remove fraudulent transactions from their records." Montgomery recounts, "It has impacted every single part of my life. I can't get a credit card. I can't get a loan. I can't get a house."[34]

The General Accounting Office estimates that identity thieves stole at least $750 million in 1997. The credit bureau Trans Union reported to the GAO that identity fraud inquiries comprised about two-thirds of consumer inquiries, with fifteen times the number of inquiries made in 1997 as in 1992.[35] Trans Union reports receiving approximately 1,200 calls per day from victims of identity theft.[36]

According to the Privacy Rights Clearinghouse, which maintains a hotline providing assistance to victims of identity fraud (and other privacy-related issues):

> Law enforcement almost never gets involved. There's just too much of this type of crime occurring for them to handle. . . . Many police and sheriff's departments refuse to issue a police report to the victims—and many victims find they need that police report to prove their innocence to the credit card companies, and the check guarantee services.

Credit grantors and bureaus and collection agencies often do not believe victims when they say that they have been the victims of identity crimes. Additionally, victims often experience great stress in dealing with such agencies and must suffer the psychological sense of invasion or violation that results from being nearly helpless in the face of identity theft. Beth Givens, the director of the Privacy Rights Clearinghouse, notes that "victims are often scarred emotionally. They feel violated and helpless—and very angry. I've heard people who've called the hotline use the word 'rape' to describe how they feel."[37]

Between October 1994 and September 1997, identity theft was either the first or second most common problem for which individuals contacted the Privacy Rights Clearinghouse's hotline. In 1994–1995, 18 percent of all calls to the hotline sought help in cases of identity theft; in 1995–1996 the number was 25 percent; and in 1996–1997, 20 percent of calls to the hotline concerned identity theft. As of August 1998, the "percentage of calls regarding identity theft is 28 percent, the highest to date."[38] (The clearinghouse receives between 4,000 and 5,000 calls per year.)[39]

CREDIT CARD FRAUD

Professional and amateur criminals using fraudulent identification documentation to make phony credit card purchases cost credit card companies and retail businesses billions of dollars each year.[40] One enterprising New Jersey man created records for more than 300 nonexistent people (giving them all excellent credit ratings), obtained more than 1,000 credit cards, and spent $600,000 before he was caught.[41] Other credit card thieves make extensive purchases by telephone before cards are reported lost or stolen. In 1997 nearly 9,500 people were arrested by the Secret Service for financial crimes involving false or stolen identities; their crimes cost $745 million in losses to banks and credit card holders.[42]

* * *

In short, even though not being required to carry an ID card may well be a mainstay of American liberty, one can hardly deny that public safety, taxpayers, and consumers all pay a hefty price for this freedom. As with other statistics on illegal activities, it is difficult to assess the precise numbers of fugitives who are free to commit more crimes, illegal immigrants, and so forth. It is clear, however, that the number of people involved runs into the millions and that the economic losses for governments, companies, and individuals run into the many billions each year. The cost in inconvenience and human suffering, while not quantifiable, is certainly not insignificant.

In terms of my first criterion for assessing the balance of privacy and the common good, the absence of universal identifiers in the United States clearly does pose a significant and macroscopic problem. Thus, although one may strongly oppose ID cards on various grounds, one cannot reasonably claim that such cards would not significantly enhance the common good, especially if new technologies are employed that make universal identifiers virtually tamper-proof, a point to which we shall turn shortly.

ARE THERE OTHER WAYS?

ID cards, as well as other means of personal identification (e.g., fingerprinting), elicit legitimate concerns about privacy in particular, and individual rights in general. Therefore one must ask whether the same goals could be achieved by some voluntary means, that is, through second-criterion treatments instead of introducing universal identifiers. The answer seems to be that other methods of trying to reduce the social costs that result from lack of secure identification pose major problems of their own, as well as threaten various rights. For instance, imposing a fine on employers who hire illegal immigrants has led the former to discriminate against all who look or sound foreign, especially those who appear Hispanic or Asian.[43]

Moreover, no viable alternative to ID cards has been widely introduced so far; otherwise, the social costs, caused in part by the inability to identify people reliably, would already be significantly lower.

True, there are already numerous cards people use to identify themselves for specific purposes, including driver's licenses, student and employer IDs, credit cards, and passports. These forms of identification meet little resistance because they seem voluntary. Even though they are often required if a person seeks to engage in a given activity, he or she is theoretically free to choose whether to engage in that activity. Thus, theoretically at least, no one must drive a car, board an airplane, enter a public building, purchase goods and services without cash, or travel overseas. People can maintain the belief that they freely choose these ID cards, that the cards are not forced on them. Also, because these semivoluntary cards are issued by numerous jurisdictions (7,000, according to one estimate),[44] they do not evoke the same Orwellian fears associated with an official ID card. (I refer to these cards as semivoluntary because as a matter of fact most people have no choice but to use them. Anybody who has had to fly in the United States since the beginning of 1997 and tried to do so without a driver's license or some other reliable form of identification has quickly discovered that he or she really has no say in the matter.)

These semivoluntary cards, though, have two major defects that prevent them from reducing social costs significantly. First, these cards are highly unreliable and very easy to forge and obtain illegally. Social Security and green cards are readily available for small sums on the streets of many American cities; a phony birth certificate can be purchased for as little as $5.00.[45] Fake-ID Web sites abound; one site, called "NIC Law Enforcement Supply," even offers discounts—any ID for $4.95, three for $11.95.[46] And when stolen, most of these documents can easily be used by people other than those to whom the cards were originally issued.

Second, because people are not required by law to possess any of these cards, public authorities cannot rely on them to identify people when searching for criminals, illegal immigrants, and others who violate the law. This is the crucial reason why proposals to introduce voluntary national identification cards will fail to solve the problems listed earlier. Those who stand to gain by being easily and securely identified would avail themselves of voluntary cards, while those who violate the law are likely to avoid them.

I refer to a full-fledged ID card that everyone is required to have, of the kind used in several Western democracies, as a "universal ID card" or, to the extent that a technology other than cards is used, a "universal identifier." To overcome the deficiencies of semivoluntary cards, a universal ID card has three attributes:

1. Unlike driver's licenses or voter ID cards, it is a general means of identification that all citizens (or residents) of a given jurisdiction, above a certain age, are required to have.
2. All citizens (or residents) are required to carry this generic identification with them at all times, and to present it when asked to do so by public authorities. Note that presenting such identification is required even when there is no specific evidence that a crime has been committed or a regulation violated, a point whose significance I discuss later.
3. The card must be linked to a database that enables authorities both to verify the information that identifies the person and to link it to other information about the person—for instance, to determine whether the person has been convicted of a felony and thus is not entitled to purchase a gun.

One advocate of this kind of universal ID card, Joseph W. Eaton, believes that such a card would elicit political opposition so great that it would not even be considered by U.S. legislators. Eaton argues that some other combination of devices should be employed to serve the same need for universal and reliable identification, devices that would entail: (1) having private profit-making corporations, licensed by the state, market highly reliable ID cards; (2) urging that private parties, from banks to employers, colleges, and supermarkets, have people identify themselves by presenting these cards; and (3) incorporating one or more features that would make these cards more attractive, such as the names of the next of kin to be alerted in the case of an emergency, or medical information that might be beneficial under emergency conditions—for instance, that a person is allergic to certain antibiotics.[47] Eaton believes that in this way nearly everyone would eventually carry a reliable ID card. Moreover, he asserts, the cards would entail no costs to taxpayers (an issue raised by the opponents of universal ID cards) because people would buy them from private vendors, and the cards would not be linked to one central databank (a prospect that evokes fears of Big Brother), but rather to several specialized ones (although those would be linked to one another).[48]

This approach has all the merits that Eaton and other proponents claim for it.[49] But it has one fairly serious flaw: Those who violate the law either will not purchase such a private ID card or will not present it when they are engaged in their illegal activities. The key missing feature is a requirement that all people in a given jurisdiction be able to identify themselves when so required by public authorities. Without this feature, the high social costs of having no universal ID cards cannot be adequately curtailed.

MAKING ID CARDS LESS INTRUSIVE AND MORE RELIABLE

If the introduction of universal ID cards is to be justified at all on the grounds that they would contribute significantly to the common good and that no viable alternatives seem to be available, one must ask whether there are ways of making these cards minimally intrusive. The evidence presented next shows that the answer seems to be in the affirmative, but only in regard to some of the features of these cards.

The near future holds ways of identifying people, ways that are extremely reliable and universal and do not require that people carry some form of ID with them. None of these methods of identification, however, overcome all, or even the most important, reasons for the objections of civil libertarians and other individualists to ID cards. Still, given that these identifiers are much more reliable and significantly less burdensome, they must be considered a less intrusive technology than ID cards.

BIOMETRICS: NEW UNIVERSAL IDENTIFIERS

Biometric technology is defined as technology that "analyzes and measures unique physiological or biological characteristics that can be stored electronically and retrieved for positive identification."[50] Various cardless biometric identification technologies are in advanced stages of development and in use by various government agencies and private corporations. These identifiers include voice recognition, hand geometry, facial recognition, retina and iris scans ("eye prints"), and above all, automated fingerprint identification systems.[51] All these means of identification are still being developed or perfected. Retinal scanning is deemed problematic because the shape of the retina changes as people age. Iris scanning avoids this problem, but both technologies are still relatively untested. Voice recognition technology has proven to be relatively expensive. Facial recognition technologies, although in use for limited private transactions in the United States, are not yet fully reliable as identifiers.[52] Measuring hand geometry is considered relatively reliable.[53] In spite of the fact that these technologies are not yet fully developed, there is little doubt that in the very near future they will revolutionize our methods of identifying people in the same way that DNA tests already have.

When biometrics is more fully developed, an individual doing something for which he or she needs to be identified (e.g., buying a gun, applying for a job, or receiving government aid) would place a hand on a machine or stand with his or her eyes near a retinal scanner that would verify whether the hand or retina matches the record in a database. If voice recognition is employed, the individual would be asked to speak. In low-risk or low-security circumstances—cashing a check at a local grocery perhaps—presentation of a physical ID card containing information that could be visually compared to the bearer (such as a photograph) might suffice. The card could also be encoded with biometric data that could be accessed and read or compared in higher-risk situations. In 1998 Wells Fargo installed an ATM-like device that allows people to cash checks on the basis of face recognition.[54]

In a card-free system, biometric data would be stored in one or more central databases only (not on a card that each individual bears).

Those who seek to identify a person would access these bases for verification purposes. As Ann Cavoukian, Canada's information and privacy commissioner, puts it, biometrics will link "the individual irrefutably to his or her identity."[55]

As of mid-1998 the Department of Health and Human Services is considering a proposal to utilize biometric identifiers as unique health identifiers for all Americans. The HHS white paper recognizes some drawbacks for issuance and verification of a biometric identifier: The individual must be present, and "special equipment to scan or read the specific biometric attribute used for the identifier" is necessary. The white paper also notes that the need for the individual's presence at issuance or verification is a drawback because "it has been estimated that 80 percent of the times when patient records need to be accessed, the patient is not physically present; for example, when the patient telephones the provider for consultation."[56]

The white paper lists the benefits of biometric identifiers, including administrative simplification and, most important, the ability of biometrics to "uniquely and positively identify the patient."[57] Above all, biometric identifiers would, of course, sharply reduce most of the social costs cited earlier. They would have one additional merit: As computers are increasingly rigged to recognize their legitimate users, there would be much less need for various access control devices such as passwords, access cards, and computer security systems, a billion-dollar-plus expenditure.[58]

MULTIPLE-QUESTION VERIFIER

Another possible universal identification system would rely on techniques that are widely employed already to verify the identity of callers seeking information about their credit cards. A person is queried about personal data that have previously been stored in a database. Questions might include birth date, address, mother's maiden name, eye color, education history, and so on. Compared to biometric technologies, this system would be less reliable but also much less costly.

Multiple-question verifiers may be less intrusive than carrying an ID card, and they may evoke fewer fears of Big Brother, but they have some weaknesses of their own. They assume that only the individual to be identified would be able to provide the correct answers to the personal questions. Although it is unlikely that another person could learn the correct answers to all these questions, it is quite possible that the information could be obtained by force or blackmail. Once such information was unlawfully obtained, this system, unlike a biometric identifier system, would no longer be secure. A criminal with access to the relevant information could easily impersonate a victim.

It is unclear to what extent people will feel that universal identifiers that rely on biometrics or personal questions are less intrusive than a requirement that they always carry and produce on demand an identifying card. The minimal opposition to cameras installed in many public places suggests that citizens may be less opposed to some kinds of biometric ID technologies than to ID cards.

* * *

What many Americans consider their right to be anonymous (unless there is a legally satisfactory reason to demand identification) would be just as violated by biometrics and by multiple-question verifiers as it would be by a universal ID card. In that sense, one may say that although certain forms of biometrics and multiple-question verifiers are less intrusive psychologically—one need not carry an ID card on one's person at all times—these other forms of identification are not necessarily less intrusive from a legal or constitutional viewpoint. These issues are next examined one at a time: Do Americans object to ID cards nearly as much as conventional wisdom has it? And are these objections raised on constitutional grounds?

PUBLIC RESPONSE TO CARDING

There is considerable evidence that Americans consider ID cards much more acceptable and less psychologically intrusive than one would assume from the high public concern about protecting privacy in general. The most reliable evidence that public objections to ID cards might well be smaller than expected is behavioral (what people actually do) rather than attitudinal (what they tell pollsters), though the latter is certainly important as well. As of 1997, for instance,

Americans had acquiesced with little protest to a requirement that they present identification before boarding a commercial airplane; others expected and welcomed the enforcement of this requirement in the wake of the crash of TWA flight 800 and the suspicions surrounding the event.[59]

Americans seem to have accepted the use of driver's licenses as a de facto ID system. We are routinely asked to identify ourselves by producing a driver's license when we want to pay for a transaction with a personal check, purchase alcohol, obtain credit, apply for a public library card, secure government services, or rent an apartment. The use of driver's licenses as IDs is so common that all state motor vehicle departments, since 1979, have also issued IDs to nondrivers. (The total number of citizens possessing nondriver's IDs is not known.)[60]

Passports are another form of de facto ID card. Millions of people each year must present a passport upon returning to the United States from most trips to other countries, and their identity is confirmed through the use of computerized databases.

Most Americans have identifying Social Security numbers. Frequently, a Social Security number is required (or expected to be provided) to gain employment or a driver's license, open a bank account, apply for a loan or mortgage, obtain a telephone number, seek a credit card or admission to a college, rent an apartment, house, or vehicle, obtain an insurance policy, and so on. Social Security numbers were originally intended, by law, to be used only to track an individual's Social Security benefits; the evolution of the many uses of the Social Security number as an identifier points not only to the great need for identifiers but also to how widely such a need is recognized and acknowledged.

Admittedly, we have seen that these de facto identification cards lack some important attributes of universal identifiers; as a result, they are far less effective, but also much more appealing to the general public. The most significant problem with de facto ID cards is that many of them are not linked to any one central databank containing extensive additional information about, or a profile of, the holder. Thus, a check on a Social Security number in the Social Security Administration's database will not reveal whether the holder of that number is being sought by the police; a motor vehicle department's check of a driver's license that has been legally obtained will not reveal whether the bearer has failed to pay child support; and so on. The fact is, however, that we are already moving toward de facto ID cards connected to central databanks that are themselves linked to one another—thus, in effect, generating extensive personal profiles—with limited public opposition despite strong objections by civil libertarians. For instance, beginning in 1982, the Social Security Administration (SSA) and the Selective Service began database matching to identify young men who failed to register for the draft. New York, Massachusetts, and California use database matching to "minimize welfare, insurance, and other frauds."[61] In September 1997, American Insurance Services Group and the National Insurance Crime Bureau announced a merger of their claims databases.[62] The FBI is designing the Combined DNA Index System to serve as a national DNA databank and clearinghouse for all state-level DNA databanks.[63]

An important exception to this trend of accepting cards with many of the features of universal identifiers is the opposition to a health card. In 1993 President Bill Clinton proposed the introduction of "health security" cards, whose purpose would be to guarantee access to health care for all Americans. Privacy advocates expressed concerns that these cards would make sensitive, personal, medical information accessible to government agencies and bureaucrats. Critics further warned that the health security card would become "a de facto national identification card." Janlori Goldman, director of the Health Privacy Project at the Institute for Health Care Research and Policy, suggested at the time that "the mere existence of a new national data base [might] prove too tempting for other applications in the future."[64] These concerns, as well as general opposition to the national health care plan, led the president to drop the idea.[65] It should be stressed, however, that this is an exception to the rule.

Looking at attitudinal data reveals that the percentage of Americans who object to ID cards exceeds the percentage of those who favor them by only 14 percent, at least according to a 1993 poll: 53 percent objected to them, 39 percent were in favor of them, and 8 percent embraced neither side.[66] A 1995 poll found that when illegal immigration was mentioned in the questioning, 62 percent favored ID cards and only 37 percent opposed them.[67] A 1994 poll that asked a similar question but placed less stress on concern with illegal immigrants still found that a larger number of Americans favored ID cards than opposed them (53 percent to 46 percent).[68] The findings of other public opinion polls on this subject range quite a bit, but even a poll conducted as early as 1984—one that made no mention of illegal immigrants or any other threat to the public well-being—found that an overwhelming majority of Americans, 63 percent, responded positively to the question "Do you believe everyone in the United States should be required to carry an identification card such as a Social Security card?"; only one-third (34 percent) were opposed.[69] In other words, what Eaton has dubbed "the honest majority" actually seems to favor identification cards.[70]

Granted that the majority's acceptance of ID cards as not excessively intrusive by no means obviates the need to determine their constitutionality. Indeed, one of the purposes of the Constitution is to guard rights that are unpopular. What, therefore, are the principled arguments for and against universal identifiers?

LIBERTARIAN OBJECTIONS TO UNIVERSAL IDENTIFIERS

Most constitutional or sociophilosophical objections to ID cards have come from libertarians and civil libertarians. The Libertarian Party notes that "carry[ing] a card to guarantee your freedom is not what the Founding Fathers had in mind."[71] The libertarian Cato Institute characterizes ID cards as "an invasion of privacy" and suggests that a "computer registry is an assault on Americans' basic civil liberties." On a proposal to create a national database that would be used only for employment verification purposes, the Cato Institute comments: "[The] history of government programs indicates that privacy rights are violated routinely whenever expediency dictates."[72]

TOTALITARIANISM

Libertarians, along with former Senator Alan Cranston (D-Calif.), warn that ID cards are "a primary tool of totalitarian governments to restrict the freedom of their citizens."[73] Robert Ellis Smith, publisher of *Privacy Journal*, expanded on this point:

> Don't we remember the Nazi experience in Europe, where identity documents listing religion and ethnic background facilitated the roundup of Jews? Don't we remember how we condemned South Africa in the 1970's and 80's for using a domestic passport to limit the movements of certain citizens but not others? Don't we realize the dangers of allowing Government to establish identity and legitimacy? Isn't it, in fact, the responsibility of the citizenry to establish the legitimacy of Government?[74]

The ACLU cautions that if a national ID card and database were introduced, "the linkage of government databases with corporate databases increases the likelihood that intimate personal information—credit histories, spending habits, unlisted telephone numbers, voting, medical and employment histories—could be easily accessed without a person's knowledge."[75] In October 1997 the Nevada gubernatorial candidate Aaron Russo criticized ID card proposals as a sign that America was "rushing headlong into becoming a socialist totalitarian society."[76]

Privacy International, a London privacy watchdog group headed by Simon Davies that monitors surveillance activities by government and corporations, contends that national ID cards have resulted in misuse and abuse in other countries. In a survey of "the problems caused by ID cards," Privacy International obtained reports from correspondents in forty countries; "among the gravest of problems reported . . . was the overzealous use or misuse of ID cards by police." Privacy International also pointed out that during the Communist regime in Afghanistan people were stopped by the government's Soviet advisers and agents and asked to produce their ID cards, placing men age sixteen to forty-five in a dangerous catch-22. "By showing it, the bearer . . . would have been immediately taken to the nearest army post and drafted into the communist army, and if he refused to show, he would have been taken to the nearest secret service station and interrogated as a member of the resistance, imprisoned, drafted in the army or possibly killed." In Argentina, according to Privacy International, men who failed to report for military service often were detected by the absence of proper army discharge records on their ID cards. "You could not even go for a walk without risking [detention] by the police, [and] being a no-show for military duty amounted to a civil death."[77] A Congressional bill that sought to use driver's licenses to curb illegal immigration, elicited the following reaction by a large coalition of public interest groups:

> This plan pushes us to the brink of tyranny, where citizens will not be allowed to travel, open bank accounts, obtain health care, get a job, or purchase firearms without first presenting the proper government papers. The authorizing section of the law and the subsequent NHTSA proposal is reminiscent of the totalitarian dictates of Politburo members in the former Soviet Union, not the Congress of the United States of America.[78]

Phyllis Schlafly added:

> Putting all that information on a goverment database means the end of privacy as we know it. Daily actions we all take for granted will henceforth be recorded, monitored, tracked, and contingent on showing The Card. [79]

Referring to the failed attempt by the Clinton Administration to provide Americans with a health security card, Schlafly comments:

> Allowing the government to collect and store personal medical records, and to track us as we move about in our daily lives, puts awesome power in the hands of government bureaucrats. It gives them the power to force us to conform to government health care policy, whether that means mandating that all children be immunized with an AIDS vaccine when it is put on the market, or mandating that expensive medical treatment must be withheld from seniors.
>
> Once all medical records are computerized with unique identifiers such as Social Security numbers, an instant check system will give all government agencies the power to deny basic services, including daycare, school, college, access to hospital emergency rooms, health insurance, a driver's license, etc., to those who don't conform to government health policies.[80]

SLIPPERY SLOPE

Libertarians also argue that even if ID cards do not immediately bring about totalitarian government, they would still lead society down a slippery slope toward a more intrusive government in which individual liberties are continually diminished. "Once established, the computer registry could be expanded in ways that would increase the size and scope of government," the Cato Institute suggests.[81] The ACLU predicts that "just as the original restrictions on the use of the Social Security card have been all but eliminated, limits on a national ID number or card would be ignored or legislated away."[82]

Ron Unz of the Center for Equal Opportunity contends:

> A national ID database represents the slipperiest of all civil liberty slopes. . . . Why not use it, at virtually no additional cost, to track convicted child molesters as well? . . . And rapists. And drug dealers and felons in general. And fathers behind on their child support. And tax evaders. And "political extremists." Members of "religious cults." Drug addicts. AIDS carriers. Gun owners.[83]

INSIDERS/OUTSIDERS AND DISCRIMINATION

ID cards will engender a "class of outcasts," warn critics of such a system. In an ominously titled essay, "Touching Big Brother: How Biometric Technology Will Fuse Flesh and Machine," Simon Davies warns that "individuals who cannot, or will not, use the prescribed system may become outcasts on the edge of society."[84] Greg Nojeim of the ACLU states, "It's an effort to separate the two groups of people . . . us from them." Daniel Griswold of the ACLU contends, "The movement toward a national ID card is another example of how ever-expanding government infringes on our basic liberties."[85] Other opponents of ID cards argue that they would engender discrimination against certain groups, such as Asians and Hispanics.[86] They point to a 1990 GAO finding that at least 451,000 employers discriminated in their hiring practices. Of these, 227,000 rejected candidates who looked "foreign"; 346,000 checked the documents only of those who had a "foreign" appearance or accent; and 430,000 employers established illegal "citizens only" hiring practices.[87] Critics argue that requirements to identify who is and is not an American resident are a significant cause of this sort of discrimination.

CHILLING EFFECT

The various individualist criticisms of ID cards have had considerable influence. ID cards have not been seriously examined as a public policy in the United States because those who have studied them, and the very few who have considered advocating their merits, know that doing so would arouse considerable criticism. Such chilling effects on advocates of various innovative public policy ideas (a phrase applied the other way around by the ACLU to those who seek limits on the exercise of individual rights) are well known from other areas of public policy. For instance, when Kurt Schmoke, the respected, highly successful, African American mayor of Baltimore, suggested that the merits of decriminalizing controlled substances should be discussed, he faced such a storm of public criticism that he and many others were discouraged from exploring the idea any further.

The same chilling effect is evident in the discussion of ID cards. In a May 1995 article in *Roll Call*, Senator Dianne Feinstein (D-Calif.) proposed biometrically secured "work and benefits IDs" with a plan that would "press forward with a single integrated system . . . requir[ing] everyone (not just immigrants) to obtain the new document within a reasonable phase-in period."[88] The proposal was sharply criticized by Feinstein's colleagues and the popular press. The *Albany Times Union*, for instance, after enumerating the benefits of Feinstein's ID card proposal, nonetheless denounced it, writing, "Despite [its] advantages, the fact remains that a national ID card carries a stigma of totalitarianism."[89] Civil libertarians have objected to illegal immigration reform proposals because they fear that they will lead to national ID cards.[90] And testifying on Capitol Hill in November 1997, Representative Stephen Horn (R-Calif.) was careful to distinguish his support for a bill authorizing a voluntary worker verification system from anything having to do with mandatory ID cards: "The bill explicitly does not authorize a national ID card or the creation of a new database."[91]

Given such criticism, it is not surprising that it is almost impossible to find, in the very rich and elaborate literature of public policy issues, more than a handful of studies that discuss national ID cards.

COMMUNITARIAN RESPONSES

Whereas libertarians decry nearly all measures that encumber individuals, communitarian thinking favors policies that balance concerns for the common good, such as public safety and health, with concerns for individual rights. For this reason, analysis of both the costs of not having ID cards and the degree of intrusion they entail is crucial to any communitarian assessment of such cards and other methods of universal identification. Given that the costs are substantial, and that second-criterion treatments do not suffice, the question of the extent of intrusion involved becomes crucial. Are there ways to make universal identifiers less intrusive?

PRIVACY-ENHANCING FEATURES

The notion of ID cards as a trade-off between individual rights and the common good is often misleading because their relationship is not one of a zero-sum game; to a significant extent, universal identifiers enhance privacy rather than undermine it.[92] The best way to prevent nosey neighbors, former spouses, fellow employees, and private detectives from perusing one's personal data, be it investment records or medical files, is to have some reliable means of establishing that the individual attempting to gain access to that information is in fact entitled to do so. Reliable identifiers could replace the existing patchwork of passwords that are often forgotten, lost, or misappropriated. The same identifiers could be used to ensure that one's vote is not forged, that one's credit card is not misused, that one's checks are not cashed by others, that one's stocks are not sold without one's authorization, and so on. In short, reliable universal identifiers—especially biometric ones—could go a long way toward ensuring that people are secure in their identity, thereby allowing others to trust that they are who they claim to be.

NOT A SLIPPERY SLOPE

Civil libertarians caution that ID cards or universal identifiers will send the nation down a slippery slope, abandoning more and more freedoms along the way. As Frederick Schauer observes, however, such critics fall into the

> fallacy of assuming that the lack of an obvious stopping point along a continuum renders imprecise the point that is ultimately chosen.

> . . . That we are on occasion forced to specify relatively arbitrary lines does not mean that the lines, once specified, are linguistically imprecise. A line that is determined "arbitrarily" rather than by tracking some natural division of the world need not be any less precise than any other kind of line, and is often more precise. There is no reason to suppose that the line, once drawn, cannot bear the burden of preventing a decision making body from going further.[93]

In other words, it is important to recognize that although universal identifiers may diminish privacy in some respects, there is no evidence or reason to assume that their implementation will set in motion a steady descent into ever-greater restrictions on privacy and autonomy.

BANKS FOR TOTALITARIANS?

In response to the claim that universal identifiers will cause a police state or totalitarian regime to arise, it should be noted that ID cards are quite common in European democracies and have been in place for quite some time without undermining these democracies. For residents of Belgium, Germany, Portugal, Spain, Greece, and Luxembourg, ID cards generally are "not an issue . . . they are simply accepted," and have provided administrative and policing efficiencies.[94] In Germany, for example, all citizens over age sixteen must carry a passport or an ID card bearing a photograph, date and place of birth, address, and signature. France and Denmark use similar systems.[95] In many European countries, any person renting a hotel room must produce an ID card or passport, and in many Western European democracies, citizens making a permanent move must register with the local police or other authorities and present an identifying document.[96] An ambassador in Belgium reports, "For Belgians, it is second nature to carry an identity card."[97] One British expatriate in Europe chronicles her experiences with ID cards:

> For nine years I have lived . . . in societies which have required me to carry their own identification papers. ID cards ensure a swift passage through immigration; facilitate bank transactions; produce registered mail from behind Post Office counters; smooth (as far as is possible) relationships with the tax man. . . . IDs offer evidence of legal entry and

> authorized residence, and satisfy policemen who use spot checks to "discriminate" against criminals, drug traffickers and illegal immigrants.[98]

Malcolm Anderson, professor of politics at Edinburgh University, is

> dubious about suggestions that [UK] ID cards would be an infringement of civil liberties. The only argument that I can take seriously is that you lose the right to disappear, which used to be regarded as quite an important right. But as it's usually men escaping family responsibilities it cannot be regarded as a conclusive argument.[99]

A colleague in Switzerland reports: "It seems to me so natural to have ID cards that I can hardly understand the objections made in your country. But as these cards go without saying, there are no studies available in Switzerland. I have asked several research institutes . . . but nobody could reply . . . in a satisfactory way."[100] Asked about ID cards in Spain, another colleague wrote, "The ID card is a non-issue here. We all have them. Most people think every country uses the ID card. How else could anybody [attest] with an official document what his/her name is? That is the reason why there is no research done on it: ID cards are common sense."[101] Indeed, I was unable to find any published study or report examining European ID systems and the similarities and differences they share.

Moreover, libertarian concerns about totalitarianism confuse cause with consequence. Although ID cards can be utilized by totalitarian governments to restrict freedoms, these cards do not transform democratic societies into totalitarian ones. Totalitarian governments do not creep up on the tails of measures such as ID cards; they arise in response to breakdowns in the social order, when basic human needs, such as public safety and work opportunities, are grossly neglected. When a society does not take steps to prevent major social ills and strengthen social order, an increasing number of citizens demand strong-armed authorities to restore law and order. By helping to sustain law and order, universal identifiers may thus play a role in curbing the type of breakdown in social order that can lead to totalitarianism. I would also point out that during the Salem witch-hunts and the McCarthy hearings—events of the sort that critics imply would be revived by the introduction of universal identifiers—numerous violations of individual rights occurred even though nobody was required to have an ID card.

Although libertarians denounce ID cards as intrusive, they fail to recognize that ID cards would provide far less personal information than Americans currently divulge, often and repeatedly, to commercial parties—information that is thus already available to public authorities, albeit for a price. If everyone who wants to market CDs, diapers, or underwear can readily purchase extensive information about most "private" Americans (not to mention those who are in the public eye), what is to stop a police department from purchasing, or a totalitarian government from grabbing, the very same information?

Today "three national credit reporting agencies—Equifax, Inc., TRW Inc. [now known as Experian], and Trans Union Corporation—maintain files on more than 90% of adult Americans."[102] Companies that engage in mass marketing either collect massive amounts of information on potential customers or purchase it from companies that specialize in doing so, including details on what a person reads (*Hustler*?), with whom they travel (secretary?), where they visit (massage parlor?), what medications they purchase (Antabuse?), and so on.[103] One can buy, from various Web sites, detailed accounts on individuals' holdings of stocks, account balances, and other financial information.[104] The information is sold to debt collectors, private investigators, and anybody else who will foot the bill.[105] Numerous companies employ an electronic device ("cookies") that allows them to trace the tastes and choices of consumers who visit their Web sites, information these companies not only use in-house to target advertising but also sell to other companies and to information brokers, who increasingly draw on such data to fashion rather full profiles of people.[106]

Extensive personal data are available in these massive commercial databases. If any details are missing, they can easily be filled in. A private investigator researching a claimant in a lawsuit against her employer

> generated a five-page computer print-out from her name alone. The private eye had found her Social Security number, date of birth, every address where she had ever lived, the names and telephone numbers of past and present neighbors, even the number of bedrooms in a house she had inherited, her welfare history, and the work histories of her children's fathers.

Anyone who has the financial means—including drug dealers, Mafioso, stalkers, and their ilk—may gain facts about individuals' personal and financial data via "information brokers": $40–80 to uncover stock, bond, and mutual fund holdings, $450 to reveal a credit card number, between $80 and $200 to provide telephone records, and $400 for access to ten years' worth of medical history.[107]

From here on, I refer to corporations that make the selling of personal information their main line of business, often information they garnered without the knowledge of those affected, as "privacy merchants." Many other corporations conduct some such business as a sideline. I am not referring to the numerous corporations that keep tabs on what their customers' preferences are the old-fashioned way or by using electronic cookies; I am referring to those who buy and sell such information to others. When I started the publication of the communitarian quarterly *The Responsive Community*, I myself purchased from list brokers the names of subscribers to various magazines whom we then invited to subscribe to *The Responsive Community*. Of course, I could have used these lists to detect who subscribes to which kinds of publications.

Some of the corporations that collect and otherwise use information about customers ask for their consent—*Reader's Digest* and Amazon.com, for instance. It is doubtful that most customers understand all the ways this information may be used (see discussion of informed consent in Chapter 5). Other corporations, such as CVS, a large chain of pharmaceutical stores, have simply sold information about clients. CVS desisted after public outcry.[108] American Express announced it would sell information about the transactions of its card holders but changed its strategy following public criticism.[109] Geocities, a popular Web site, stopped only when the Federal Trade Commission accused the company of lying to its customers.[110]

There are more than 30,000 commerically available lists in North America, profiling more than 100 million business and consumer buyers, according to Edith Roman Associates, a names list broker.[111] Another source estimates the number of lists on the market as 40,000.[112]

List Brokers, Inc. of San Antonio, maintains homeowner lists containing millions of records pertaining just to the State of Texas. The lists contain information on the age of the home, square footage, age of the occupant(s), and whether the occupant(s) is married or single.

The company's "occupant lists" of deliverable residence addresses also contains income level.[113]

Three major corporations that administer prescription data in the U.S. are PCS Health Systems, owned by Eli Lilly & Co., Merck-Medco, and Diversified Pharmaceutical Services, a SmithKline Beecham company. These companies use patients' prescription and personal data to market drugs, for example, to urge doctors to switch their patients' to drugs these companies sell or to advertise drugs directly to patients, so that they will ask their doctors about them by name.[114]

Merck-Medco covers more than 51 million people and manages more than 291 million prescriptions for clients. PCS Health Systems covers approximately 56 million people, and maintains a database of 1.5 billion prescriptions.[115]

CMG Information Services maintains a product/service called Engage. Several larger commercial sites on the World Wide Web have agreed to feed information about their customers' reading, shopping, and entertainment habits into the Engage system.[116]

The title of a *Wall Street Journal* article summarizes well the activities of privacy merchants that deal with information about the status of one's personal finances: "Prying Eyes: With These Operators, Your Bank Account Is Now An Open Book."[117]

Public authorities who need information about a person can purchase it from the very ample private databases rather than snooping around for it themselves. For several years the FBI has been seeking the cooperation of corporations that operate cell phones to enable the FBI to pinpoint the location of callers. The companies have refused, on privacy grounds, to develop such a capacity and to make it available to public authorities. The Federal Trade Commission (FTC) has been reluctant to require the private companies to collaborate. Meanwhile, however, consumer demand for such location devices is developing.[118] Soon the FBI will be able to simply stop by a Radio Shack, or some other electronic device store, and purchase the "Big Brother" tools it seeks.

If a totalitarian regime were to arise, and no universal identification system was in place, the new secret police would have only to consolidate existing private databases and add existing public ones (those maintained by the IRS, INS, FBI, and SSA, among others) to have a very elaborate description of most Americans. Some homeless persons and a few criminals, those who have never held a regular job or have always used false IDs, might escape detection for a while. But there would hardly be enough of them to slow down a determined despot. Authorities in a democratic society are checked by the need for subpoena power, but a totalitarian state would not bother with such niceties.

In short, we Americans now have a system in which citizens *suffer the drawbacks of ID cards* (as many point out, we have precious little privacy left when it comes to marketers, employers, private investigators, insurance companies, and health care providers—and potential totalitarian governments if such a threat really exists) *but enjoy none of the communal benefits of a public-service universal identification system*, which could significantly reduce crime, child abuse, tax cheating, and other such losses and costs.

One may argue that this evidence points to the opposite conclusion: Instead of granting law enforcement access to the same information we already grant to profit makers, we should deny the information to both sectors. Indeed, there is a continuous critical rumble about the excesses of private databanks and a chorus of calls to curb them. Unfortunately, these privacy merchants are very unlikely, for political and technical reasons, to be truly reined in. Although some new limitations might be imposed on private databases (for instance, to better protect children), as long as Americans wish to enjoy the convenience of using credit cards and checks (as opposed to paying cash) and of ordering merchandise over the phone and the Internet (rather than shopping in person), they will leave data trails that are difficult to erase or conceal. And there are sizable and powerful commercial forces arrayed against the imposition of meaningful restrictions on the sources of data that commercial interests depend on to increase their profits. To be realistic, the probability of returning the genie to the bottle is nil. Therefore, the real question is: Will this capacity be available only for the profit makers or also for public protection and other social purposes?

ARE ID CARDS A SOURCE OF DISCRIMINATION?

Privacy International contends that "the irony of the ID card option is that it invites discrimination by definition."[119] Although it is not entirely clear how ID cards invite "discrimination by definition," the report went on to ask:

> Do ID cards facilitate discrimination? Yes. The success of ID cards as a means of fighting crime or illegal immigration will depend on a discriminatory checking procedure which will target minorities. . . . Discriminatory practices are an inherent part of the function of an ID card. Without this discrimination, police would be required to conduct random checks, which in turn, would be politically unacceptable.

Actually, universal identifiers could serve to eliminate discrimination in some key areas. All job applicants would be identified, not just those who look or sound "foreign." Currently, labor laws require employers to verify that the people they plan to hire are legal residents of the United States. But in a catch-22, legal residents of the United States are not required to have documents that could attest to their legal residency. Hence, these laws unwittingly encourage employers to check only those who look alien. Universal identifiers would solve this problem and, by being universal, would be *non*discriminatory. It is not surprising that 61 percent of legal immigrants favor ID cards to help distinguish citizens and legal immigrants from illegal immigrants.[120]

BREAKING WITH LEGAL TRADITION?

Libertarians point out that ID cards constitute a form of suspicionless search. The cards obligate a citizen to produce identification upon demand by proper authorized public agencies (police, immigration service, FBI, etc.), even if the citizen has not violated the law and is not a criminal suspect. In effect, though, there is no break with legal tradition here. For quite some time innocent Americans have been routinely "searched" in an analogous manner, and legal challenges to many public policies that entail so-called suspicionless searches have been rejected by the courts. These measures include drug testing of whole categories of people (e.g., train engineers) without any prior suspicion of drug use; sobriety checkpoints that stop all drivers randomly rather than stop only those who weave or otherwise show signs of being intoxicated; and the millions who pass each day through metal detectors in airports, public buildings, and many other places. In short, requiring people to identify themselves does not break new legal ground.

When all is said and done, individualists' objections to universal identifiers do not seem compelling on constitutional, sociological, or any other grounds.

SIDE EFFECTS AND TREATMENTS

The main danger posed by universal identifiers is not their potential to aid domestic or foreign tyrants, but their potential use by private parties as well as the possibility that their databases might contain inaccurate information.[121]

ABUSIVE UTILIZATION

Abusive use of data can take several forms. One form is that of electronic Peeping Toms, curious civil servants who open the files of people whose lives they wish to get a glimpse of,[122] or nosey staff members who inquire into the intimate details of the lives of fellow workers and family members (checking whether they are married to the person they say is their spouse, for example).

Another major form of abuse is committed by invasive public authorities. A case in point is the use of IRS data for harassment of political opponents, as occurred during the Nixon era.[123] During the 1992 election campaign, Bush supporters in the State Department sped up a Freedom of Information Act request to examine Clinton's passport data, looking for embarrassing information.[124]

Several steps can be taken to curb such abuses. Penalties can be increased for those who intrude. For example, in 1997 Congress enacted the Taxpayer Browsing Protection Act, criminalizing IRS employees' browsing of taxpayers' files.

One may also, as Joseph Eaton suggests, provide "feedback to the individual whenever a privacy sensitive personal file is accessed," in the hope of reducing unauthorized access by enforcing the reporting requirements.[125] Such an approach might also help private parties who could show they had been damaged by such unauthorized access to bring civil suits against the violators of their privacy.

Computer technologies now allow configurations whereby all persons accessing restricted files leave a trace that identifies them. A system of this sort would deter unauthorized access and allow offenders to be traced and punished. (For additional discussion of these access-tracking and other privacy-protecting devices, see Chapter 5.)

Abuse by the White House or other federal agencies may well be more difficult to deter. However, in the past the press has uncovered such abuses, and the ensuing storms of public protest, as well as the subsequent congressional hearings, seem to have had a limiting effect on further intrusions. All this is not to make light of such abuses, but rather to suggest that new technologies and democratic controls are the best antidote to abuse of data.

UNRELIABLE DATA

A very serious problem that confronts all databases is the possibility that incorrect information will be logged in or information will be placed in the files of the wrong individuals. Problems of this sort plague many sizable data systems, including those managed by credit bureaus and the IRS. Error rates in sizable credit agency databases have been estimated to be as high as 48 percent.[126] A Consumers Union study found an error rate of 48 percent in 161 credit reports randomly selected, and 19 percent of those reports contained a major inaccuracy that would have damaged the consumer. Most of the errors were the result either of incorrect reports given to the credit reporting agency by credit grantors or of improperly merged files.

Another major study conducted in 1988 by Consolidated Information Services reviewed 1,500 reports from the three major credit reporting agencies and found errors in 43 percent of the reports. "Many of these reports contained multiple inaccuracies. Nineteen [percent] contained an inaccuracy that could negatively affect a consumer's eligibility for credit, employment, or insurance."[127] Reports by consumers who, when unable to obtain a credit card, loan, or mortgage, discover that they have inexplicably and incorrectly been assigned a bad credit rating are far from unusual. Often they are unable to determine why they received a bad credit rating, or from whom, and are at a loss as to how to remedy the problem.[128] A physician in private practice was puzzled about her troubles obtaining insurance for her office until she found out that she had been miscoded in a national medical records database as a victim of Alzheimer's disease and heart disease.[129] (My own credit file lists me as twenty years younger than I am; drastically misspells my first name; gives me a middle name I never had; and lists my previous address as that of one of my sons. The information about my credit and debt is equally inaccurate.) Clearly, new ways of correcting such misinformation must be introduced if universal identifiers are established. Otherwise, such a system would simply cause many more people to be damaged more severely than is the case now with semivoluntary systems.

One partial remedy is to follow the example of those systems that enable individuals to access copies of their files. These include those of credit agencies, the Social Security Administration, the FBI, and the CIA. If individuals find that information in these files is incorrect, procedures are now in place—for some databases at least—that allow citizens to correct the mistakes or to include in the same file their explanation of the situation.[130] It could be made still easier, in this computer age, for citizens to review their own files.

Admittedly, it might not be possible for some citizens suspected or convicted of crimes to examine all the information in their files because doing so might reveal the source of information about their illegal conduct. (The FBI and the CIA omit such items when files are released.) Also, if a citizen claims that an item of information is incorrect—that he never was arrested for drunk driving, for example—that item cannot automatically be deleted. To clear up all such claims would impose considerable costs. However, without such vetting of the data, databases pose serious dangers to civil rights through erroneous arrests, deportations, and fines. These costs may be mitigated by allowing citizens, as I have already suggested, to file counterinformation about minor items in the data file. (For instance, if the file says that an individual did not live at a certain address, the individual may file records proving that she or he did). Also, some information could be marked as challenged or disputed. However, when it comes to information that may cause serious harm to the subject of the file, the costs of vetting are fully justified, not only by the need to make the databases on which universal identifiers rely compatible with the values of a free, fair, communitarian society, but also by the need to ensure that these databases will be relied on by potential users, and that mistakes in the data will not trigger a political backlash that undermines the future of universal identifiers.

OVERSIGHT BY AN OMBUDSPERSON

The integrity and reliability of universal identifiers might be much further enhanced if the federal government, and possibly the states, were to establish an ombudsperson's office whose task would be to process complaints and difficulties registered by citizens regarding their identifiers.[131] This ombudsperson would ideally serve in a proactive role rather than only respond to citizens' inquiries and complaints. By systematically analyzing citizens' inputs, and by studying samples of files, the ombudsperson could recommend improvements to the system and ensure that these are made. An annual ombudsperson's report would help focus attention on the work of this new office and its achievements.

Eaton describes the way ombudspeople functioned in the former West Germany:

> [Ombudspeople] have the staff and the legal powers to review complaints about the misuse of data in both private and public databanks. They and their staff also can investigate how databanks exchange information with one another. They are empowered to become involved in approving both social and medical research studies which involve access to public records.

Based on this experience, Eaton suggested that an American "ombudsman would be both an administrative watchdog and someone with quasi-judicial powers . . . with a judicial appeals process similar to the relationship between the Internal Revenue Service and the U.S. tax court system."[132]

Privacy ombudsperson's offices have also been established in Canada, on both the national and provincial levels.[133] Though German, Canadian, and future American ombudspeople cannot be expected to overcome all the flaws of universal identifiers, they can certainly be expected to reduce significantly the undesirable side effects of the system.

Marc Rotenberg of the Electronic Privacy Information Center advocates the establishment of a permanent privacy agency that would serve a similar purpose:

> We simply do not have the expertise, commitment, or understanding in the federal [government] necessary to develop the policies necessary to address the enormous challenges that we are facing. Many of the decisions that are made with significant consequences for privacy protection lack adequate representation of privacy concerns.[134]

Rotenberg also highlights a significant European data privacy directive that not only establishes privacy rights and regulations covering all European Union citizens but also forbids the exchange of personal data with countries deemed to have insufficient privacy protections—such as the United States.[135]

IN CONCLUSION

American society is one of the few democracies that has no universal identification system. The costs to society are considerable. New technologies make it possible to render such a system less intrusive and much more reliable than old-fashioned ID cards. Their threat to privacy would be limited given that much of the information they would contain is already banked in private databases and sold to all comers.

Stopping these private usages is not practical; using the data for public purposes is. We should be concerned about the possibility that data will be abused and that unreliable information will find its way into the system. However, notions that universal identifiers will help usher in a police state are based on fundamental misconceptions about how such regimes arise.

5

MEDICAL RECORDS

BIG BROTHER VERSUS BIG BUCKS

MEDICAL PRIVACY CONCERNS PEOPLE more than practically all other privacy issues. Naturally we worry more about others finding out about diseases we have contracted or our genetic "flaws" than about our shopping habits or even our reading preferences. Moreover, the privacy of sex offenders or encrypted messages may not be of direct personal interest to everyone, but we all have medical records and cherish their privacy. In spite of this, legislation to protect medical privacy, which once in a while receives a flurry of media attention, has been blocked in Congress for more than twenty years. If no such legislation is enacted by August 1999, the secretary of Health and Human Services is supposed to promulgate medical privacy regulations on her own.[1] The opposition to medical privacy, largely composed of insurance companies and other businesses, argues that no legislation is needed and that the private sector can regulate itself.[2] Following the criteria laid out as the framework for our analysis, I make it clear in this chapter that there *is* a major problem that demands attention, and I also take a look at the best ways to address it.

I will show that the privacy of medical records is often violated. Some violations are random and capricious, and others are more systematic violations that are said to serve various common goods, including cost reduction, medical research, public health, public safety, and ensuring the quality of health care. Unlike the other public policies studied in the preceding chapters, the following analysis suggests that *these common goods can be served to a very considerable extent without violating privacy;* indeed, they can be served even if medical privacy is greatly enhanced. I also show that *to the extent that common goods must be sacrificed to better respect medical privacy, these sacrifices can be minimized.* Doing so requires a shift from relying on individualistic doctrines—gaining the "informed" consent of millions of people for all uses of information about them—to relying much more on new technologies and institutional safeguards.

We turn first to the question: Are violations of medical privacy significant in scope and consequence?

UNAUTHORIZED USE OF MEDICAL INFORMATION

There are numerous reports of unauthorized use of medical records. A database created by the state of Maryland in 1993 to keep the medical records of all its residents for cost containment purposes was used illegally by state employees to sell confidential information on Medicaid recipients to sales representatives of health maintenance organizations (HMOs), and it was also used by a banker to call in the loans of those bank customers whom he thus discovered had cancer.[3] While visiting her mother at the hospital at which she worked, the thirteen-year-old daughter of a nurse walked up to a computer terminal and accessed the hospital's online patient files. The girl then used the information to call female patients and tell them they were infected with the HIV virus or were pregnant. After receiving such a call, one teenage victim tried to obtain her father's gun to commit suicide before being stopped by her family.[4] A medical student in Colorado sold the medical records of patients to malpractice lawyers who were looking for promising cases.[5]

In Newton, Massachusetts, a convicted child rapist working at a local hospital used a former employee's computer password and then accessed nearly 1,000 patient files to make obscene phone calls to young girls.[6]

In Florida a state health department worker using state computers compiled a list of 4,000 people who tested positive for HIV and forwarded it to a local health department and two newspapers, the *St. Petersburg Times* and the *Tampa Tribune*.[7]

The fact that one's personal medical information could be publicized is frightening. There may be some exceptional instances when the public has a legitimate right to such information. For example, there has been considerable debate about whether the president's medical condition is so vital to national interests that its disclosure to the public should trump his right to privacy. Possible exceptions notwithstanding, one of the most criticized episodes of media intrusion stemmed from the 1992 disclosure that the former tennis star Arthur Ashe was HIV-positive.[8] Ashe, one of the most respected figures in sports, had sought to keep his condition private, hoping to keep it from his young daughter. He was forced to reveal his HIV-positive status because *USA Today* was on the verge of printing the information.[9]

When Nydia Velazquez was running for Congress in 1992 to represent New York City's Twelfth Congressional District, someone obtained hospital records detailing her 1991 suicide attempt and forwarded them to the press. The *New York Post* published the story, forcing Velazquez to acknowledge publicly something even her family did not know: She had tried to kill herself with sleeping pills and vodka.[10]

All these instances of people's medical records being publicized, and many others that have been reported,[11] have several attributes in common: They are isolated acts, often committed by a single person; they violate the policies and ethical codes of the institutions in which they took place; and they are sometimes in violation of federal or state laws as well. Hence I refer to them as "unauthorized use." As troubling as some of these incidents are, their ill consequences pale in relation to the fallout from what might be called "authorized abuse." However, before turning to this massive form of abuse, I must digress to report briefly on the major technological changes that have made these abuses possible.

PRIVACY-DIMINISHING DEVELOPMENTS IN THE CYBER-AGE

There has been a powerful trend in the United States in recent years, as we have entered the cyber-age, to gather and record in greater detail and volume the information in medical records, including genetic information and lifestyle details.[12] The health insurance industry now collects much larger amounts of information from physicians than it gathered in the past, amassing very large databases of personal information. Until recently, insurance companies usually received only an abstract of a patient's record, containing information on diagnoses, tests performed, and treatment provided. Nowadays it is not uncommon for insurers to demand to see a patient's entire record.[13] The shift to managed care programs (run by HMOs) has generated considerable additional demand for detailed patient information by groups other than doctors and other treating personnel.[14] For instance, representatives of managed care companies have required psychiatrists, as a condition of payment, to reveal a great deal of detail about their patients to verify that treatment was necessary.[15] One study found that 37 percent of respondents to a survey of psychologists and psychoanalysts by the Santa Clara County Psychological Association said they "had a client who either decided against therapy or interrupted it 'because of confidentiality concerns.'"[16]

Equally important are technological developments, especially the move by health care organizations to switch the format of their medical information from traditional paper-based files to computerized records stored in online databases.[17] In 1992 the prestigious Institute of Medicine, part of the National Academy of Sciences, advocated the wide-scale transfer of medical records into online health databases.[18] Since that time, the move to electronic medical records has surged. Fifty-six percent of hospitals had invested in electronic databases by 1995.[19] Electronic medical records make retrieval and access much easier than with paper records.

The increasing use of electronic medical records has been compounded by moves to link health care databases. These, in effect, turn numerous databases into one.[20] This often takes place within a single entity—for example, in the hospitals, clinics, and outpatient services all located within one medical center. Of a greater order of magnitude are the linkages among organizations that render personal medical information accessible to a large number of institutions with distinct purposes, such as pharmaceutical marketers, employers, and research centers.

A report issued by the congressional Office of Technology Assessment (OTA) states that "as a result of the linkage of computers, patient information will no longer be maintained, be accessed, or even necessarily originate with a single institution, but will instead travel among a myriad of facilities. As a result, the limited protection to privacy of health care information now in place will be further strained."[21] There is reason to believe that the trend will lead to one central storehouse of health care information, a national health database, an idea that was proposed as part of President Clinton's health care reform initiative in 1993 (the Health Security Act) and has actually begun to be implemented in Britain.[22] As a matter of fact, whether the data are stored in a single place or in several linked databases makes little difference for the issues at hand.

Electronic medical records also differ from traditional paper-based records in the ease with which longitudinal records can be created, forming what the OTA's report terms "a cradle to grave view of a patient's health care history."[23] One can easily imagine how difficult such an endeavor would be under the old paper-based system for a patient who has lived in several cities and thus has records scattered among many physicians and hospitals in different locations and with no ties to one another. One can just as easily imagine the relative ease of compiling such information when the separate records are entered into online databases. As a result, there is no escaping earlier facts, from drug abuse as a teenager to a family history of mental illness. The great gains in efficiency of electronic systems have caused a very considerable loss in privacy.[24]

Additional concerns are raised by the fact that once online, health information can be linked with other, non-health data sets—such as an individual's credit report—to create encompassing personal dossiers.[25] In 1995 Equifax, the giant consumer credit reporting agency, announced it would supply computerized medical records systems in addition to consumer credit reports.[26] Already privacy merchants are obtaining and selling individual, personal data on a large scale (see Chapter 4).[27] These consolidated personal data may be used by employers, private investigators, lawyers, or others who may have a nonbeneficent interest in an individual's personal health or lifestyle—or most anything else.

The Institute of Medicine concluded that said developments

> raised numerous issues, including (1) worries on the part of health care providers and clinicians about use or misuse of the information health database organizations will compile and release, and (2) alarm on the part of consumers, patients, and their physicians about how well the privacy and confidentiality of personal health information will be guarded.[28]

It is not, however, an explosion of unauthorized use to which these developments are giving rise, but a much more widespread and systematic violation of privacy through *authorized* abuse.

AUTHORIZED ABUSE OF MEDICAL PRIVACY

Although there is justifiable concern about unauthorized access to or disclosure of electronic medical records, the main problem lies elsewhere. Most violations of privacy of medical records are the result of the legally sanctioned—or at least tolerated—unconcealed, systematic flow of medical information from the orbit of the physician–patient–health insurer and health management corporation to other non–health care parties, including employers, marketers, and the press. I refer here not to the occasional slip-up or the mischief of a rogue employee, cases that often violate ethical codes or laws, but to authorized abuse—the daily, continuous, and very numerous disclosures and uses that are legal but of highly questionable moral standing.

One major problem is *the disclosure of information by some health insurance companies to employers*, which employers then use to the detriment of prospective or current employees.[29] In 1996, 35 percent of the Fortune 500 companies acknowledged that they drew on personal health information in making employment decisions.[30] These companies employ many millions of people.

Authorized abuse also occurs when *corporations that self-insure* (provide their own health insurance plans to their workers) *draw on their personnel departments or medical claims divisions for privacy-violating data.* According to recent figures, as many as 48 million people are enrolled in such plans.[31] A 1991 OTA survey found that one-third of employers used their personnel departments to examine the medical records of their employees without notifying these employees.[32]

Another avenue of *employer access* to personal medical information is exemplified by the Southeastern Pennsylvania Transit Authority (SEPTA). SEPTA had contracted with Rite-Aid Pharmacy to provide prescription benefits to its workers. The contract included a requirement that the pharmacy provide SEPTA with systematic access to employees' prescription records. One supervisor was told that an employee was taking AIDS medications.[33] It is unclear how the supervisor made use of this information, if at all, but one can imagine how such information could be abused.

Although information about people's genetic predispositions is collected much less often than other medical information, its collection is on the rise. A 1996 study conducted by Harvard and Stanford documented 206 cases of genetic discrimination against asymptomatic individuals. The individuals involved suffered loss of employment, loss of insurance coverage, or ineligibility for insurance based on their genetic potential for disease—not on any current maladies or symptoms.[34] In another survey, 550 people were found to have been denied jobs or health insurance owing to their genetic predisposition to certain illnesses.[35] Nearly one-third (31 percent) of members of families with inherited diseases were found to have been denied insurance coverage, even though they displayed no symptoms, in a survey cited in congressional testimony by Dr. Francis Collins, the director of the Human Genome Project.[36] It is safe to assume that there are many more cases, not recorded, of people being fired, not hired, and so on, for reasons of which they remain unaware.

Data from the Equal Employment Opportunity Commission (EEOC) on discrimination cases filed under the Americans with Disabilities Act (ADA) suggest the extent of possible abuses. Between 1992 and 1996 nearly 1,700 HIV-related charges were filed with EEOC under ADA; in nearly 60 percent of these cases, a firing was at issue.[37] In the same period, approximately 13 percent of the ADA-related charges filed with EEOC were based on claims of psychiatric or emotional disability.[38]

In all of these situations, the employers did not misappropriate medical information; their access to it was contractual and legal.

Fear of improper use of medial records is harming medical research and may endanger treatment. Senator Olympia J. Snowe (R-Maine) reported:

> One-third of high-risk women refused to participate in a Pennsylvania study to understand how to keep women healthy with a breast cancer gene. They refused to participate because they feared losing confidentiality with respect to genetic information. [At] the National Institutes of Health . . . 32 percent of women eligible to undergo genetic testing for a breast cancer gene refused to do so, again for fear of losing privacy and confidentiality with respect to genetic testing and genetic information.[39]

Regarding treatment, A. G. Breitenstein, director of the Health Law Institute, a Boston advocacy group, said, "People are not going to feel comfortable going to the doctor, because now you are going to have a permanent record that will follow you around for the rest of your life that says you had syphilis, or depression, or an abortion or whatever else."[40]

Thirteen percent of 332 people in a Georgetown University study believed they were denied employment or fired from a job based on leaked genetic information.[41] In another study, one-fourth of the therapists surveyed reported that they had lost a client because the client feared a breach of confidentiality.[42] The threat of public disclosure has also been found to deter people with mental or emotional problems from seeking needed treatment: 33 percent of nonpatients in a survey said the possibility that a psychiatrist might divulge confidential information (to a health plan, for example) would deter them from seeking therapy.[43]

It is not only employers who engage in authorized abuse of private medical information; commercial forces have discovered that such information is a lucrative commodity. According to Kathleen A. Frawley, vice president of the American Health Information Management Association, "There is a whole market of people buying and selling medical information."[44] One such marketing firm is IMS America of Totowa, New Jersey, which buys patient records—with personal identifying information attached—outright from state governments, medical clinics, and drugstore chains.[45]

The Medical Information Bureau (MIB) is a clearinghouse of personal medical information whose members include 680 life insurance companies and most major issuers of health and disability insurance in the United States and Canada. Member companies are required to submit any information about the individuals they insure or who have applied for insurance that pertains to their life expectancy. This includes medical information such as high blood pressure and obesity, and other information that may affect insurability, such as a reckless driving record or participation in hazardous activities. Whenever an individual applies for health, life, or disability insurance, the company obtains the record that MIB has compiled on him or her.[46]

Pharmaceutical companies have obtained medical records to discover which prescription drugs individuals are using and which physicians are prescribing them so that they can solicit the physicians to prescribe their drugs.[47] These companies also obtain patient lists and medical information from pharmacists in order to advertise prescription drugs directly to select patients. Metromail, known for its National Consumer Database profiling approximately 92 million American households, has a medical database, Patient Select, that contains 15 million names. For about thirty cents per name, large drug companies can pitch their products directly to angina sufferers, diabetics, or arthritics.[48] CVS Corporation and Giant Food, the largest pharmacy chain and grocery retailer, respectively, in the Washington, D.C., metropolitan area, sent confidential prescription information to a database marketing and prescription tracking company, Elensys. Elensys used the data to send personalized letters to CVS and Giant pharmacy customers, reminding them to follow their doctor's prescriptions and to refill their prescriptions. Elensys also arranged for pharmaceutical companies, such as Glaxo Wellcome, to pay the pharmacies for the right to send marketing materials to the pharmacies' customers. This practice was stopped only after it was revealed to the press.[49]

Some companies even provide specialized software to pharmacists—for example, embedded with programs that gather personal health data (type of prescription, diagnosis, demographic information, duration of prescription, etc.). "Switchers," who transfer claims from pharmacists' computers to those of insurers, gather and resell these data. Pharmaceutical plan managers provide claims data to employers as well as sell it to other data merchants. All these practices currently are legal.[50]

All this sharing of information occurred *without* customers' knowledge or consent. George Lundberg, the editor of the *Journal of the*

American Medical Association, calls these arrangements "a gross violation" of privacy, wondering, "Do you want . . . the great computer in the sky to have a computer list of every drug you take, from which can be deduced your likely diseases—and all without your permission?"[51] Notably, when Janlori Goldman, herself an authority on medical privacy, was pregnant, she received by mail coupons for parenting magazines and baby merchandise. She never was able to find out how the marketers knew about her condition.[52]

A report by the National Academy of Sciences notes that the committee heading its investigation "quickly learned from its research that the primary threats to the confidentiality of patient information" do not originate from unauthorized access or disclosure, but from "the lack of controls over the legal (and generally legitimate) demands for data made by organizations not directly involved in the provision of care, such as managed care organizations, insurers, public health agencies, and self-insured employers."[53]

The National Committee on Vital and Health Statistics, a committee of health care experts that serves as the statutory public advisory body to the secretary of Health and Human Services—a committee not given to hyperbole—concluded that the "United States is in the midst of a health privacy crisis" and urged the Clinton administration to "assign the highest priority" to dealing with the matter. This committee, like other organizations that focus on medical privacy—such as the Institute of Medicine, the National Academy of Sciences, and the Office of Technology Assessment—expressed concern that unless the privacy of medical records is enhanced, the value and efficacy of the medical records system, as well as patient trust in physicians and more generally in the health care system, may well be undermined.[54]

These conclusions are further supported by the concern expressed by large numbers of patients about improper use of their medical records. A 1993 public opinion poll found that 60 percent of Americans were worried that the establishment of computerized medical records would result in mistakes in medical conditions being placed in patient records; 75 percent said they were concerned that a computerized health information system would be used for non–health care purposes.[55] Eighty-five percent of those surveyed said that protecting the confidentiality of medical records was "absolutely essential" or "very important."[56]

THE PRIVACY PARADOX

The preceding evidence points to a conclusion that is both obvious and often ignored: The main danger to privacy for people who live in free democratic societies in the cyber-age comes from within the private sector, not the government. This is highlighted by the sources of systematic authorized abuse just reviewed. It is further supported by an examination of the lineup of those who oppose new measures that seek to protect privacy in general and medical privacy in particular. The opposition is led by major industry groups such as the Health Benefits Coalition, which has financed an advertising and lobbying campaign to stop congressional passage of the Patients' Bill of Rights "dead in its tracks,"[57] and the Healthcare Leadership Council (HLC), comprising approximately fifty large pharmaceutical companies, trade groups, and managed care plans, which "hosted dozens of meetings in the districts of Republican Members of Congress who support the legislation. The HLC wanted the Members to hear local leaders' complaints [about the proposed legislation]."[58] The opposition also includes the Health Insurance Association of America (HIAA), "along with the U.S. Chamber of Commerce, the Blue Cross Blue Shield Association, and others, pledged to oppose any effort to legislate patient rights."[59] This opposition is one major reason a proposed Patients' Bill of Rights, like many other privacy-protecting acts before it, was not enacted in 1998.

Still, leading libertarians persist in their focus on the government as the great enemy to individual privacy. Writing about this issue (although without specific reference to medical records) in the libertarian publication *Reason*, Brian Taylor stated, "While private-sector surveillance is commonplace and widely accepted . . . the trends of placing cameras in public areas for use by law enforcement is a new and disconcerting variation on the established practice."[60] Solveig Singleton staked out this anachronistic position more starkly in a Cato Institute report:

> We have no good reason to create new privacy rights. Most private-sector firms that collect information about consumers do so only in order to sell more merchandise. That hardly constitutes a sinister motive. There is little reason to fear the growth of private-sector databases. What we should fear is the growth of government databases.[61]

Other privacy advocates call for new federal legislation to protect privacy more effectively, without fully realizing the paradox of, on the one hand, characterizing the government as Big Brother, the enemy of privacy, and on the other hand, hoping to rely on it to protect privacy.[62]

In short, the privacy of medical records is endangered, not so much by unauthorized probing or disclosure as by the much more systematic and frequent authorized abuses in which data about a very large number of individuals are released to parties who are not part of the treatment community. There may or may not be a health care privacy "crisis," but medical privacy clearly is often and systematically violated. To put it in the terms used here: Violations of private medical records, especially authorized abuses, constitute a macroscopic problem.

THE COMMON GOODS SERVED BY COMPUTERIZED MEDICAL RECORDS

There is no doubt that computerized medical records serve the common good. They play a role in ensuring public safety; improving the quality of health care and reducing costs; promoting medical (and more generally, health care) research; and improving public health. Two questions arise in regard to each of these goods: Does the violation of the privacy of medical records serve the particular good in a major way? And could we protect privacy much better while minimizing the negative impact on the particular common good?

PUBLIC SAFETY

In 1997 the Clinton administration suggested legislation that would allow any law enforcement authorities "quick, confidential, unhindered" access to medical records, without the prior consent of the patient and without notifying the patient that his or her records are being examined.[63] The administration claimed that such access is necessary for two reasons: First, in time-sensitive cases law enforcement officers may need, for example, to examine emergency room records in the search for someone who has just fled a crime scene; and second, the government may need to scan records to curb medical and financial fraud. Health and Human Services Secretary Donna Shalala recommends that actions taken to improve protection of the privacy of medical records impose no new hindrances on law enforcement access to medical records.[64]

Consider two scenarios in which access to medical records might be required. In the first, there is a specific indication that a crime has been committed. Here the American legal system already allows the search of records if a reasonable case can be made for doing so. If the FBI or a local police force seeks to examine any private records, say a person's or a corporation's financial files, that authority needs to provide evidence to a magistrate that there is reasonable suspicion that a crime has been or is being committed. There seems to be no reason that medical records, correctly considered more intimate and hence having a higher claim to privacy, should be accessed more easily. In this scenario, if there is a legitimate need, a warrant can be obtained, but otherwise privacy can be well guarded.

In the second scenario, the police need access but there is no time to gain a warrant. For instance, the police may be looking for a killer believed to have been stabbed and treated in an emergency room, and they want to comb the records of local hospitals before he disappears. The law, however, already allows for such "hot pursuit" searches that can be justified after the fact. In the frequently cited case of *United States v. Santana*, the Supreme Court ruled that police could pursue a suspected drug dealer even after she fled into the privacy of her home. The Court observed that police had probable cause to arrest the woman (they had seen her dealing drugs in the doorway), and that officers were therefore justified in following her into the house without having first secured a warrant. The Court explained its position by saying "there was likewise a realistic expectation that any delay would result in destruction of evidence."[65] The same would hold for medical privacy. Again, there is no need to tolerate extra intrusions.

A different situation arises when law enforcers need to comb a large number of records to determine whether fraud has been committed. Because the "suspects" in these cases typically are not the patients but the health care providers (nursing homes, profit-making hospital conglomerates, and providers of home health services have particularly troubling records), the searches conducted by law enforcement authorities can be limited in scope so that they can obtain the facts they need without violating the privacy of patients, as I demonstrate later in the chapter. (If it is a patient, on the other hand, who is suspected of committing or participating in the commission of a crime—say, having conspired with a physician to defraud an insurance company—the rules of specific suspicion would apply.) In short, in all these situations, there seems to be no reason to conclude that better protection of the privacy of medical records would undercut public safety. The mechanisms for setting privacy aside—when justified—are already in place.

QUALITY AND COST CONTROL AND RESEARCH

Three related, but far from identical, health care goals are served by allowing access to medical records.

Quality control seeks to ensure that care is given in line with established practices. Hospitals typically maintain internal mechanisms to ensure quality of care. For instance, committees routinely review patient charts to determine whether the performed surgery was required, the correct procedure was performed, and the proper aftercare was provided. Some outside agencies, such as accreditation organizations and some HMOs, review the data for the same purpose.

Cost control seeks to curb waste and fraudulent use and to promote the utilization of effective and efficient products and procedures. "Utilization reviews" are conducted routinely by HMOs, health insurance companies, and federal and state government agencies, and they routinely encompass a great deal of information, such as the costs and nature of drugs prescribed, the number of days a patient stayed in a hospital, the specialists assigned to the patient, and the number of X-rays conducted.

Medical research aims to discover better treatments, often by comparing one intervention to another or to a control group. Medical researchers also monitor the population's health, identify populations at high risk for disease, determine the effectiveness of treatments, obtain accurate estimates of prognosis, assess the usefulness of diagnostic tests and screening programs, and monitor the adequacy of care.[66]

Dr. David Korn of the Association of American Medical Colleges emphasizes that it speaks well for medical records research that nearly all cases of unauthorized use of which researchers and the media are aware "have involved trespass into medical records used in health care operations; none of them has involved the leakage of medical information obtained, maintained or created in the course of research."[67]

The fact that these three health care goals benefit greatly from access to the medical records of individual patients is self-evident. One point, though, should be emphasized: All three goals become much easier to reach as a result of the cyber-age technological and organizational developments that constitute a major source of the new threats to privacy. Instead of laboriously piecing together information from thousands of paper records maintained in physicians' private offices or in numerous hospitals and clinics, new computerized and linked databases in principle provide much more expeditious and efficient resources to those who seek to evaluate care, control costs, and advance medical knowledge. As Dr. Korn writes:

> [This point] cannot be overemphasized: archived medical records of individuals and populations are the essential life blood of a vast array of medical research that has been of enormous public benefit in the past and will continue to be so in the future, unless misguided legislation or regulation driven by excessive privacy concerns makes such research impossible.[68]

One example will stand for all the others. The quality of medical care has long suffered from grossly deficient evaluations of doctors and their treatments.[69] Medical treatments often still rely on notions transmitted from masters to apprentices (during medical training), notions whose effectiveness often has been poorly evaluated, if at all. Medical history, including that of recent decades, is replete with accounts of interventions used on a mass scale and for long periods that later were discovered to be useless, if not harmful. Examples include radical mastectomies, prolonged bedrest after surgery and child delivery, and the prescription of drugs such as Fen-Phen and some anti-arrhythmic drugs. Some techniques have been found to be not only nonbeneficial and harmful but sometimes fatal, such as pulmonary artery catheterization, a technique "performed daily around the world."[70]

In the late 1980s and early 1990s, a RAND Corporation study found that only 56 percent of the coronary bypass operations examined in the study appeared justified.[71] RAND estimated in 1991 that as much as one-third of the financial resources devoted to health care was spent on ineffective or unproductive care.[72] The fact is that many interventions take place in physicians' offices in which small numbers of people are treated, and hence it often is impossible to assess statistically the outcomes of the interventions.

Medical evaluators have long sought to improve the quality of care by collecting information from private practices and hospitals in order to determine which interventions are effective and which are not. This often has proved rather difficult because of poor access to data. In the new cyber-world, such "outcome" studies are becoming, and will continue to become, much easier, promising great advances in the quality of care, and that is obviously a major common good.[73]

All this suggests that ready access to medical records is essential for the advancement of major health care goals, and that privacy may have to yield if these important common goods are to be served better. However, I will shortly show that these health care goals can be largely achieved even as privacy is being much better protected.

PUBLIC HEALTH

Public authorities make concerted efforts to improve the community's health by encouraging inoculation, food inspection, fluoride programs, provision of flu shots, and similar endeavors. Several key public health efforts require access to information about individuals. The most difficult case, in terms of the balance between privacy and the common good, concerns information about those afflicted with HIV and the public health measures that must be taken. This issue is explored extensively in Chapter 1; all that needs to be noted here is that the communitarian profile in public health is rather distinct. The reconciliation of privacy and public health is much more difficult than in the service of other health-related goals, and in this arena it is more often privacy than the common good that needs to yield. Public health is the exception, not the rule.

NON-INTRUSIVE AND MINIMALLY INTRUSIVE MEASURES

Having established that medical privacy needs enhancing and that it can be done without significantly intruding into most health care goals, the next question is: What is the best way to proceed? To what extent can we rely on second-criterion treatments rather than on third-criterion interventions?

To proceed, I must first show that the measures most favored both by the private sector and by privacy advocates are based on an individualistic paradigm that is unrealistically and ethically highly questionable. I turn then to examine one communitarian suggestion, drawing on self-regulation by the business community, before I turn to the main communitarian approach, that of institutional recasting.

THE UNDERLYING PRINCIPLES: INFORMED CONSENT OR INSTITUTIONALIZED REFORMS?

Oddly, both the prevailing suggestions for dealing with the tension between privacy and health care goals and a major source of that tension are based on the same legal-ethical doctrine, that of informed consent. This notion is based on legal, philosophical, and moral individualistic assumptions.[74] Individualists argue that people are autonomous agents and that using information about a person without explicit consent is a violation of that autonomy.[75] Some also suggest that medical information about a person is that person's property and should not be used for any purpose unless the person gives explicit consent.[76]

This individualist position reflects the classical liberal view of a person as a free agent who knows his or her preferences and is able to act on them rationally. It reflects the ideology that to the extent that shared, inter-individual arrangements are necessary, they ought to be based on voluntary agreements or contracts between individuals—hence the notion of consent. Privacy is not violated, accordingly, if patients freely consent to disclosure of information about themselves—for instance, by signing an authorization form provided by the physician, the hospital, or the insurance company. As Daniel Lin and Michael Loui succinctly put it: "Informed consent is sufficient for the collection of information to be ethical."[77]

In order for patients to give consent, the individualist doctrine stresses, they not only need to do so voluntarily but must also be informed about the consequences of their act. The OTA report emphasized that "the act of consent," whether it involves receiving a specified medical treatment or allowing the disclosure of one's personal medical information, "must be genuinely voluntary, and there must be adequate disclosure of information to the patient about what is to be done."[78] This is what is meant by the ubiquitous concept of "informed consent." Although it is rarely explicitly stated as such, the prevailing doctrine assumes that if a person was informed and then voluntarily consented to release information from his or her medical records, privacy was not violated and the tension between privacy and the common good has been resolved.

However, the consent forms that contain the "contracts" or agreements that patients routinely sign are neither voluntary nor informed. To receive health insurance or join a managed care health plan, a person often must sign a form that authorizes the provider of health care (whether an individual physician or a medical care facility such as a hospital, clinic, or nursing home, or even the welfare department) to disclose any medical information that is requested for the payment of the individual's claims.[79] These forms impose no limits on what is to be disclosed or to whom, or on the release of personal health information to third parties or the sale of such information to all comers.[80] Under most circumstances, people de facto have no choice: No health insurance is available unless they sign these forms.

A typical form reads:

> I authorize any medical professional, hospital, medical or medically related facility, pharmacy, government agency, insurance company, or other person or firm to provide (the insurer) information, including copies or records, concerning advice, care or treatment provided the patient above including, without limitation, information relating to mental illness, use of drugs or alcohol, upon a presentation of the original photocopy of this signed authorization.[81]

Most people seem not to realize that, as the OTA report noted, "usually no restriction is placed on the amount of information that may be released, the use to which these parties may put the information, or the length of time for which the consent form is valid."[82] Once an individual has signed a payment provider's blanket consent/authorization form, the floodgates have been opened. From this point forward, the individual exercises no control over how much health information may be disclosed from his or her records to other parties—parties that did not come to mind when the consent forms were endorsed—and no control over what these parties may do with that information once they receive it (such as sell or otherwise redisclose it).

Most significantly, the health insurance company, managed care company, hospital, or treatment facility may redisclose the information to companies and people that do not serve the patient. As the IOM report indicated: "Once patients have consented to an initial disclosure of information (for example, to obtain insurance reimbursement), they have lost control of further disclosure. Information disclosed for one purpose may be used for unrelated purposes without the subject's knowledge or consent (sometimes termed secondary use)." This may take the form of sharing an individual's medical records within different departments of a single organization (e.g., the health and life insurance divisions of a single company, or the clinical and research wings of a hospital) or between different organizations (e.g., between the insurance company and an employer that provides the insurance).

Moreover, once in the hands of external parties, the information may be redisclosed again (e.g., between an individual's current employer and a prospective one). Given open-ended consent forms, as the IOM report correctly pointed out, "consent cannot be truly voluntary or informed . . . because the patient cannot know in advance what information will be in the record, who will subsequently have access to it, or how it will be used."[83]

Furthermore, because "many patients are neither granted access to their medical records, nor appraised of which portions of the record are accessible to others, most patients are ill-equipped to make intelligent choices about authorizing disclosures."[84] In addition, because this authorization is blanket in nature, it covers all subsequent redisclosures by insurers, physicians, and hospitals. The Institute of Medicine notes that redisclosure to external parties is also "*rationalized* as being conducted by consent of the patient or a patient representative."[85]

Theoretically, one can refuse to sign the consent form and, as a libertarian might say, live with the consequences, which is to forgo health care insurance benefits, most often those provided by one's employer or government programs such as Medicare and Medicaid. However, as an OTA report notes, "individuals for the most part are not in a position to forgo such benefits, so that they really have no choice whether or not to consent to disclose their medical information."[86] The Institute of

Medicine concurs: "Such authorizations are not *voluntary* because the patient feels compelled to sign the authorization or forgo the benefit sought." The institute concluded that "consent [to disclosure of medical information] is so often not informed or is given under economic compulsion that it does not provide sufficient protection to patients."[87]

In short, because the consent that is said to be given for disclosure of information to third parties is often neither informed nor voluntary, it does not provide a legitimate basis for disclosure of personal medical information to external parties. As the OTA report put it, the idea of informed consent is "largely a myth and the mechanism of informed consent has no force."[88]

As a solution, individualists, including many champions of privacy, have suggested a remedy that is also based on the consent theory: Patients would have the right to grant a *specific consent* for each use of information about themselves.[89] The National Academy of Sciences advocates the development of authorization forms that make it clear to patients the organizations to which their medical information will be released and that limit the time period for which the authorization is valid. "These forms should be separate from other consent forms (e.g., those requesting consent to provide care), should inform patients of the existence of an electronic medical record, and . . . should explicitly list the types of organizations to which identifiable or unidentifiable information is commonly released."[90]

The 1973 Code of Fair Information Practices and legislation based on it already require that when the federal government collects information of any kind in a database, specific consent must be given for every use of information (not for every item of information, but for every purpose for which information is used). A privacy act proposed by the Clinton administration seeks to apply the same notion to collection of information by private agencies. The American people strongly support this version of consent. According to a *Time*/CNN poll, most Americans (87 percent of respondents) believe patients should be asked for permission *every* time *any* information about them is used.[91]

The difficulties in relying on this approach are immense. One example will suffice. Minnesota enacted a law on 1 January 1997 requiring specific informed consent from each individual whose medical records are accessed in the course of research of any kind. When medical researchers have tried to gain consent, however, for each and every specific use of medical records, they have found that a significant segment of the population does not mail back the needed consent forms. Mayo Clinic researchers then spent considerable resources locating and contacting those who did not respond. Still, many former patients either could not be found or refused to participate, further distorting the database.

The difficulties multiply when dealing with old data (many patients will have moved) and with data about deceased patients. Obtaining needed consent "would be impossible to accomplish in the retrospective studies that are so vital for assessing trends in disease over time and the long-term outcomes of treatment; such studies often involve thousands of subjects who may have last been seen many years ago."

In addition, studies conducted using only live patients (because the deceased cannot consent, or their living kin did not consent or were unreachable) may produce distorted results, reflecting outcomes primarily among the younger and living population.[92] Another suggestion that would have even more deleterious effects comes from the Health Law Institute: Individuals should have the right to keep their medical records out of online databases altogether.[93]

Alarmed by the damages that specific consent imposes on health care goals, medical authorities have advanced a third notion of consent, that of *implied, presumed, or constructed consent.* According to this doctrine, anyone who comes to a physician's office or health care facility is treated as if he or she has given consent for the data generated to be released to third parties, without the need for explicit consent. Some versions of this concept at least sound rather nonthreatening to privacy and autonomy. For instance, Arnold J. Rosoff defines the concept of implied consent as "that which arises by reasonable inference from the conduct of the patient." He adds, "If a patient voluntarily submits to a procedure with actual or apparent knowledge of what is about to transpire, this submission will constitute implied consent even though there was no explicit oral or written expression of consent."[94] A physician at the Mayo Clinic's health sciences research department suggested that "since the vast majority of patients agree to the broad use of their medical-records data for research . . . the overwhelming preponderance of agreement is consistent with the notion of 'constructed consent' from the whole patient population."[95] Robert

Veatch also has introduced the notion of constructed consent to permit access to medical records and to conduct some innocuous forms of research.[96]

Although a widespread introduction of concepts such as constructed or implied consent would serve various health care goals, it may not so much diminish or redefine medical privacy and autonomy as abolish them. Some researchers may not abuse the privilege that such "consent" grants, but others may convince themselves all too readily that patients would have consented to whatever they seek to do with the data. Still other researchers would draw on the concept of implied consent to conduct medical experiments and order treatments for their patients that they know their patients would be very likely to refuse if they were truly asked to grant their consent.

In short, none of these forms of consent—old-fashioned, specific, or presumed—provides the properly sought-after balance between health care goals and privacy. I cannot stress strongly enough that I do not mean to imply that "empowered" individuals have no role to play in helping to protect the privacy of their records, while taking into account legitimate communal needs. My thesis is that the burden patients can carry is much smaller than is presumed by the individualist paradigm, which relies largely on consent, and that other means are required if the balance is to be found.

SELF-REGULATION?

One communitarian approach seeks to draw on the business community to introduce and enforce new and stronger privacy-protecting measures. Esther Dyson has written in favor of self-regulation, which is also favored by the Department of Commerce, a Clinton White House group headed by Ira Magaziner, and several others.[97] This model relies largely on those who collect the information to regulate themselves and one another, rather than on government regulations. It is a second-criterion treatment rather than a third-criterion intervention.

The model, it should be noted, is being advanced as a way to deal with information about consumers' choices in general and is not specifically tailored to deal with medical information.

Under self-regulation, providers of consumer goods and services would display their privacy policy when a consumer enters cyberspace (queries a Web site, sends an e-mail message to providers of goods or services, and so on). For instance, a marketer may promise not to sell or otherwise release information about the consumer to others, or not to collect information about children without parental consent.

Rather than having to consent to each specific use of information, consumers can choose those providers whose policies are compatible with their preferences. Individuals could even set their computers to consent automatically or refuse to share information about themselves according to patterns; for instance, their computer would be programmed to consent to information requests from medical researchers but to refuse requests from marketers.[98]

To ensure that those who gain the information abide by their stated policies, Dyson suggests marking Web sites with various seals of approval that would indicate the scope and specific nature of their privacy commitments and how strictly they adhere to various privacy-protecting standards. The integrity of these seals would be monitored by private trustees. More than one kind of seal would be available, so that consumers could decide which they trusted most. By 1998 two such seals were available and widely used—"TRUSTe," and one provided by the Better Business Bureau.

Far from being an abstract idea, self-regulation was favored in 1998 by the Direct Marketing Association, a major representative of the private sector, several large corporations (including Kellogg and Disney), and the White House. By contrast, various privacy advocates and the Federal Trade Commission viewed it as woefully inadequate, if not defective, and called for strong new government protections of privacy.[99]

Attempts to bridge the gap led to various suggestions for more robust self-regulation. Suggested measures included auditing corporations to ensure that they are adhering to the policies they display; expelling those members of the marketing association or particular industry group who fail to abide by the posted privacy policies; compensating individuals who have been harmed when the said policies were violated; and, drawing on the FTC's antifraud powers, subjecting violators to penalties on the ground that they have engaged in fraudulent business practices.[100]

INSTITUTIONALIZED PROTECTION

Several important generalizations arise from the preceding discussion. Together they lay some of the groundwork for a communitarian approach to the issues at hand. First, an examination of policies on private medical information shows that second- and third-criterion approaches are not stark alternatives: We are not compelled to choose one or the other; they can be combined in various ways. For instance, the more self-regulation (a second-criterion treatment) is backed by the government (which often relies on third-criterion interventions), the less government intervention is needed in toto.

Second, the intricate dynamic between second-criterion treatments and third-criterion interventions strongly suggests that the common tendency to view them as alternatives is often invalid; balancing privacy with the common good is not a matter of relying either on mores, the moral voice, and informal controls such as self-regulation, on the one hand, or on government control and command systems on the other. Frequently an industry's fear of third-criterion interventions enhances its willingness to engage in second-criterion treatments. This is the case here. The private sector has become willing to post privacy policies and to honor them in part because the demand for legislation has intensified.

Third, the focus of many policy discussions on privacy in general rather than on specific areas of concern (e.g., medical information) raises a difficult question: Should all kinds of information be treated in basically the same manner? Or should some types, such as medical information, be treated differently?

Although rarely stated explicitly, the new approaches are based on the assumption that all information should be treated the same way, on the grounds that in the cyber-age one can use insensitive information about a person (for example, his or her name and zip code) to generate a highly invasive profile by drawing on other items of information available in various databases (a practice referred to as "triangulation" of databases). And information that seems innocent at one point in time may turn out to be highly sensitive at another, and hence all information should be treated as subject to the same rules.

The following case underscores this point. A man used a charge card for many years at the same supermarket. He fell in the market and needed expensive knee surgery. He sued the market, which used information it garnered from his card indicating that he bought a lot of liquor to argue that he was at fault. He could not have considered when he obtained the charge card that insensitive information he generated in the process would one day be used against him in a court of law.[101]

At the same time, it is not possible to treat all information as highly sensitive, to demand that information about one's shoe size, for instance, be kept under lock and key, or that information about the cereal one buys be treated with the same level of confidentiality as information about one's HIV status. Some kind of compromise is needed, one that combines better protection for privacy, when it does not seriously undermine the common good, with special protection of highly sensitive information.

Most important, a communitarian approach to privacy protection, although strongly supportive of self-regulation, considers it insufficient when applied to medical privacy. Although self-regulation has much to recommend it—being based on social mechanisms that opportune virtue, which communitarians favor[102]—additional mechanisms that draw on largely institutional changes, as well as some new legislation, are needed.

The communitarian approach advanced here is based on the concept that people, far from being free-standing agents, able to form and follow their own preferences at will, are profoundly affected by *prevailing social institutions.*[103] As Robert Bellah and his colleagues noted:

> Institutions form individuals by making possible or impossible certain ways of behaving and relating to others. They shape character by assigning responsibility, demanding accountability, and providing the standards in terms of which each person recognizes the excellence of his or her achievements. Each individual's possibilities depend on the opportunities opened up within the institutional contexts to which that person has access.[104]

When these institutions affect people in ways that offend our values or raise considerable resentment or opposition, often the most effective way by far to treat such ethical or sociopolitical problems is to modify or recast the institutions rather than rely on changing the behavior of millions of individuals—say, by granting them new information. To provide one example of this general principle from a non-health-related area—if the nation concludes, after a proper dialogue and election, that the savings rate must be raised, it is much more effective to reduce the public deficits (or to run a budgetary surplus) than to convince or try to motivate millions of individuals to change their behavior, that is, to save more.

Another great advantage of changing institutions is that such actions tend to be preventive. American individualism favors a cops-and-robbers approach to social issues: We wait for individuals to transgress and then try to catch and penalize them. (Often the result is political theater: A few transgressors are strung up and dramatically punished, while many others continue to cross the line. This is particularly evident in our war against substance abuse.) In contrast, institutional changes seek to encourage people to do what is right in the first place.

Significant modifications in the current institutional setup could significantly alleviate what the National Committee on Vital and Health Statistics has called the "health privacy crisis" without significantly setting back the desired health care goals. Specifics follow.

LAYERING RECORDS

Better protection of records' privacy requires complex treatment because it is affected by numerous technical, economic, and political considerations. Any policy suggestions have to be tested carefully. However, each of the reforms suggested next is based on at least some current practice; they are not cut out of newly spun cloth. The suggested changes are organizational and technical; legal and ethical considerations follow. The main suggestions are centered on *layered records and graduated release; access and audit trails; smart cards; inner-circle interface; and capping as an option.*[105]

To clarify the discussion, I have made two distinctions among the various parties involved. I refer to all those who are directly involved in the treatment of a patient, especially his or her physician and nurses, as the *inner circle*. These people obviously need ready access to medical records, although some layering (or sectorialization) of access may be possible with little or no damage to health care goals. (This is already often done regarding HIV tests, which are treated as more confidential than other information, even in the inner circle.[106]) Although these inner circle personnel are far from immune or indifferent to financial considerations or the profit motive, they tend to share a culture and mores that include a high respect for privacy issues and a tradition of confidentiality.

The *intermediary circle* includes health insurance and managed care corporations. They are much more driven by profit considerations and much less imbued with a medical tradition or culture that emphasizes confidentiality. However, unless the current modes of reimbursement are changed radically, those in the intermediary circle will continue to need extensive information about individual patients.

The *outer circle* includes parties not directly involved in health care, such as life insurers, pharmaceutical companies, employers, marketers, and the media, whose access to medical records may be legal but raises grave concerns because such access, as a rule, does not advance the health care goals of either the patient or society.

Institutional Remedy A: Layered Records and Graduated Release. In the past, all patients had paper records (or "charts") that included most of the information about them available to the treating physician. (Many patients still have such charts.) A typical chart includes medical history, records of treatment, and lab results. Hospital charts are similar and typically are centrally filed. When a patient is moved from department to department or from one area of specialization to another, the whole chart typically accompanies the patient. Indeed, charts are often deposited in a box close to the entrance of the patient's room, as they have been for generations, and can be examined by any member of the inner circle who passes by.

The underlying assumption of this highly routinized arrangement is that the inner circle is an extension of the personal physician and its members are bound by the same legal, ethical, and socially enforced mores of confidentiality. And indeed, violations of privacy by the inner circle seem to be relatively rare and largely of the unauthorized kind. Sometimes staff members have seen the name of someone they know posted on the board or door and have reviewed the chart out of concern for the patient or mere curiosity. But such incidents seem to be rare and not particularly harmful.

The introduction of computerized medical records makes it possible to enhance the privacy of the medical records, even within the inner circle, by layering the records. The traditional division of medical records into distinct segments, such as medical history, treatments, lab results, and so on, makes such layering rather easy. The segments could be assigned different passwords with the understanding that some segments would be open only to the treating physicians; other segments might be more accessible—open, for instance, also to a rehabilitation worker or a dietitian. In the future, physicians and nurses would directly input information into computerized databases either by using a keyboard or by addressing the computer instead of talking to a dictation machine or scribbling handwritten notations. Filing clerks would rarely be needed, and those remaining might need no more than a relatively low level of access.

Institutional Remedy B: Access and Audit Trails. Much wider use of technologies such as access and audit trails and smart cards (discussed in the next section) could almost eliminate unauthorized access, although with greatly disparate effects on various public health goals. The need for access and audit trails is underscored by the frequent absence of even basic protections for patients' health data. In February 1998 I called the office of a Washington, D.C., radiology practice and asked that the results of my chest X-ray be sent to a physician other than my regular doctor. The radiology practice readily complied without asking for proof of my identity. In contrast, when I call my credit card or mutual fund company, I am almost always asked for some evidence that I am indeed the person entitled to receive the information requested. There is no reason medical privacy should be looser than commercial privacy; in fact, if anything, the opposite should be true. Medical providers should request some form of identity validation both for the person asking that information be passed on and for the party receiving said information. (The recipient of the Washington radiology X-ray, for instance, could have been a trial lawyer, a divorce lawyer, or a reporter.)

Access and audit trails are computer technologies that record the identity of people who access files. To access information, a user must log in with his or her unique password, as recommended by the National Academy of Sciences.[107] Such procedures already are in effect or in the planning and design phases in many hospitals, including those at the University of Pennsylvania and the Cleveland Clinic Foundation. Such passwords would obviously block a good number of unauthorized log-ins.[108]

Audit trails further enhance privacy by forming a record of the details of all accesses to a database. Such a record may include the dates and times of access, the information or particular patient record accessed, and the IDs of those who examined the information.[109]

Some suggest that if individual patients, not just a medical facility's privacy committee, were able to review audit trails, an additional privacy-protecting enforcement mechanism would be built into the system. Even without patient review, however, access and audit trails provide a fine example of how privacy can be protected, especially from unauthorized use, with minimal losses to the common good—and without waiting for each patient to act, consent, or even be personally involved. The privacy of dying or weak patients, of those with few social skills, or of those who are simply timid would be honored in about the same way as the privacy of those who are in a more robust or privileged condition.

Institutional Remedy C: Smart Cards. Smart cards are credit card–sized devices that can store health information and/or serve as the key to accessing personal health information stored in a computer network. A patient visiting a doctor, clinic, or emergency room hands the card to the treating personnel, who can display the information on their computer screens and encode in the card additional information—for instance, about tests conducted and the findings. As the technologies improve, visuals such as X-rays, EKGs, and sonograms also could be encoded. Smart cards remain in the possession of patients and hence greatly enhance privacy by affording patients effective control over who has access to their medical information. Access by anyone other than the patient is to occur only with the patient's full knowledge and consent. The card could also be layered so that the patient could determine which segments to open to whom.[110]

In emergency situations, of course, difficulties might arise if the patient is not carrying the card or is unable to provide the needed accessing passwords for some of the segments (one would expect patients not to password-protect elementary information). This problem, however, is not limited to smart cards. After all, patients today typically do not carry their charts with them when they are rolled into the ER. At the very least, a person could share key passwords with a close relative or friend, whose names and phone numbers would be noted on the card's open segment.

A very serious defect of smart cards is that they will severely curtail researchers' and health care professionals' ability to serve the common goods of quality and cost control as well as medical research, because of limitations on access to the data.[111]

Institutional Remedy D: Interface and UPNs. A major method that protects medical privacy much more effectively than is currently the case and does not entail breaking with legal or ethical tradition has, in fact, some precedent. I refer to an interface that turns most of the information in medical records into personally "unidentifiable" information at the point where it is transmitted beyond the inner or intermediary circle. Using such an interface greatly enhances privacy but does not hinder the use of the data in the service of several, albeit not all, of the common goods at issue here.

By "interface" I refer to individuals and processes that transmit information in medical records to users other than members of the inner or intermediary circle by conducting various coding procedures to remove patients' names, addresses, phone and Social Security numbers, and a few other such items that could enable outsiders to identify them. The transmitted information is coded instead by unique patient numbers (UPNs).

The 1996 Health Insurance Portability and Accountability Act mandated the establishment of a "unique health identifier" or "federal health identification number" for every individual in the United States that would be used for all paid health care encounters and would serve as the basis of a national medical and health database. The Department of Health and Human Services, whose charge it is to establish the identifier, is examining several possible formats, including the use of a composite number (e.g., one comprising date of birth, longitude and latitude of a patient's hometown, and additional numerals), or a biometric identifier, such as a thumbprint or iris scan.

Opponents contend that such an identifier "smacks of Big Brother" and caution that health data might be linked to personal data (such as criminal or financial records) in other databases. Dr. Donald J. Palmisano, a medical privacy expert for the American Medical Association, warns, "We have very grave concerns about the unique patient identifier. If this information ended up in some central repository, some giant clearinghouse, what protection do we have that some vandal would not break in?" Dr. Richard Sobel of Harvard Law School contends: "What ID numbers do is centralize power, and in a time when knowledge is power, then centralized information is centralized power. I think people have a gut sense that this [UPNs] is not a good idea."

Alternatively, proponents note that the major benefit of UPNs is that they would allow the storage of all the information available on one patient—from numerous sources, such as different doctors, emergency rooms, or cities—in one database, without endangering the patient's privacy. This, in turn, would allow any doctor a patient sees to tap into a detailed, complex medical profile and provide highly informed care. Above all, it will make possible medical research that requires neither individual consent nor exposure of patient identity, because researchers will know most, if not all, they need to know about a patient without knowing who she or he is. The alternative is to "rely on folklore and anecdote in health care," according to Dr. Christopher Chute of the Mayo Foundation.[112] So far the opposition has succeeded in blocking UPNs. The Clinton administration has announced that "because the availability of these identifiers without strong privacy protections in place raises serious privacy concerns, the Administration is committed to not implementing the identifiers until such protections are in place."[113]

Dr. David Korn suggests that this very powerful tool for protecting medical privacy will not be acceptable to the public unless its introduction is accompanied by proper federal privacy-enhancing legislation.[114] This may well be true, but as I discuss later, such legislation itself faces some serious problems.

Medical privacy would be better served if institutions relied on *in-house* interfaces in transmitting information from personal files to UPN records, using inner circle personnel, such as medical records personnel, coding clerks, and nurses and physicians. These professionals are preferable to outsiders, such as utilization reviewers and auditors, because the very introduction of outsiders to the original medical files exposes those records to an additional set of people; if the interface is internal, the interfacers mainly are personnel who already have access to the data. Moreover, insiders are more likely to share the values of the medical culture, which, in an extension of the traditional physician-patient confidential relationship, tends to discourage violations of privacy.

Personally unidentifiable information may at first seem useless, but for many purposes this type of information suffices. For instance, for *medical research* it is often sufficient to know from a patient record that the individual scored *x* on variable *y*, had certain scores on other variables, and so on. True, some personal attributes may need to be known, such as race, gender, or age—but not name, address, and other details that point to a specific identity.

In the rare cases when information contained in a patient's address or some other such highly personal detail is critical for the research, those who provide the interface could "code" such details as well. Thus, instead of including the person's address as, say, 240 Central Park West, New York City, the address could be coded as a highly affluent, urban neighborhood in New York City. Instead of providing birthdays, the month and year of birth would suffice, and so on. It should be noted, though, that if the interface leaves out personal details such as names and Social Security numbers, it will be difficult, although far from impossible, to correlate these databases with data from non–health care databases.

To the extent that such a correlation is legitimately called for, special provisions are best made to allow *inter*-database analyses by computers, releasing only the correlations and not individuals' identities. Bonded inter-databank agents, whose specific job is linking databases, could be employed to carry out such correlations.

The issues posed by *quality control* often are similar to those presented by medical research. A typical question is: If the patient's condition includes *x*, *y*, and *z*, were proper procedures *a*, *b*, and *c* undertaken, and in the correct sequence given the patient's age, gender, and so on? One does not need personal information to address these questions. This is especially true outside the inner circle. A hospital quality control committee, still part of the inner circle, may benefit from knowing a patient's identity, because some inner circle members of the committee may be able to contribute facts not detailed in the record, based on an intimate knowledge of the patient. When the information travels beyond the inner circle, however, there is no reason, as a rule, to include personal identity.

The same can be said about several *cost control* procedures. If a patient presented with condition *x*, and his other attributes included *y* and *z*, was a less costly or more costly procedure used? Most often, an examiner would be seeking to establish a rate or identify a pattern of diagnoses, procedures, and referrals (for example, how often does a physician or hospital err in the direction of expensive and unneeded procedures?) rather than trying to second-guess every case.

Although UPNs currently are not widely relied upon, they have been tried in two states for HIV and AIDS reporting. In Maryland, when HIV is reported to public health authorities, a UPN is fashioned by combining the patient's birth date with a digit representing his or her racial or ethnic group, a digit representing his or her gender, and the last six digits of his or her Social Security number.[115] Texas relies on a similar unique-identifier HIV reporting system. Both Maryland and Texas have "found that their data contain a substantial number of incomplete or difficult-to-match records."[116] It would be a mistake, though, to conclude from these preliminary findings that this approach cannot be made to work.[117] Clearly a UPN system would require some debugging, but it would work better and better as more health care providers introduce such numbers: UPNs would then allow collection of more information and better reward the efforts to shift to such a system. It is noteworthy that even a group deeply concerned about privacy, the Gay Men's Health Crisis, reversed itself in 1998 and called for doctors to report HIV-positive individuals to the state via a UPN.[118]

Critics may suggest that it would be easy for those who command considerable financial and technical resources and have access to the data that contain only information without individual identifiers, to correlate UPNs with other databases that contain individual identifiers and thus establish the identity of those whose medical privacy is being protected by UPNs. This may well be true. Still, UPNs would prevent many kinds of unauthorized use because they prevent casual perusal of records by people seeking to find out who is impotent, pregnant, and so on.

Moreover, the introduction of an interface of the kind suggested here would establish a new, clear line between legal and (what from then on will be) illegal use of data. Members of the intermediary and especially the outer circle could no longer commit authorized abuse of data that are legally generated by tapping into existing databases. If they persist, under the new arrangements they would have to engage in an activity whose only purpose would be to violate the confidentiality built into the data—in effect, to engage in code-breaking. Granted, even after such activities were defined as a violation of the law, abuse would not cease; completely airtight databases cannot be created. But the introduction of the interface would largely halt these penetrations. If audit trails also are used, attempts to crack the codes would leave the "fingerprints" of those who violated patients' privacy, and help defend privacy even better.

Institutional Remedy E: Capping as a Compatible Option. UPNs would not work for managed care and other health insurance programs that reimburse health care providers on the basis of procedures performed, time spent with patients, and drugs or equipment (such as wheelchairs or special beds) dispensed to the patient. These programs work by linking the identity of the person who purchased the insurance policy, is enrolled in the HMO, or is entitled to Medicare or Medicaid to the one for whom the said measures were taken. In the current system, millions of times each month payment to providers is conditioned on delivering highly detailed, specific, and individually identified medical information to members of the intermediary circle. Thus, if a person is tested for depression, syphilis, or cancer, this information is reported and care providers are paid accordingly. Every medical episode—

whether a paranoiac attack, a pregnancy loss, or a prescription for Valium—is not only noted in the patient's record but also reported to a reimbursement agent who is not a part of the medical institution or culture. Indeed, precisely because reimbursement differs according to the nature of the treatment, payers engage in the cumbersome and costly procedure of either seeking to approve before the fact the right of specific patients to gain specific interventions or haggling with the provider over how much intervention to provide (no more than six weeks of psychotherapy, only *x* days in the hospital after major surgery, and so on). In short, UPNs—a major privacy-enhancing measure—and most reimbursement schemes are basically incompatible.

The particularly costly reimbursement arrangement of the American medical care system, however, is not one of the common goods that have been identified. Indeed, the prevailing reimbursement system is a major reason the United States spends a much greater proportion of its health care dollars on administration than do most other developed nations. In fact, many would regard a simplification and streamlining of the system as a major service to the common good. How this might be done raises ethical, administrative, and political issues that would take us well beyond the scope of the current study. It should be noted, however, that within the existing medical care system there is a way to protect privacy much more effectively while still relying on the existing reimbursement arrangements.

UPNs can be employed in those reimbursement schemes that use "capitation"—providing a fixed payment per member, per month, to a health provider or plan, regardless of the amount of care that person receives. In capitated systems, there is no need to report to anyone outside the inner circle on the medical procedures undertaken because reimbursement is not tied to the specifics of the care given. Capitation is a method of paying primary care physicians as well as some specialists and hospitals, and it is far from an esoteric method: "On average, in markets with high HMO penetration, capitation is the method of paying primary care physicians (PCPs) for 63% of enrollees." In addition, specialists are paid by capitation "for 46% of HMO enrollees in large markets" (typically through "carve-outs" from the pool of money available to compensate PCPs), as are some hospitals (under an arrangement sometimes referred to as global caps).[119]

Capitated payment systems carry certain advantages over other common reimbursement schemes, as well as disadvantages. None of these are discussed here, however, because my purpose is not to evaluate this form of reimbursement but only to note that, in principle, capping is much more compatible with medical privacy than other prevailing medical care reimbursement systems.

* * *

To recap the argument so far: Individualist informed consent has some limited merit, but to rely on it as the main protector of medical privacy is both impractical and morally dubious. Communitarian measures, including robust self-regulation, institutional recasting, and the introduction of new technological devices, can carry a good part of the burden, although some third-criterion interventions may well be required. For instance, to keep firewalls between the intermediate and outer circles of users of medical information, new penalties on those who breach those walls may be necessary. As I see it, however, the legislation currently most widely considered provides neither an effective approach nor one that is compatible with communitarian principles.

PROPOSED LEGAL REMEDIES: HIGHLY INTRUSIVE OR PUBLIC RELATIONS?

Over the last twenty-five years, a broad consensus has been established concerning the principles that new comprehensive privacy protection legislation ought to follow. These ideas draw on many sources, including the legislation already in place governing the information collected and used by the government but not yet the private sector; policies of international groups such as the Organization for Economic Cooperation and Development (OECD) and the European Community (EC); and the deliberations of numerous private groups, commissions, scholars, and activists.

GUIDING PRINCIPLES

While there are numerous specific differences in the policies advanced by these various bodies, they basically reflect the following principles:

1. Notice/awareness: Patients should be given notice of an entity's information practices before they divulge any personal information. Without notice, a patient cannot make an informed decision as to whether and to what extent to disclose personal information. Moreover, three of the other principles of privacy protection—choice/consent, access/participation, and enforcement/redress—are meaningful only when patients have learned an entity's policies, and their rights with respect thereto.
2. Choice/consent: Patients should be given options as to the uses of any personal information collected from them. Specifically, choice relates to secondary uses of information—uses beyond those necessary to complete the original transaction. Such secondary uses can be internal, such as placing a patient on the collecting company's mailing list in order to market additional products or services, or external, such as transferring information to third parties.
3. Access/participation: A patient should be able both to access data about himself or herself—that is, to view the data in an entity's files—and to contest that data's accuracy and completeness.
4. Integrity/security: Collectors must take reasonable steps to ensure data integrity, such as employing only reputable sources of data, cross-referencing data against multiple sources, providing consumer access to data, and destroying untimely data or converting it to anonymous form.
5. Enforcement/redress: Privacy protections can be effective only if a mechanism is in place to enforce them.[120]

These principles mainly reflect the individualistic notions of consent whose validity I have already questioned; rather than focus on prevention, they are backed up by some post-hoc punitive legislative measures. To the extent that these principles undergird the new federal laws now under consideration, I shall try to show, in some detail, that such laws would severely undermine several important health care goals. To the extent that such laws are meant to assuage public angst, they will contribute to the distrust in which the government often is held. I focus on the two major, rather typical, efforts in this realm. One is a code that was originally introduced in 1974, and the other is legislation suggested by the Clinton administration but not yet enacted.

The Code of Fair Information Practices developed by the Department of Health, Education, and Welfare in 1973 governs the collection and use of information by the federal government.[121] The principles of the code were, in turn, incorporated into the Privacy Act of 1974, which governs all personal information collected and stored by any federal government agency.[122] This legislation is considered a model for what is now believed to be needed for the private sector.[123]

The legislation drafted by the Clinton administration seeks to protect individuals against the collection of information by private bodies, as well as against redisclosure of such information to third parties; this area is currently governed by a patchwork of state laws and common law precedents, superimposed on a federal regulatory framework. "The result," according to a report by the Workgroup for Electronic Data Interchange (WEDI), is "a morass of erratic law, both statutory and judicial, defining the confidentiality of health information."[124]

The existing legal patchwork is ineffective for three reasons:

1. Not all states or jurisdictions have the same laws or even any relevant ones.[125] For example, only twenty-eight states even grant individuals the right to have access to their medical records, let alone some measure of control over their redisclosure.[126]
2. The computerization of medical records has led to frequent interstate transmissions, often making state laws protecting privacy irrelevant and creating confusion over which state's laws apply.[127]
3. Most state laws purporting to protect privacy do not go far enough and specifically do not outlaw what is now considered authorized abuse.[128]

As a result, calls for federal legislation to protect the privacy of medical records have become frequent and pronounced. Both the Institute of Medicine and the Workgroup for Electronic Data Interchange recommend such legislation.[129] Secretary of Health and Human Services Donna E. Shalala concurs that

> every day, our private health information is being shared, collected, analyzed, and stored with fewer federal safeguards than our video store records. . . . To eliminate this clear and present danger to our citizens and our health care system, we must act now with national legislation, national education, and a national conversation.[130]

I turn now to examine in some detail the 1973 Code of Fair Information Practices and the Clinton administration proposals for federal legislation more than twenty years later.

FAIR INFORMATION PRACTICES (1973)

The federal 1973 Code of Fair Information Practices states: "There must be a way for an individual to find out what information about him [or her] is in a record and how it is used."[131] "Must be" does not deliver the groceries or do much of anything else.

The code further states: "There must be a way for an individual to prevent information about him [or her] obtained for one purpose from being used or made available for other purposes without his [or her] consent."[132] I have already argued that this notion of relying on specific consent is likely to do serious damage to health care goals, especially research, and that less damaging options are available.

The OTA report cites health professional organizations and privacy advocates who also recommend imposing the very onerous requirement that "when health care personnel request information, the individual must be given notice as to the authority of the collection of data, whether the disclosure is mandatory or voluntary," and that "health care personnel [be] required to request information directly from the individual to whom it pertains, whenever possible."[133]

Statements of policy that include "whenever possible," like those that feature the phrase "must be," if not taken as the blandishments of public relations and the politics of vacuous reassurance, would impose severe burdens on medical research, and very likely on cost and quality controls as well. The simple reason is that if one purpose or one use of information (for which a patient is said to have given consent) is broadly defined (say, "the common good," or "improving health"), it will be so open-ended as to do precious little to protect privacy. If these terms are construed to mean that information released by a patient for one purpose (e.g., treatment) cannot be used for another purpose (e.g., research) without the patient's specific consent, severe burdens would thus be imposed on other health care goals, as the earlier discussion of the findings of the Mayo Clinic study has already illustrated. The threat of such burdens is far from hypothetical; several states have already enacted laws that at least on paper provide such rights to their residents.

Another principle included in the code suggests that "there must be a way for an individual to correct or amend a record of identifiable information about him [or her]."[134] Such a measure might have some deterrent effects on privacy violations: If a patient were to find out that the hospital or physicians had conducted tests or engaged in procedures of which he or she was unaware, this would be considered a violation of the patient's privacy. This is illustrated by the case of workers at a government laboratory on the campus of the University of California at Berkeley. Only when an employee requested her records did she discover that she had been repeatedly tested for syphilis without her consent. It was later discovered that the lab had systematically tested its employees for pregnancy, syphilis, and the sickle-cell trait, never obtaining their consent or notifying them of the results.[135] However, unlike most other files about a person, there are very few limits on what a patient's medical record may include—anything from sexual preferences to drinking habits may legitimately show up—and because of this the importance of this corrective for the *protection of privacy* is rather low. Ensuring patients' ability to make corrections in their files, however, might well help ensure the higher accuracy of those files.

At the same time, the capacity to correct one's file raises numerous issues for health care goals. Considerable efforts would have to be made to translate abbreviations used by physicians—such as codes that indicate whether a patient smokes or is alcoholic—as well as numerous Latin words, in order for patients to be able to understand notations in the files. Furthermore, many patients, galled by the discovery of unflattering information, whether it be their weight or descriptions of their violent tendencies, might demand to "correct" the "erroneous" information. Physicians would then have to either convince patients of the accuracy of the notations or delete material that they consider relevant, to avoid conflicts with those who are, after all, their customers.

The same privacy advocates who favor the onerous patient notification procedures discussed here also champion a policy requiring that health care personnel make a decision on a patient's request to have his or her record amended within a fixed time, such as thirty days. If a request for change is denied, "the individual may file a statement of disagreement, which must be included in the record and disclosed along with it thereafter," and the individual may seek a formal review of the denied request.[136]

These all add to the burden on health care providers while, for reasons already discussed, providing little benefit. The difficulties are much greater than those involved in ensuring the accuracy of the databases used for national ID cards, because medical information is much more complex, professional, and intimate. The difference is so large that what might be quite achievable in the case of ID systems may well impose unacceptable costs on the health care system.

CLINTONIAN REMEDIES (1997): THE SAME APPROACH

The Clinton administration outlined in 1997 six standards to be included in any comprehensive privacy bill. These recommendations were substantially detailed in a report issued by Health and Human Services Secretary, Donna Shalala, who summarized them well in a speech delivered to the National Press Club.

1. Medical records should, with few exceptions, be disclosed only for the purpose of health care.

Exceptions cited by Secretary Shalala include the national priorities of promoting public health and research, ensuring quality care, and fighting health care fraud and abuse.

Limiting the legal distribution of medical information makes a great deal of sense, for reasons already discussed. One question remains, however: Do we largely and initially rely on legal penalties to enforce this dictate, thus going after the horse after it is stolen from the barn, or do we first (although not only) strengthen the locks on the barn (by the means already discussed)?

2. Patients should be able to view and correct their records, and also find out who has had access to them.

I have already discussed the limited merits and high costs of such a policy.

3. Employers who receive medical information in the process of reviewing claims should not be able to use the information to make employment-related decisions or for any other purpose unrelated to health care.

This seems a highly commendable recommendation, one of special importance given the large number of employees who work for corporations that self-insure and the many others who work for corporations that process their claims or have contracts for release of information with companies that handle such processing.

4. Organizations that collect patient information, such as hospitals, should be required by law to take appropriate measures to safeguard its security.

This seems a reasonable measure, but it largely aims to prevent unauthorized use, which is not the main problem, as we already have seen.

5. Those who gain access to medical information in the course of doing business, such as insurers, drug distributors, and billing service companies (companies that handle physicians' billing, often serving as a conduit between a doctor's office and an insurer), should be held to the same standards of confidentiality and limits on disclosure as hospitals and doctors.

A worthy aim, but one unlikely to succeed because of the difference in culture. It is best if the personally identifiable information provided to outer circle parties is as limited as possible. It is also desirable if the alternative reimbursement options described earlier are offered to patients so that much less identifiable information is released to these entities to begin with.

6. Criminal punishments should be imposed on those who use medical information improperly.[137]

The penalties on corporations typically are fines, and these, under the pressures of lobbies, are set at levels so low that they often are disregarded, if not considered part of the cost of doing business.[138] Again, the danger is that such legislation, which focuses on retroactive steps, would be more reassuring than effective.

In conclusion, the effective protection of the privacy of medical records will have to rely mainly on institutional changes (largely using UPNs and new technological devices such as audit trails), self-regulation backed up by various private-sector and public means, and, possibly, changes in the reimbursement systems that would curtail sharply the information needs of the intermediary circle, the major source of redisclosure to the outer and most problematic circle. These efforts could meaningfully enhance privacy without significantly burdening efforts to enhance health care goals, including quality and cost control, research, public health, and public safety.

Legislation has a role to play, largely in fostering and backing up other means. Two main categories of legislation illustrate this approach. One is legislation that requires the introduction of institutionalized safeguards—for instance, the use of audit trails or some other technology that allows privacy accountability (by tracing those responsible for violations). Such legislation does not rely on individual patients to make choices but deters privacy violators by relying largely on institutions to hold accountable those who gain illicit access to information and abuse it.

Another category is legislation that penalizes those institutions that pretend to have in place privacy safeguards but actually do not. Such legislation would allow individuals not to consent to specific actions, which can run into many thousands per file, but to give or withhold consent based on their perception of general patterns—something people can do as long as society does a good part of the homework for them, so to speak. This may not be as flattering a view of human nature as the individualists hold, but it is one that is much more valid.[139]

CLEANING UP SIDE EFFECTS

The side effects of these interventions have already been discussed as the various privacy-enhancing measures were introduced. Some concern the costs of changing the system. We saw that costs are relatively low for some measures (e.g., patients' review of audit trails) and high for others (e.g., patients' right to review and then correct their medical records). Obviously, given that the health care system already is very costly, first preference should be given to those measures that are less costly.

In addition, we must recognize that some research projects, especially those that require older data, would be made more difficult through the approaches suggested here. It seems advisable to establish a special human subject review committee that would determine when it is justified to suspend or modify the new rules in order to carry out a significant research project. For instance, a research project carried out at the University of Washington required tracing the effects of treatments carried out long ago on cancer patients. The only way to locate these patients was to use their names and addresses, and perhaps even their Social Security numbers. Given the importance of fighting cancer, if such a search is limited to a sample of the patients, and if the data collected are properly protected, such a proposed review board may well allow such disclosure. This does not mean that everyone wishing to conduct a longitudinal study would gain such an exemption. The review board might find that some other procedures that violate privacy to a lesser extent could be used to the same effect. And, of course, with every year that passes more data will be coded with UPNs, rendering such forays less necessary.

Telemarketers, employers, and credit organizations who seek to use medical data for their profit-making activities are likely to experience a loss when they are no longer able to target the ill. This is a side effect we can learn to live with.

IN CONCLUSION

Medical privacy is full of abnormalities. It is in a fundamentally different condition than the other four areas of public policy studied here. Although there is an imbalance here, too, it tilts in the opposite direction: Privacy is unnecessarily compromised without serving any important common good.

The violations of privacy we have seen are not those that have attracted much attention—unauthorized uses of medical information by some rogue individual—but highly systematic and authorized abuses of personal information.

The violators are not the individualists' usual culprit, the government, but are mainly privacy merchants, profit-making companies that grow rich by selling information about people's medical conditions to all comers.

The most effective treatments to shore up medical privacy cannot rely on the legal fiction of informed consents by millions of patients for every use of every piece of information about them, but on new privacy-enhancing technologies (e.g., audit trails) and institutional arrangements (e.g., changing reimbursement systems).

Above all, we need to rethink the public policy, normative, and constitutional assumptions that underlie our conception of privacy, the subject of the next, concluding chapter.

mation—have we seen that privacy is invaded without yielding significant gains to the common good.

Behind these observations lies the assumption that good societies carefully balance individual rights and social responsibilities, autonomy and the common good, privacy and concerns for public safety and public health, rather than allow one value or principle to dominate. Once we accept the concept of balance, the question arises as to how we are to determine whether our polity is off balance and in what direction it needs to move, and to what extent, to restore balance.

In Fourth Amendment cases, courts often rely on the criteria articulated in *United States v. Katz* to determine reasonable expectations of privacy by individuals and by society. In this court case, the defendant, a gambler who made calls from a public phone booth, won on the grounds that he had a reasonable expectation of privacy that his phone calls would not be intercepted by the police or FBI agents and that society shares this expectation.

To one untrained in law, and especially to a sociologist, this twin criterion is difficult to comprehend, let alone apply. How, for instance, is a court to determine whether a person who grows marijuana on his private property, concealed by some bushes, has a "reasonable" expectation of privacy, say, when a police helicopter flies overhead? Is it legitimate for police to search someone's street-facing porch, when no public good is served, just because the individual and his community may have no, or only a low, expectation of privacy there?[1] A leading lawyer, in a private conversation, referred to the criteria articulated by *Katz* as "bizarre." Another pointed out that *Katz* is tautological: Once the Supreme Court rules that there is an expectation of privacy regarding a certain area of conduct, there is such an expectation—whether or not it existed prior to the ruling.

Rather than drawing on a pseudo-sociology of expectations, I have articulated four criteria in the opening part of this volume and have applied them throughout, to guide the analysis of the public policy areas under study from ethical, social, and legal perspectives.

The first criterion asks: Is there a compelling need for corrective action? Or are we about to recalibrate privacy unnecessarily? Tampering with ethical, social, and legal traditions—and with the public philosophies that underlie them—endangers their legitimacy because once tradition is breached it is difficult to prevent it from unraveling, a phenomenon often referred to as the slippery slope problem.[2] Changes in these matters, therefore, should not be undertaken unless there is strong evidence that either the common good or privacy has been significantly neglected. By this criterion, we saw in an analysis of the AIDS epidemic and sexual offenses against children that additional efforts on behalf of public health and safety are needed, even if privacy must be reduced a peg or two. A similar conclusion reached in the analysis of ID cards and biometrics is based more on an accumulation of several desiderata rather than on any one in particular. Encryption poses a special problem: Although many of the dangers are hypothetical (for instance, a terrorist holding a nuclear bomb, threatening a city), the disutility of any such dangers is so high that greater attention to public safety seems justified. In my analysis of medical privacy, the evidence ran the other way around: Privacy needs more protection.

After determining that the common good (or privacy) needs shoring up, the second criterion examines whether that goal can be achieved without recalibrating privacy. (Or conversely, can privacy be enhanced without recalibrating the common good?) My examination of HIV testing of infants shows that the need for such testing can be reduced by encouraging pregnant women to consent to be tested and treated but that such voluntary measures do not suffice and that hence some intrusion into privacy may be justified.

Similarly, although child sex offenders might benefit from therapy, that possibility is not sufficient to obviate the need for Megan's Laws or even stronger public safety measures. While we use voluntarily more and more ID cards, they are rather inadequate because they do not satisfy a primary public safety need—namely, that all people be required to identify themselves when asked to do so by public authorities. And as we saw, we cannot possibly rely on voluntary disclosure of encrypted messages. We also observed that medical privacy could benefit greatly from the employment of new technologies and social arrangements, but that these will not obviate the need for changes in law and public policy. In short, second-criterion treatments have a role to play in all five public policies studied here, but they must be supplemented by third-criterion interventions.

The third criterion points to the merit of minimally intrusive interventions. With HIV testing of infants, we saw that the legalization of disclosure of infant HIV test results to the mothers is vital and not overly broad. Courts have considered Megan's Laws and determined that they do not entail excessive state interventions; indeed, I demonstrated that these laws are too weak to serve their purpose. As far as ID cards are concerned, we have not even seriously considered making the legal, policy, and normative changes that would allow the introduction of universal identifiers. And my analysis found that enabling public authorities to engage in decryption only under conditions very similar to those under which phones can be legally tapped, in service to public safety, to be reasonable and not excessive. Finally, enhancing medical privacy, as I noted, would require some additional legislation.

The fourth criterion asks whether the suggested changes in law and public policy should include treatments of undesirable side effects of the needed interventions. These measures are required both to protect people from unnecessary injury and to sustain public support for the needed policies. Thus, the HIV testing of infants and disclosure of the results to their mothers requires new and stricter measures to protect the confidentiality of medical records; Megan's Laws require extensive community education to prevent vigilantism; and the introduction of universal identifiers should be accompanied by an elaborate system of ombudspersons to correct and protect individuals from mistakes and abuses.

Application of the four balancing criteria, as the preceding analyses have sought to show, helps ensure that correctives to a society's course are both truly needed and not excessive. True, even when these criteria are applied, one cannot pinpoint with complete precision the proper or optimal course to follow. Societies have rather crude guidance mechanisms,[3] and may need constantly to adjust their course as they oversteer first in one direction and then in the other. However, the criteria do provide a basic measure of the extent of the imbalance between privacy and the common good, and the direction and nature of the necessary corrections.

The preceding explorations of five public policy areas have further illuminated the four criteria by suggesting that, far from being mutually exclusive, treatments and interventions can often complement one another. For instance, self-regulation has been urged on private actors such as marketers on the Internet (a second-criterion treatment) as a way to protect the privacy of consumers. Corporations have been urged to post their privacy policy on their websites. Critics argue that such self-regulation has little effect because there is no way to ensure compliance. Champions of self-regulation have responded with the suggestion that such sites could be audited (a second-criterion treatment), but they also have agreed that corporations that violate their posted policy may be considered to have engaged in fraudulent business practices and will be subject to legal claims (a third-criterion intervention).[4] Many other examples come to mind in which it is better to consider combining treatments and interventions rather than view them as stark alternatives.

In what might be called the "privacy paradox," most civil libertarians and many other privacy advocates keep railing about third-criterion alternatives, as they view Big Brother—the government—as the enemy of privacy. As Justice William O. Douglas stated in *Osborn v. United States*, "We are rapidly entering the age of no privacy, where everyone is open to surveillance at all times; where there are no secrets from the government."[5] I have found, however, that to the extent that privacy is grossly and wantonly violated in contemporary American society, more often than not it is violated by privacy merchants rather than by Big Brother government. Nowhere is this more true than in the area of medical privacy (Chapter 5), but this fact is also evident in the uses of new, huge databases that contain detailed information about numerous aspects of the lifestyles of most Americans and are maintained for profit-making purposes (Chapter 4). As a result, privacy advocates have sought to stop massive and encompassing privacy violations by these profiteers—by drawing on new *legislation*—that is, on the government.[6] Moreover, my analysis of infant HIV testing, Megan's Laws, and encryption—all areas in which the government is involved—did not find intrusions into people's privacy that are not justified by concerns for public safety and public health.

The tendency to allow privacy considerations to take precedence over concerns for public safety and health is not accidental. It reflects fundamental conceptions that are deeply embedded in our civic culture, public policies, and jurisprudence. The evidence presented in this book points to the need for a different conception of privacy, one that accords it equal standing with the common good, without privileging either value.

To reconceptualize privacy, a highly revered right, may seem offensive, almost sacrilegious. We traditionally view individual rights as strong moral claims with universal appeal, indeed we perceive them as inalienable rights. Although we also realize that individual rights were formulated under certain historical conditions, we tend to conceive of these formulations as truths rather than mores fashioned for a given time that are open to amendment as conditions change.

I argue in the following pages that privacy is a contingent concept. Although some vague notion of privacy exists in most, if not all, societies,[7] the specific way we treat privacy in our law and culture is a recent phenomenon, and one that has already been recast at various times. In other words, privacy is hardly a near-sacred concept that cannot be reformulated.

I also show that the governing formulation of privacy in our society and time treats it as an unbounded good, privileging it over the common good. This conception was well suited to the sociohistorical conditions that prevailed from the formulation of privacy as a legal concept until roughly 1960. However, in the wake of the rise of radical individualism between 1960 and the 1990s, a new conception of privacy is called for, one that does not privilege privacy over the common good but rather is open to balance with concerns for social responsibilities, a communitarian concept.[8]

PRIVACY ARGUMENTS REEXAMINED

A reexamination of the often-told legal history of privacy in American society helps to illuminate the nature of the arguments used to "extrapolate" privacy as a right from the common law and the Constitution.

In examining the arguments that were used to formulate the legal doctrines that support privacy in American law, I discuss three stages of development: pre-1890 (utilizing principles derived from property rights to protect privacy); 1890 to 1965 (generally considered the era during which a right to privacy was developed, largely as a part of tort law); and post-1965 (a period that has seen a major expansion of the right to privacy, particularly with regard to its constitutional basis). Although my discussion focuses on legal concepts, I cannot stress enough that, as the preceding analyses indicate, these concepts have parallels in civic culture and play a major role in the decisions of policymakers.

Before 1890 American society, like many others, had a vague social concept of privacy, albeit one that was not embedded in a distinct legal doctrine or constitutional right.[9] Although there were several legal cases defending some aspect of what later would be called privacy, these typically relied on the well-established right to private property.[10] For example, harming a person's reputation through the revelation of private details was deemed legally redressable because it was thought to do damage to something one owned (i.e., one's reputation), rather than because it was viewed as an invasion of privacy.[11]

The right to private property was, in turn, treated as semisacred: a reflection of a natural law, an inalienable right, and an unmitigated, or at least strongly privileged, good. John Locke, who heavily influenced American thinking on these matters at the time, wrote that property is based in "an original law of nature" that "still takes place" even though societies "have made and multiplied positive laws [laws created by humans] to determine property."[12]

Classical liberals did recognize that the rights of an individual could be asserted only up to the point where such exercise intruded on the liberties of others, and thus individual rights were, in a sense, "limited." But such limitations were not, as a rule, considered for the common good. It was thus typically assumed that property owners were free to do with their property as they deemed fit unless and until their actions plainly impinged on the rights of others. Even then, the burden of proof fell on those who would limit the use of private property, and no principled concessions were recognized to serve socially formulated conceptions of the good.

The next marker in the legal history of privacy is an 1890 essay by Samuel D. Warren and Louis D. Brandeis,[13] which served as the basis for hundreds of legal cases in the century that followed and is considered "the most influential law review article ever published."[14] Warren and Brandeis advanced the novel claim that the right to privacy is conceptually distinct from other freedoms, particularly the right to private property. (As others have observed, the authors were far more explicit in rejecting the notion that privacy is derived from other rights than they were in articulating any specific legal foundation for privacy.[15])

Warren and Brandeis framed their argument in terms of "the right to be let alone," a right the two assumed to be self-evident. Indeed, Warren and Brandeis referred to the "precincts of private and domestic life"—implying the capability to isolate oneself from public spheres and the community—as "sacred,"[16] a term typically employed to designate values or precepts of the highest authority, ones that should not be touched, let alone reined in. (It is indicative of the reverence for rights in general and for privacy in particular that the term "sacred" is frequently employed by people who otherwise draw on no religious images, terminologies, or beliefs.[17]) As invoked, the right to be let alone stands supreme and apart from other considerations; it presumes that all people can be left alone as much as they desire—completely if they so prefer—without restricting other persons' abilities to exercise their own right to be left alone to the fullest extent. Nor is there any apparent recognition that if the members of a community exercise this liberty in full, the common good will be shortchanged.[18]

Later authorities referred to privacy as an "inalienable right,"[19] thereby denoting its powerful claim and trump standing. (Trumps are defined as "reasons that can be played against any and all ethical concerns."[20]) Indeed, as Justice Holmes stated: "Rights tend to declare themselves absolute to their logical extreme."[21] As the right to privacy is viewed as an inalienable right, it does not yield to the common good. "Moreover," William Lund observed, "any citizen who manages to get an interest wrapped in the cloak of a right appears to have an absolute claim against other considerations."[22] Henkin has made the communitarian point that "consideration has focused on defining the private right of privacy, with little regard to our other balance, the competing 'public good.'" He added that although this lack of balance characterizes applications of the Bill of Rights generally, the public good has been given particularly short shrift in the area of privacy.[23]

Moreover, there has been a strong tendency to treat privacy either as a cardinal element of autonomy (or liberty), or to treat these concepts as if they were synonymous with privacy, further extending the reverence for privacy. Charles Fried adds that "men feel that invasion of that right injures them in their very humanity," and in regard to respect, love, friendship, and trust, "without privacy they [respect, love, etc.] are simply inconceivable."[24]

Others have claimed that privacy is intimately associated with our most profound values, our understanding of what it means to be an autonomous moral agent capable of self-reflection and choice, and that its violation is "demeaning to individuality [and] an affront to personal dignity," that is, its violation offends the core of Western values.[25] Jean Cohen adds that "a constitutionally protected right to personal privacy is indispensable to any modern conception of freedom."[26]

All of these arguments paint a picture of the right to privacy as an unmitigated good, at least as a strongly privileged value. Indeed, few individualists (a term used here to refer to civil libertarians, libertarians, classical liberals, and contemporary classical liberals) even broach the question of whether there can be excessive privacy. Avishai Margalit, for instance, simply states that "the institutions of a decent society must not encroach upon personal privacy," recognizing no principled situations in which the common good might require some limitations on privacy.[27] Glen O. Robinson points out that, in "controversies over regulating communities and community activities, most legal scholars and judges start with a [classical] liberal bias."[28] This legal approach is particularly well summarized by Stanley I. Benn:

> The liberal . . . claims not merely a private capacity—an area of action in which he is not responsible to the state for what he does so long as he respects certain minimal rights of others; he claims further that this is the residual category, that the onus is on anyone who claims he is accountable. . . . There is room for a good deal of disagreement about the extent to which considerations like those of general economic well-being, social equality, or national security justify pressing back the frontiers of the private, and thus holding men responsible for the way they conduct their daily business. For the liberal, however, every step he is forced to take in that direction counts as retreat from a desirable state of affairs, one in which, because men may please themselves, what they are about is properly no one's business but their own.[29]

The third stage of the development of the legal foundations of privacy is commonly recognized as commencing with cases such as *Griswold v. Connecticut* (1965), *Eisenstadt v. Baird* (1972), and *Roe v. Wade* (1973), all of which deal with reproductive choices. Using the early 1960s as a baseline, the period before the cases that lay the foundations of a constitutional right to privacy were decided, one sees that the prevailing conceptions of the common good were very strongly privileged and left relatively little room for considerations of privacy and autonomy. Thus, the use, distribution, and sale of contraceptives was outlawed even for married couples. Abortion was banned by law in most states; it was allowed only to save the life of the mother.

Following these landmark court decisions of the 1960s and 1970s, the situation changed drastically. To a large extent, age-old prohibitions that had been imposed in the name of what was considered the common good were struck down. A new constitutional conception of privacy, a right that is not so much as mentioned in the Constitution, was generated—and privileged.

Griswold, the first of these reproductive choice cases, is commonly credited with establishing a general constitutional right to privacy. In that case, the Supreme Court ruled that a Connecticut statute forbidding the use of contraceptives violated the right of marital privacy. Thus, overnight, behavior that had been banned (as far as the law was concerned) was transformed into one that married couples could engage in without limitations. Privacy was now honored. (To note that no limitations were set on this new right is not to suggest that they should have been set, but rather to highlight the dramatic nature of the reversal of the previous position.)[30]

This new right was soon extended. In *Eisenstadt*, the Court went further and invalidated a ban on the *distribution* of contraceptives, even to unmarried couples. In a subsequent case, *Carey v. Population Services International* (1977), limitations on the sale of contraceptives to minors were removed.[31] In these cases, too, the Court did not introduce or explicitly acknowledge any qualifications or limitations on the liberty in question. Protection for privacy had become almost absolute. As Louis Henkin observes, "The Court paid virtually no attention to the State's possible purpose or motive in outlawing contraception."[32] And although *Griswold* was limited to the use of contraceptives by married couples, *Eisenstadt* created a new, much broader conception of privacy, that of the individual: A person could carry this right anywhere; it was a freedom that would no longer be confined to one's bedroom or house.[33]

To reiterate, I am *not* suggesting that the various prohibitions on the use and sale of contraceptives or on abortion should have been allowed to stand. My argument only points to the unbounded nature of the position embraced. No limits on the right to privacy in the name of some other consideration—for instance, respect for community values or special considerations for parents' responsibilities for minors—were allowed to stand.

In *Roe v. Wade*, the Court further expanded the right of privacy by striking down bans on abortion. This case, however, was arguably somewhat less comprehensive than the others. Although the Court did not let stand any limitations on terminating pregnancies, it explicitly stated that it rejected the unbounded approach and formulated some criteria under which states could ban abortion. Justice Harry Blackmun wrote:

> Some amici argue that the woman's right is absolute and she is entitled to terminate her pregnancy at whatever time, in whatever way, and for whatever reason she alone chooses. With this we do not agree. . . . A state may properly assert important interests in safeguarding health, in maintaining medical standards, and in protecting potential life.[34]

The Court ruled that the states may override a woman's decision "whether or not to terminate her pregnancy" if the state's interest is "compelling."[35] And the Court, by introducing distinctions between the trimesters of pregnancy, indirectly legitimated more regulation of the third trimester than of the second, and more of the second than of the first.

One may side with those who believe the Court should have allowed the bans on abortion to stand or with those who hold that the ruling was too restrictive; neither position alters the observation here about the basic nature of the argument at issue: *Roe v. Wade* is an important case in which a behavior that had previously been controlled by the state was freed to be subject to personal choice.

In short, the approach to privacy that evolved, first in tort law and then in Supreme Court decisions concerning reproductive choice cases, treats privacy as an unbounded good. In its more moderate form, this approach lays the burden of proof on those who seek consideration for other claims, thus treating the common good at best as secondary.

HISTORICAL CONTEXT FOR THE PRIVILEGING OF PRIVACY

The nature of these individualist arguments is best understood in the historical context in which they arose. The extrapolation of a legal right to privacy from common law cases, from newly fashioned arguments, and ultimately from the Constitution took place late in the long development of legal individual rights, a process that was itself an indication of the growing value accorded to individual dignity and liberty. Indeed, one can read the writings of John Locke, Adam Smith, and some of those of John Stuart Mill as arguments for individual rights and liberty that were formulated in authoritarian and excessively communal historical periods and as arguments for rolling back extensive and oppressive societal controls imposed by both the state and the community. Not surprisingly, social philosophers whose societies experienced these highly restrictive conditions did not concern themselves with the danger of legitimizing individual rights to excess—no more than one is concerned about overusing a town's water supply in the depths of the rainy season after decades of more than ample rainfall, indeed flooding.

Historically, the formulation of privacy is a late addition to the long list of rights. Its development took place several generations after the first recognition in American law of the rights to free speech, freedom of association, and freedom of worship, among others. In fact, Warren and Brandeis are explicit about this point in their 1890 article. They open their renowned essay with a discussion of their belief that it was time for the common law to "grow to meet the demands of society," much as it had done on previous occasions when social circumstances had shifted.[36] The same approach is reflected in the work of T. H. Marshall, who viewed Western history as a relentless march toward increasingly expansive spheres of rights, growing from legal to political to socioeconomic rights, with little concern or suggestion that rights might be overextended or intrude on other common goods.[37]

SAME ARGUMENTS—IN A NEW WORLD

Contemporary champions of privacy often still employ arguments that treat privacy as either an unbounded or privileged good. Although they may recognize that rights in general, and privacy in particular, are significantly better protected in contemporary America than they were in the 1890s and earlier, contemporary individualists nonetheless marshal arguments similar to those of their ideological ancestors because they continue to fear that the state is, or may grow to be, overbearing. Moreover, these individualists are concerned that new technological and social developments may lead to the diminution, if not the destruction, of privacy. Legal scholars as well as others make statements like: "The dossier and computer bank threaten us with victimization and persecution by unscrupulous, intolerant, or merely misunderstanding officials." "Trade-offs where privacy has been sacrificed are now so common that, for all practical purposes, privacy no longer exists."[38]

The negative consequences, however, of treating privacy and other individual rights as sacrosanct have been largely ignored by those who draw on legal conceptions fashioned in earlier ages. As has been demonstrated by Robert Bellah and his associates, Mary Ann Glendon, and myself, American society after 1960 entered an era of growing individualism and neglect of the common good; expressive individualism (of the countercultural variety) was followed by instrumental individualism (of the sort championed by Margaret Thatcher and Ronald Reagan and other laissez-faire conservative thinkers).[39] The realms of rights, private choice, self-interest, and entitlement were expanded and extended, but corollary social responsibilities and commitments to the common good were neglected, with negative consequences such as the deterioration of public safety and public health. The new sociohistorical context, as we see it, calls for greater dedication to the common good and less expansive privileging of individual rights.[40]

THE QUEST FOR A COMMUNITARIAN BALANCE

There is no widely accepted communitarian conception, let alone definition, of privacy. I suggest that a sound communitarian treatment of privacy views it as the realm in which an actor (either a person or a group, such as a couple) can *legitimately* act without disclosure and accountability to others. Privacy thus is a *societal license* that exempts a category of acts (including thoughts and emotions) from communal, public, and governmental scrutiny.[41] For instance, contemporary American society largely exempts from scrutiny most acts that occur inside the home, especially the bedroom, and to a lesser extent those that occur within the automobile. Exceptions include child abuse, domestic violence, and illegal drug use. Even in these situations, respect for privacy typically requires that the state act only after the consequences of acts that took place in the home or auto have become visible outside the space exempted from scrutiny—for example, when a violent fight inside a house is heard from the outside, or when a child comes to school or a physician's office showing clear signs of abuse.

In addition to legitimately exempted action,[42] privacy encompasses behaviors that members of a particular social entity are positively *expected*, by prevailing social mores or laws, to carry out so as not to be readily scrutinizable. For instance, defecating is expected or required to take place out of sight in many societies. Such privacy aims to shore up the common good or certain social virtues (modesty, for instance) rather than individual autonomy. Mandated privacy is reflected in the so-called moral laws that prohibit people from bathing nude on many public beaches, limit public drinking in some communities, and so on. This is a topic rarely treated and not developed here, but it deserves much additional study for those who are concerned about the good, and not merely a civic, society.[43]

In many societies public spaces are scrutinized to ensure that conduct and acts characterized as private are not carried out there. For example, the moral squads of Iran's police ensure that women's hair and bodies are exposed only at home. This kind of privacy can be referred to as mandated or positive privacy.

Considering its normative nature, mandated privacy is, on the face of it, not a right but a social obligation. This kind of privacy is at issue in discussions of, for instance, bans on nudity on beaches; privacy in this context is typically treated, however, as a protection of the right to be nude rather than of the social requirement to be clothed. Given the prevalence of rights talk, one should not be surprised to find that positive privacy rarely is mentioned, let alone studied, in the vast literature on legal privacy.[44] It is certainly a topic that deserves a treatment all of its on.

Many discussions of privacy ignore the normative component and simply define privacy empirically as an avoidance or absence of surveillance, the kind of protection a wall or curtain provides.[45] In contrast, the definition of privacy provided here has a normative element because it includes an exemption from scrutiny and, in some instances, the requirement to close to view or hearing those elements considered normatively appropriate or inappropriate by the relevant society. At issue, then, is not merely whether there are barriers that block visibility and audibility, but also which barriers are legitimate and which are not. The concept of privacy implicitly denotes the existence of *legitimate* barriers; illegitimate barriers are seen as fostering concealment or secrecy, terms that imply illicit, if not illegal, behavior. That is, both the scope of privacy and the nature of the specific acts that are encompassed by definitions of privacy (e.g., sexual behavior, voting) rather than excluded (e.g., office mail, including e-mail, the private lives of public figures) reflect a society's particular values. I discuss the implications of this point later.

I will draw on a critical distinction in the following pages between accountability (matters the government is or is not entitled to "watch") and control (the "decisional" realm, choices the government is or is not entitled to make).[46] But let us look first at the roots of this suggested definition of privacy in communitarian thinking and in the sociohistorical context.

Roots in Responsive Communitarianism

The definition of privacy I advance here reflects a particular brand of communitarian thinking sometimes referred to as responsive (or new) communitarianism.[47] Responsive communitarians seek to balance individual rights with social responsibilities, and individuality with community. They differ from early communitarians such as Ferdinand Tönnies and contemporary Asian communitarians, who celebrate community and authority but ignore (at best) individual rights.[48] Responsive communitarians do not view community or social harmony as an unbounded or privileged good but rather treat social formulations of the common good as values that need to be balanced with concerns for individual rights and subgroup autonomy.[49]

The responsive communitarian approach reflects historical circumstances decidedly different from those Warren and Brandeis faced in the 1890s. It evolved in response to the dramatic shift in American society between 1960 and 1990 toward egoism after decades of strong communalism and even a measure of authoritarianism (especially in the treatment of minorities and women). During the 1960s the United States experienced various social movements that emphasized many previously neglected rights, particularly in the areas of race and gender. Such movements also placed new limitations on police powers (e.g., the *Miranda* ruling in 1966 and the introduction of guidelines limiting the FBI in the 1970s) and glorified countercultural expressions of self, which often involved the flouting of traditional communal mores. These movements were followed by the celebration of self-interest during the 1980s. What started as an individualistic correction of excessive communalism led to excessive individualism, wanton manufacturing of presumed rights (such as a right to a credit card or a right to use the men's room if there is even a small line in front of the women's room), neglect of social responsibility, and the waning of commitments to the common good.[50] At this point, to move toward a state of equilibrium required a communal shoring-up—hence the rise of the new communitarian movement in the early 1990s.[51]

The simple image of a bicycle rider who must constantly adjust her balance captures the essence of the responsive communitarian public philosophy: The rider pulls the bicycle back to the center when it tilts too far to the left or to the right.

It follows that the necessary societal adjustments in the scope and specific nature of any right—in the case of privacy, how much and what kinds of conduct are legitimately exempted from social scrutiny?—are deeply influenced by their sociohistorical context. Consequently, privacy is not treated in this paradigm as a good one seeks to maximize in and of itself.[52] Privacy cannot be extended to the point where it undermines the common good; conversely, duties set to maintain social order cannot be expanded to the point where they destroy privacy. Thus, policymakers and citizens who advocate the communitarian ideal of equilibrium between privacy and the common good may seek to limit privacy when doing so will yield major gains in public safety and health and no viable alternatives are available. By the same token, people who live in societies where their mail is scrutinized by the police, their phones are tapped without warrant, and files are kept about their sexual proclivities may (and should) legitimately fight to expand the scope and protection of privacy. Moreover, within the same society and time period, achieving balance may necessitate better protection of privacy in some social spheres (for instance, acting to stem the disclosure of sensitive medical information to employers) while curtailing it in others (for example, requiring individuals who have the lives of others directly in their hands, such as school bus drivers, to be drug tested).

Fred Cate puts it especially well:

> Privacy is not an absolute. It is contextual and subjective. . . . Moreover, the privacy interests at stake in any given situation may vary from the profound to the trivial, and that valuation will depend significantly on who is making it. For example, if privacy protects the combination to my safe or the location of a key to my house, it is extraordinarily valuable to me and, in most circumstances, to society more broadly, which shares my interest in avoiding theft and other criminal conduct. . . . If, however, privacy permits me to avoid paying taxes or obtain employment for which I am not qualified, it may be very valuable to me, but extremely costly to society as a whole. It is clear, therefore, that neither privacy val-

> ues nor costs are absolute. . . . What is needed is a balance, of which privacy is a part. Determining what that part is in any specific context requires a careful evaluation of subjective, variable and competing interests.[53]

Alan Westin observes:

> Each individual must, within the larger context of his culture, his status, and his personal situation, make a continuous adjustment between his needs for solitude and companionship; for intimacy and general social intercourse; for anonymity and responsible participation in society; for reserve and disclosure.[54]

Although the detailed justification of each effort to achieve or restore balance is, by necessity, complex, the basic approach is straightforward: Privacy is to be treated as a value that needs to be balanced with concerns for the common good, and the question of which of these two needs shoring up depends on the sociohistorical context.

SOURCES OF LEGITIMACY FOR PRIVACY: ALTERNATIVE PUBLIC PHILOSOPHIES

The responsive communitarian public philosophy has strong foundations in social science and social philosophy. It builds on the sociological observation that although ideologies can be structured around a single organizing principle—like liberty, or a particular social virtue—societies must balance values that are not fully compatible.[55]

Furthermore, the responsive communitarian position reflects the finding that the scope and legal standing of privacy, like that of private property, is contingent on sociohistorical context.[56] The right to private property, the initial basis for the legal concern with privacy, fails to provide a strong or privileged ground for privacy because property itself is a social construct rather than a natural or innate quality of objects.[57] Different societies define different objects and spaces as legitimate subjects of private—as opposed to public—ownership. In the early kibbutzim, all property, even the shirt on one's back, was considered communal. Grave ideological debates and condemnation arose when members of kibbutzim started to get their own coffee cups, which they kept in their rooms. In this context, the onus rested on those who sought an exception from the prevailing rule to justify the right to hold an object privately. And certain countries define land, certain minerals, and beaches as inappropriate for private ownership. Large tracts of land in Israel are owned by the state or the Jewish National Fund and can be leased for forty-nine years, with an option to extend for another forty-nine, but they cannot be owned outright.[58] All these examples make it clear that the definition of property is itself based on socioeconomic facts and on that which a society considers legitimate, and hence cannot be simply an expression of some overarching, universal "nature." In short, relying on private property rights to serve as a legal basis for privacy hardly gives this right the privileged standing that individualists claim for it.[59]

It is reported that Warren and Brandeis's fashioning of privacy as a legal concept was a response to an increasingly intrusive press, which was giving wide circulation and a semblance of credibility to gossip by spreading it to large groups.[60] As for the post-*Griswold* era, it is commonplace to note that privacy is not even mentioned in the Constitution; rather, it was derived from "penumbras" and "emanations" of the specifically detailed guarantees of the Bill of Rights.[61]

Carl Schneider put it so effectively that I quote him at length:

> The case [*Roe*] turns on the constitutional "right to privacy," a right inferred from the fourteenth amendment's provision that no state may deprive a person of life, liberty, or property without due process of law. Since little in the language, structure, or intent of the clause establishes the nature or limits of that right, since the Court has never defined those limits, since the right has little to do with "privacy" in the colloquial sense, and since the right of privacy is a "greedy" one, the right has long seemed menacingly capacious. The Court in *Roe* opens its discussion of the right to privacy with a sentence that acknowledges that the Constitution mentions no such right. In its next two sentences, the Court attempts to identify the origin of the right:
>
> "In a line of decisions . . . going back *perhaps* as far as . . . [1891], the Court has recognized that a right of personal privacy, *or* a guarantee of certain areas *or* zones of privacy, does exist under the Constitution. In varying contexts, the Court *or* individual Justices have, indeed, found *at least* the roots of that right in the First Amendment . . . ; in the Fourth

> and Fifth Amendments . . . ; in the penumbras of the Bill of Rights . . . ; in the Ninth Amendment . . . ; *or* in the concept of liberty guaranteed by the first section of the Fourteenth Amendment. . . ."
>
> After this disjunctive jumble of precedent (which may establish no more than "the roots of that right"), and after adding that the right has "some extension to activities relating to" various family law issues, the Court closes its attempt to define and defend the right, having established neither the principle that justifies nor the principle that limits it.
>
> Nevertheless, the Court next says, "This right of privacy . . . is broad enough to encompass a woman's decision whether or not to terminate her pregnancy." *Why* that right is "broad enough" the Court does not say. The Court does follow this sentence with a list of "detriments" a woman would suffer who could not have an abortion, and one may infer that it is the severity of the detriments that gives rise to the right. But while the Court cannot mean that "detriments" create rights—since all statutes impose "detriments," and since most "detriments" do not give rise to a legal right—the Court does not say why detriments create a right here, or why these particular detriments create this particular right.[62]

Others have used harsher terms in describing the Court's finding of a constitutional right to privacy. Hyman Gross, for instance, declares that the right of privacy defined in *Griswold* was "a malformation of constitutional law which thrives because of the conceptual vacuum surrounding the legal notions of privacy."[63] Indeed, Justice Douglas's reasoning reportedly provoked "not only giggles but guffaws" by clerks in the office of the concurring Justice Goldberg.[64]

It is often suggested that Douglas went through such legal contortions to avoid the charge that he was relying on substantive due process—the original sin of constitutional interpretation. Indeed, Douglas took great pains at the beginning of his opinion to distance his reasoning from this discredited doctrine.

The lack of a clear basis for an absolute or "natural" right of privacy brings us again to the idea that privacy varies with context. Social scientific comparative studies leave no doubt that the scope of what is considered a matter of privacy varies greatly not only across societies but also within a given society over time, including democratic societies.[65] In Britain, for example, privacy is much more restricted in many social domains than it is in the United States. Camera surveillance of public spaces and searches of bodies and belongings are carried out much more readily there. At the same time, Britain protects privacy to a greater extent in the domain of libel law.[66] On the Continent, people are routinely required to carry some form of identification and to identify themselves at police request, without any special cause. In other parts of Western Europe privacy is a highly contingent right whose scope and standing vary sharply with the sociohistorical context.[67]

THE FOURTH AMENDMENT AS THE CORNERSTONE FOR PRIVACY LAW

The communitarian conception of privacy advanced here is not founded on a stretched interpretation of a curious amalgam of sundry pieces of various constitutional rights but instead rests squarely on the legal conception contained in the Fourth Amendment. In this amendment, *the Constitution provides a clear and strong foundation for acts that serve the common good and take precedence over privacy* considerations by establishing a whole category of legitimate, "reasonable" searches. In effect, this amendment is the only one that explicitly qualifies a right, although the Second Amendment does as well, in some interpretations. A comparison of the texts of the First and Fourth Amendments underscores this point: If the Fourth had been written in the same strongly privileging language as the First, it would have read: "*Congress shall make no law* violating the right of the people to be secure . . . against searches and seizures. . . . "

The *extent* to which the Fourth Amendment does not privilege privacy as much as the legal texts examined earlier is open to interpretation. On the face of it, the first clause seems balanced between privacy and legitimation of reasonable searches. The amendment's further requirement that "no Warrants shall issue, but upon probable cause, supported by Oath of affirmation, and particularly describing the place to be searched, and the persons or things to be seized," can be read merely as providing a mechanism for sorting out which searches are unreasonable or reasonable, rather than further restricting them. Admittedly, if one applies the criterion of original intent it leaves little doubt that the Fourth Amendment was conceived as one of a list of rights, meant to protect individuals from an overpowering government. The same holds for a fair number of historical interpretations and an even larger number of court cases that have very much tended to put the burden of proof on those who sought to limit privacy rather than the other way around. However, changed historical conditions, the rise of radical individualism, and the erosion of authority[68] have already led to a much more even-handed interpretation of the Fourth Amendment in our own time. More and more legal searches are conducted for which neither warrants nor even specific suspicion are required. Examples include drug testing, screening gates in airports, and field sobriety checkpoints.[69] This is a trend that one might argue should be further extended to make future interpretations of the Fourth Amendment more even-handed, although obviously we should not automatically favor every single case that points in this direction.

When all is said and done, however, it is debatable whether current interpretations of the Fourth Amendment are even-handed or simply less privileging of privacy than other governing texts. In either case, the treatment of privacy under the Fourth Amendment is closer to a balanced approach than the jurisprudence that grew out of the reasoning of Warren and Brandeis and the reproductive choice cases. This balance is what a communitarian position calls for.

The Fourth Amendment is mentioned as an afterthought in many earlier discussions of the evolution of the legal doctrines of a right of privacy,[70] and even those that are dedicated to analyzing the constitutional basis of privacy either give it short shrift or do not mention it at all.[71] The focus instead is on the cases involving reproductive choices because, it is stated repeatedly, the Supreme Court did not treat privacy as an independent right before *Griswold.* Rather, the decisions in those earlier cases treated privacy concerns through other rights, with different rights supporting the claim in different cases.[72] In *Boyd v. United States,* for instance, the Court held that the Fourth and the Fifth Amendments protected papers as within a person's "zone of privacy" but did not treat privacy as a distinct right.[73]

The question may be asked: Why did the Supreme Court, when it did fashion a constitutional right of privacy in *Griswold* and the subsequent reproductive choice cases, not rely squarely on the Fourth Amendment? We need not inquire into either the scholarly and normative motives of those involved or the institutional and doctrinal constraints on them to be able to discern one compelling reason: A straightforward reliance on the Fourth Amendment would not have led to free choice—the right of a person to control her reproductive life that the Court was evolving in *Griswold*, *Eisenstadt*, and *Roe*. In the Fourth Amendment, privacy is conceived as the right legitimately to avoid being subject to public *scrutiny*, to being "watched" by the government—not the right to *control* the action at stake, to make the driving decisions. Searches make public what had been kept private, in the sense of being protected from disclosure. They help determine whether that which was deliberately or unwittingly kept from scrutiny is a matter of subordination, concealment, or even illegality and therefore no longer subject to privacy rights. Thus, if a person is suspected of having purchased a stolen painting, a search (based on a proper warrant) helps determine whether this suspicion is valid. The question as to who has a right to own (to control) the painting must be resolved by other means and considerations.[74]

Usually, the chief criticism of *Griswold* et al. is that reproductive rights are poorly founded on privacy grounds (or that there are no such rights); the argument advanced here runs the other way: *A concept of privacy fashioned to fit reproductive rights is not soundly crafted.* I will justify this statement after making several more points about the public philosophy that emanates from the Fourth Amendment; here I would add only that I favor reproductive rights but join others who hold that these rights would be much better protected if they were based on different legal grounds than those currently used to support them.

My examination of the Fourth Amendment seeks to make one observation and one observation only: That the Fourth Amendment provides a conception of privacy that does not privilege it. I do not seek to explore the many other important issues that arise from studying the specifics of the relationship of the Fourth Amendment to privacy. This would entail examination of the text, the intentions of the founding fathers,[75] and Supreme Court interpretations of the amendment, specifically in *Boyd v. United State*, *Olmstead v. United States*, and

Katz v. United States. A fine place to start would be the many law review articles on privacy and the Fourth Amendment.[76] There is only one observation, however, that I wish to make here about the Fourth Amendment: It provides a balanced conception of privacy.[77]

The public philosophy that emanates from the Fourth Amendment is an enormous subject that can be visited only briefly here. Although the jurisprudence evolved by Warren and Brandeis and those who have built on them focuses on a privileging of the "right to be let alone," the conception reflected in the Fourth Amendment suggests that we can identify a significant category of situations in which a violation of privacy is reasonable and serves the common good. Legal scholars correctly stress, however, that the Fourth Amendment deals with the relations of citizens to the government, not to one another. I would merely suggest that the idea of balance contained in the Fourth Amendment can also be applied to relations between private individuals.[78]

Think of the many situations in which one private party searches the property of another, and the question arises: Is this behavior legitimate, ethically speaking? Although these are not searches in the Fourth Amendment sense, because they are not conducted by the government, they clearly are searches as commonly understood. Cases in point would be shippers who, without consent or prior notice, open packages entrusted to them by private parties, or the husband who rummages through his wife's office drawers. It seems clear that these are acts whose legitimacy ought to be judged in part on the basis of the extent of the common good served, not just the extent of the violation of privacy. Thus, if the shippers are seeking to ensure that no explosives are being shipped (assuming there is no law requiring them to so examine the packages), and they do not unnecessarily display or disclose what they see when examining packages entrusted to them (for instance, they do not call the attention of coworkers to sexual toys they come across), such an examination would be fundamentally different from the act of opening parcels to satisfy voyeuristic curiosity.

One important person-to-person situation in which we are justified in attempting to balance privacy with the common good is the media's violations of people's privacy in order to keep the public informed and to invigorate the marketplace of ideas.

In many other situations that do not involve a direct government-citizen relationship, the common good is properly privileged over privacy, including situations in which client-psychiatrist confidentiality can legally be set aside, mail addressed to someone else can be opened, and polygraph tests can be conducted. For example, in *Tarasoff v. Regents of the University of California*, a California judge ruled that mental health professionals have a duty to provide adequate warning if a patient threatens the life of a third party during counseling sessions.[79] At the same time, courts have staunchly protected patient-psychiatrist confidentiality in cases where such compelling interest cannot be shown, even extending such confidentiality rights to communications with social workers.[80]

Last but not least, it should be noted that the Fourth Amendment model reflects the issues raised by the tension between privacy and the common good. That is to say, it reflects the profound tension between two core American visions: the virtue and public-spiritedness fostered by republicanism, and the liberty and individualism championed by classical liberalism. It is a conflict between those who see American society as a community dedicated to fostering a specific set of social virtues (or social formulations of the good) and those who see it as one that promotes the free choices and actions of individuals (and favors only individual formulations of the good).[81] While each of these camps has claimed that it represents the true conception of American values, and while in some ages one or the other of these two conceptions has been stressed more, the uneasy conjunction of the two is what constitutes the American creed, the core set of values that guides American society and nurtures its laws. It follows that whenever American society tilts too far in one direction or the other, balance needs to be restored by shoring up the neglected core value.[82] The same holds for privacy: Balance can be achieved by redefining what is considered reasonable versus unreasonable under the Fourth Amendment.

PRIVATE CHOICE VERSUS PUBLIC CONTROL: A PIVOTAL DISTINCTION

Making the conception embedded in the Fourth Amendment the cornerstone of the public philosophy of privacy allows us to limit privacy to the bounds of legitimate scrutiny. Doing so clears away a great deal of intellectual, normative, and legal confusion that has arisen because the Supreme Court created a right of privacy that encompasses both the right to be exempt from scrutiny and the right to make choices—that is, the right to be exempt from state control.[83] The inclusion of decisional matters in the constitutional conception of privacy has been criticized by a number of authorities, including strong supporters of reproductive rights of women, such as Ruth Bader Ginsburg.[84]

The important distinction between exemption from control (granting a freedom to choose) and exemption from scrutiny is highlighted by the very behavior at issue in the reproductive choice cases. The question is not whether couples should be expected to make decisions concerning the use of contraception, or women concerning abortions, in public view. Indeed, those whose values are offended by such behavior would be even more perturbed if such conduct were not carried out behind closed doors, or if such choices were widely publicized. What is at stake in these cases is who *controls* the decision—the persons involved or the state.

There is room for disagreement as to whether *Griswold* deals with privacy as an issue of scrutiny or of private choice. Several eminent constitutional scholars, such as Gerald Gunther and John Hart Ely, have taken the position that it deals with transparency.[85] Others see *Griswold* as concerned with control. Louis Henkin, for instance, has noted that "the issue was whether the state could bar the use of contraceptives not whether it could intrude into the bedroom for evidence of its use."[86]

True, Justice Douglas's argument in *Griswold* was not that the Court ban was unconstitutional because it sought to control what a couple does, but rather that the surveillance procedures necessary to establish whether contraception is used would be unacceptably intrusive.[87] Note, however, that the result of the Court ruling was not to move contraceptive behavior from being conducted in public view to spaces not subject to scrutiny; the behavior was not public to begin with! The ruling did change the designation of the behavior from one that the state could control to one that was from then on a matter for individual decision. As Henkin emphasized: "In a word, the Court has been vindicating not a right to freedom from official intrusion, but to freedom from official regulation."[88] Indeed, the Douglas argument seems somewhat difficult to comprehend given that there are no particular difficulties in devising procedures for determining whether people use contraceptives without intruding on their homes. For instance, if a person regularly purchases contraceptives and has no medical prescription for them for noncontraceptive purposes, there would be strong circumstantial evidence that he or she was using them. (Also, sellers of contraceptives could be judged as accessories.) Indeed, Douglas himself at one point argues in reference to *Griswold* that the "government purpose to *control* or prevent activities constitutionally may not be achieved by means" that the Court finds too sweeping.[89] Most important, there is widespread agreement that the subsequent reproductive choice cases, including *Roe*, dealt with control, not scrutiny, issues.

In contrast, the voyeurist nature of some media reporting, which purportedly prompted Mrs. Samuel D. Warren to encourage her new husband to act to curb such intrusion,[90] gives rise to issues of privacy violation but not of state control. Mrs. Warren feared that gossip about her would be spread widely by the press. She was *not* afraid that if details about her personal life were to become public she would be subject to arrest, or that her private choices would be preempted by the government.[91]

In short, the Supreme Court's crafting of the right to privacy in the reproductive choice cases *conflates notions of scrutiny and control, and privacy and private choice.*[92]

Once we agree that much is to be gained, both in clarity of thought and judgment as well as for the communitarian balance, if we draw the distinction between exemption from scrutiny and exemption from control, there are at least two ways we can proceed.[93] We can refer to the first category as "privacy" and to the second as a matter of "private choice," or we can recognize two different kinds of privacy. The first approach makes a great deal of sense given the meaning of these terms in common parlance and the appropriateness of their intellectual and normative associations. "Private choice" correctly brings to mind unregulated economic behavior, deregulation, school choice, and reproductive choices. The second approach, establishing two different rights of privacy, is especially attractive to those who are concerned that if choice is not deemed a matter of "privacy" it may lack constitutional protection until a new legal foundation can be formulated; this is a serious consideration.

In either case, each category requires, and in effect already implicitly contains, a strong and distinct rationale. Although both implicate human dignity and liberty—the independence of a person within the communal context—two rather different facets are involved. The first—privacy in both approaches—deals with the value of being able to be legitimately different, with being able to *individuate* without activating legal (governmental) or moral (communal) pressure—a respite from the social. A useful image here is that of a veil or cloth with which an individual can drape parts of his or her self when there is legitimate reason to keep those parts—such as his or her mastectomy scar, genitalia, or bank account—invisible to some or all others. (That the individual lifts such a veil for certain others, say a physician or a nurse, should not mean that he or she gives up the right to be draped where others are concerned, a key issue in the area of medical privacy.) The second category—private choice or privacy II—concerns autonomy in the profoundest sense—the definition of the spheres in which one can legitimately direct one's own life.[94]

The first category is characterized by *trust:* Society deems that a person will not be under surveillance, but it does not forgo its right to act—for example, in cases where a person uses his or her privacy to molest a child or make bombs. The second category, in contrast, is characterized by societal indifference and hence *full individual (or group) liberty.* It concerns all those numerous matters about which the society rules that these are matters in which the individual is free to act as he or she deems fit, whether or not the action takes place out of sight and audibility.

The following examples serve to further highlight this pivotal distinction. The government may have a right to determine what a person cannot carry in a car (contraband, human corpses, etc.) and what a person must carry (e.g., a flare or a spare); that is, it can *control* certain acts and choices. But the government does not have a right to examine a trunk or glove compartment without specific cause; that is, it does not have a right to *scrutinize* spaces legitimately cordoned off in the name of privacy.

Buying items in a supermarket is a matter of personal choice, not a state-controlled action. It is a private act, but one that cannot be said to implicate privacy because its commission is quite visible to the public. Generally, the advocates of the private sector and the opponents of government interventions are concerned with who controls the act rather than whether the action is visible (or audible). In contrast, preparing a tax return is legitimately carried out in privacy, but it is not a matter about which one has a choice: Filing a tax return is required by the state and in this sense is a public act typically carried out under the condition of privacy.

Indeed, only relatively few acts are both under individuals' control and legitimately conducted in ways that defend them from scrutiny—voting for public offices, for instance. Few others, such as standing trial for criminal activity, are both expressions of government control and acts carried out in full public view, even on television.

One might argue that even though privacy and private choice (and publicness and public control) are clearly distinct conditions, the second presumes the first—a state that seeks to control certain kinds of behavior must be able to scrutinize them and thus cannot allow them to take place in privacy. Yet this is not the case. Precisely in order to respect the privacy of certain acts and yet to control them, the state often waits before taking action until there are publicly visible consequences of behavior that took place in privacy. Thus, the state typically acts to rescue a child from abuse only after some signs of ill treatment are noticed at school or at a clinic, or when someone files a complaint before a public authority and backs it up with evidence. In free societies, the state does not scan homes preemptively to ensure that no child abuse is taking place.

There are many other important matters in which the law calls for public scrutiny but not state control. The legal requirement that many meetings of elected officials, corporate stockholders, and others be held in open session is one example; there are also numerous disclosure requirements about data that must be revealed in the annual reports of publicly held corporations and about personal financial details that people running for certain public offices must provide. (Although some of the disclosures are required to facilitate governmental controls—audits, for instance—in other instances it is presumed that the very exposure to the "sunshine" of the public and the press will suffice to prevent antisocial conduct, thereby precluding the need for state-controlling acts.)

Especially telling is a considerable category of laws, mores, and behaviors—typically not even mentioned in this context, at least in part because it does not fit the conflated and overexpansive conception of privacy—that refers to acts mandated by the state to be carried out in privacy. Nudity, sexual intercourse, and toilet functions all fall into this category. Those who treat privateness and privacy as synonymous, as many do, would be in the odd position of saying that these are acts that are public and private, which, of course, makes no sense.

Although there is certainly some initial awkwardness in drawing a distinction between privacy and privateness, and between publicness and public control, many issues cannot be properly conceptualized and examined unless such a distinction is made and separate legal rationales for both kinds of cases are provided. The particular term used is, of course, a much less important matter. Whatever course is followed, there is a pressing sociohistorical need to consider adopting in both areas the Fourth Amendment model of balance rather than privileging privacy.

MORE PUBLICNESS—LESS PUBLIC CONTROL

At issue here is much more than an accurate definition of privacy; at the very heart of this discussion is the appropriateness of social formulations of the good, the point of contention that separates communitarians from both individualists and social conservatives. For individualists, who strongly oppose social formulations of the good and believe that each person should be free to form and pursue his or her own good, and who thus seek to maximize both private choice and privacy, the distinction matters little. For social conservatives, especially religious fundamentalists who would rely on the state to enforce their values—for instance, to suppress pornography—and who are willing to curtail both private choices and privacy, the difference between these two concepts is also of limited import. In contrast, the distinction is crucial for communitarians (at least for responsive ones), who hold that important social formulations of the good can be left to private choices—provided there is sufficient communal scrutiny! That is, *the best way to curtail the need for governmental control and intrusion is to have somewhat less privacy.* This point requires some elaboration.

The key to understanding this notion lies in the importance, especially to communitarians, of the "third realm."[95] This realm is not the state or the market (or individual choices), but rather the community, which relies on subtle social fostering of prosocial conduct by such means as communal recognition, approbation, and censure. These processes require the scrutiny of some behavior, not by police or secret agents, but by friends, neighbors, and fellow members of voluntary associations.[96]

Indeed, crimes are best prevented when a community abhors the behavior that is considered criminal by lawmakers; conversely, law enforcement works poorly when not supported by the community's moral and informal enforcement systems.[97] For instance, abuse of controlled substances and alcoholism are very rare in religious communities that object to such behaviors, such as in Mormon, Hasidic Jewish, Amish, and black Moslem communities, and relatively rare in much of the Bible Belt and small-town America.[98] The reason is not simply that internalized values lead individuals to avoid these behaviors; these prosocial values also find much support in their communities—support that entails a measure of scrutiny by others. The extent to which many professionals, such as physicians and lawyers, conform to their ethical codes is largely determined by the values upheld by their particular community, and mostly by informal enforcement mechanisms that require social *scrutiny* but reduce the need for government *control.* The same holds true for honor codes among students in military academies and select colleges.

In fact, continual efforts by groups such as the ACLU to extend the sphere of privacy paradoxically force increases in governmental interventions. We saw a sterling example in Chapter 3 in the examination of encryption. As the ACLU and other individualistic groups have blocked the introduction of public key recovery, which would have enabled the government, with proper court authorization, to decode encrypted messages, the government has been pushed to use more invasive procedures for the same kind of criminal investigations—for instance, planting microphones in the homes of suspects.[99]

William Donahue effectively highlights these self-defeating tendencies:

> The ACLU is driven by an atomistic vision of liberty. It envisions solitary individuals, armed with rights and unencumbered by duties. This vision does not conform with reality. When we look at society we do not see solitary individuals. Rather we see constellations of people in associations. . . . These groups arise naturally when people are left alone. This explains the great paradox of the ACLU. Its atomistic ideal is so unnatural that its realization (if possible) would require a great coercive power. Thus it is that an organization devoted solely to individual rights seeks in practice the total aggrandizement of the state.[100]

In short, if we hold constant the values involved and the level of adherence we seek, publicness reduces the need for public control, while excessive privacy often necessitates state-imposed limits on private choices.[101] Admittedly, each community and society determines the scope and content of its particular formulations of the good, the normative claims it makes, and the intensity with which it fosters compliance. However, once these matters are settled, higher levels of communal scrutiny facilitate compliance better than higher levels of public control and often allow that control to be kept at a lower level.[102]

It might be argued that these matters are of no concern to the legal realm. Yet there are numerous laws that affect the level of communal scrutiny rather than public control. For example, laws that limit the right of the press to report the scandalous behavior of public officials, corporate executives, foundation officials, and others, or make it too easy to win libel suits against ordinary citizens, not only raise First Amendment concerns but also may extend privacy too far, diminish community scrutiny, and undermine the common good. The same holds for laws that limit the scrutiny of professionals by one another and the disclosure of immoral conduct.

IN CONCLUSION

The conception expressed in the Fourth Amendment provides a solid foundation for a communitarian public philosophy of privacy, one that has significant implications for our social mores, public policy, and jurisprudence as we struggle to adapt our institutions to the cyber-age. This philosophy recognizes as justified a whole category of acts in which concerns for the common good take precedence over privacy, rather than strongly privileging privacy a priori, implying that a balance between these two core values must be worked out.

Another reason to rely on the conception embodied in the Fourth Amendment, rather than on the amalgam of various constitutional rights used to construct a constitutional right to privacy in the reproductive choice cases, is that the Fourth Amendment focuses on scrutiny rather than on control. Thus, it avoids the major conceptual and ethical confusion between privacy and privateness (or autonomy) that has affected mores, policy, and legal doctrines. Most important, the Fourth Amendment, by introducing the distinction between searches that are unacceptable violations of privacy and those that are justified by public needs, recognizes the need for balance between privacy and the common good rather than treating privacy as privileged.

Above all, a communitarian approach to privacy avoids the failings of static conceptions by taking into account sociohistorical changes. For instance, it recognizes that the more privacy is granted from informal social controls in a given period, the *more* state controls will be necessary in following years to sustain the same level of social order.[103] It follows that the best way to defend against the theocratic tendencies of religious fundamentalism and right wing extremists, both foreign and domestic, as well as authoritarianism and tyranny, is not through a relentless expansion of permissiveness, but through endeavors to ensure that society's elementary needs for public health and public safety are not neglected.

NOTES

INTRODUCTION

1. John T. McQuiston, "Sex Offender Sues Neighbors over Protests," *New York Times*, 20 June 1997, A23.

2. Matt Bai, "A Report from the Front in the War on Predators," *Newsweek*, 19 May 1997, 67. See also Rick Hampson, "Notification: Reason for Law Is Its Biggest Problem," *USA Today*, 14 May 1997, A1.

3. 1996 Equifax/Harris Consumer Privacy Survey, 20–29 July 1996, available from: http://www.equifax.com/consumer/parchive/svry96/docs/summary.html; 1997 *Money* magazine poll, cited in Barnet D. Wolf, "Computers' Spread Heightens Consumer Privacy Concerns," *Columbus Dispatch*, 7 September 1997, 1H; 1997 Harris-Westin survey for the Center for Social and Legal Research, cited in Lawrence A. Ponemon, "Privacy Needs Protection," *Journal of Commerce*, 23 March 1998, 7A; 1998 Harris-Westin Survey on Privacy and the Elements of Self-Regulation, presented by Alan Westin at Department of Commerce Privacy Conference, 23 June 1998, Washington, D.C.

4. For an overview, see Center for Public Integrity, "Nothing Sacred: The Politics of Privacy" (Washington, D.C.: Center for Public Integrity, 1998).

5. The term "cyber-age" is rather unfortunate, but no better term seems available.

6. Carol W. LaGrasse, "Ex-Con Caregivers," *City Journal* (Summer 1998): 8–9. A new congressional law bars background checks from reporting criminal convictions that are more than seven years old for positions that will earn less than $75,000—a figure that includes most positions in child care centers. Del Jones, "Background Check Rule Change Contains Flaws," *USA Today*, 24 February 1998, 4B; Fair Credit Reporting Act of 1970, 84 stat. 1128, *codified* at 15 U.S.C. s. 1681(c).

7. LaGrasse, "Ex-Con Caregivers," 8.

8. There are those who object to formulations that balance rights and the common good, arguing that privacy, and more generally rights, *are* the common good. But this is largely a semantic issue. If one considers rights a common good, one needs to balance it with other common goods. The issue at hand does not change by calling privacy a common good rather than a right. For an important book that treats privacy as a social good—but not the only one—see Priscilla M. Regan, *Legislating Privacy* (Chapel Hill: University of North Carolina Press, 1995). For a major, seminal work on privacy and the common good that has withstood the test of time, see Alan Westin, *Privacy and Freedom* (New York: Atheneum, 1967).

9. Jennifer Lenhart, "Keeping an Electronic Eye on the Kids; Day-Care Cameras Let Parents View Children Via the Internet," *Washington Post*, 29 May 1998, A1.

10. Amitai Etzioni, *The New Golden Rule: Community and Morality in a Democratic Society* (New York: Basic Books, 1996).

11. Robert Bellah, Richard Madsen, William M. Sullivan, Ann Swidler, and Steven M. Tipton, *Habits of the Heart: Individualism and Commitment in American Life* (Berkeley and Los Angeles: University of California Press, 1985); Mary Ann Glendon, *Rights Talk: The Impoverishment of Political Discourse* (New York: Free Press, 1991); Amitai Etzioni, *The Spirit of Community: The Reinvention of American Society* (New York: Simon & Schuster, 1993).

12. American Civil Liberties Union, ACLU "Take Back Your Data" campaign, February 1998, available from: http://www.aclu.org/action/tbyd.html.

13. Thomas Nagel writes about "the culmination of a disastrous erosion of the precious but fragile conventions of personal privacy in the United States over the past ten or twenty years." Thomas Nagel, "The Shredding of Public Privacy," *Times Literary Supplement*, 14 August 1998, 15.

See also Joshua Quittner, "The Death of Privacy/Invasion of Privacy," *Time*, 25 August 1997, 28–35; Roger Rosenblatt, "Who Killed Privacy?" *New York Times Magazine*, 31 January 1994, 24–28; John Riley, "The End of Privacy?" *Buffalo News*, 28 April 1996, 7F; Jonathan Franzen, "Imperial Bedroom," *New Yorker*, 12 October 1998, 48–53.

Bob Herbert writes that our financial information is traded like baseball cards; medical privacy cannot be eroded because it does not exist; employers monitor e-mail and phone calls; and surveillance cameras are all over the place. Bob Herbert, "What Privacy Right" *New York Times*, 27 September 1998, 4, 15.

Lawrence Lessig refers to "the increasing Sovietization of our personal and private life." Jeffrey Rosen, "Is Nothing Private?" *New Yorker*, 1 June 1998, 36–41.

14. Brian J. Serr, "Great Expectations of Privacy: A New Model for Fourth Amendment Protection," *Minnesota Law Review* 73 (1994): 584–585.

15. David Brin, *The Transparent Society: Will Technology Force Us to Choose Between Privacy and Freedom?* (Reading, Mass.: Addison-Wesley, 1998).

16. Scott E. Sundby, "Everyman's Fourth Amendment: Privacy or Mutual Trust Between Government and Citizen?" *Columbia Law Review* 94 (1994): 1751–1752.

17. Richard A. Spinello, "The End of Privacy," *America* 176 (1997): 9–13, reprinted in Robert Emmet Long, ed., *Rights to Privacy* (New York: H. W. Wilson Co., 1997), 25–32; see also Beth Givens and the Privacy Rights Clearinghouse, *The Privacy Rights Handbook* (New York: Avon Books, 1997), especially 1–12.

18. Louis Harris and Associates, Inc., and Equifax, 1996 Equifax/Harris Consumer Privacy Survey, available from: http://www.equifax.com/consumer/parchive/svry96/docs/summary.html.

19. Lawrence A. Ponemon, "Privacy Needs Protection," *Journal of Commerce*, 23 March 1998, 7A.

20. Scott E. Sundby, "'Everyman's Fourth Amendment: Privacy or Mutual Trust Between Government and Citizen?" *Columbia Law Review* 94 (1994): 1789–1790.

21. For instance, the introduction of home testing for HIV. Documentation concerning this development may be obtained from the Communitarian Network, Washington, D.C., available from: http://www.gwu.edu/~ccps.

22. John Kifner and Jo Thomas, "Singular Difficulty in Stopping Terrorism," *New York Times*, 18 January 1998, 23.

23. Randall Coyne contends that the images captured by such public-space cameras constitute a search by Fourth Amendment standards. Brian J. Taylor, "The Screening of America: Crime, Cops, and Cameras," *Reason* (May 1997): 45.

24. Steven Yarosh, "A Place for Safe Housing in the Fourth Amendment," *The Responsive Community* 4 (1994): 29–41, adapted from *Northwestern University Law Review* 86 (1992): 1103–1129.

25. Ronald Bayer, *Private Acts, Social Consequences: AIDS and the Politics of Public Health* (New York: Free Press, 1989).

26. Roger Conner, "The Checkpoint at Inkster: Reasonable or Unreasonable?" *The Responsive Community* 1 (1990): 88–91.

27. Ronald Bayer, "Public Health Policy and the AIDS Epidemic," *New England Journal of Medicine* 324 (1991): 1500–1504. See also Gabriel Rotello, *Sexual Ecology: AIDS and the Destiny of Gay Men* (New York: Dutton, 1997), and Michelangelo Signorile, *Life Outside: The Signorile Report on Gay Men: Sex, Drugs, Muscles, and the Passages of Life* (New York: HarperCollins, 1997).

28. Daniel Bell, "Together Again?" *Times Literary Supplement*, 25 November 1994, 5–6.

29. For details, see Hanna Rosin, "Bad Blood," *New Republic*, 27 June 1994, 12; Ronald Bayer, Jeff Stryker, and Mark Smith, "Sounding Board: Testing for HIV Infection at Home," *New England Journal of Medicine* 332 (1995): 1296.

30. For additional discussion of these criteria, see Etzioni, *The Spirit of Community*, 177ff.

31. For an editorial on the topic, see "Saving Swordfish," *New York Times*, 21 January 1998, A22.

32. A notable exception is a coding in the National Practitioner Data Bank for payment made in settlement of a medical malpractice action, which the data bank cautions "shall not be construed as a presumption that medical malpractice has occurred." See "Interpretation of Data Bank Information" in the *National Practitioner Data Bank's Guidebook*, 6 November 1996, available from: http://www.hrsa.dhhs.gov/bhpr/dqa/factshts/fsnpdb.htm#1.

33. For documentation, see Chapter 5.

34. See Amitai Etzioni, "Making Policy for Complex Systems: A Medical Model for Economics," *Journal of Policy Analysis and Management* 4 (1985): 383. See also Etzioni, "Policy Research," *The American Sociologist* 6, supplementary issue (1971): 8.

CHAPTER ONE

1. Michael A. Stoto, Donna A. Almario, and Marie C. McCormick, eds., *Reducing the Odds: Preventing Perinatal Transmission of HIV* (Washington, D.C.: National Academy Press, 1998). The IOM issued its report, as this book goes to press, on 14 October 1998.

2. Randy Shilts, *And the Band Played On* (New York: Penguin Books, 1988).

3. Ronald Bayer, *Private Acts, Social Consequence: AIDS and the Politics of Public Health* (New York: Free Press, 1989).

4. R. J. Simonds, "Prophylaxis Against Pneumocystis Carinii Pneumonia Among Children With Perinatally Acquired Immunodeficiency Virus Infection in the United States," *New England Journal of Medicine* 332 (1995): 786; Centers for Disease Control and Prevention, "Guidelines for Prophylaxis Against Pneumocystis Carinii Pneumonia for Children Infected with Human Immunodeficiency Virus," *Morbidity and Mortality Weekly Report*, 15 March 1991, 40; Leonardo Renna, "New York State's Proposal to Unblind HIV Testing for Newborns: A Necessary Step in Addressing a Critical Problem," *Brooklyn Law Review* 60 (1994): 407, 415; Colin Crawford, "An Argument for

Universal Pediatric HIV Testing, Counseling, and Treatment," *Cardozo Women's Law Journal* 3, no. 31 (1996): 39–41.

5. Nettie Mayersohn, letter to the author, 25 August 1997.

6. American Academy of Pediatrics, Committee on Infectious Diseases, *Report of the Committee on Infectious Diseases,* 22nd ed. (Evanston, Ill., 1991): 121; Stephen Arpadi and William B. Caspe, "HIV Testing," *Pediatrics* 119 (July 1991): S8; Margaret H. Burroughs and Paul J. Edison, "Medical Care of the HIV-Infected Child," *Pediatric Clinics North America* 38 (February 1991): 47.

7. CDC, *HIV/AIDS Surveillance Report* 9 (June 1997): 11.

8. Institute of Medicine, *Reducing the Odds: Preventing Perinatal Transmission of HIV* (Washington, D.C.: National Academy Press, 1998), 6. According to one source, the annual number of perinatal AIDS cases was 1,500; Andrew Helfgott, "HIV Infection in Women and Children: Where Are We Headed?" *Pediatric AIDS and HIV Infection* 8 (April 1997): 86.

9. Estimates as to the number of infants infected perinatally range from as low as 20 percent to as high as 30 percent; Catherine Wilfert et al., "Evaluation and Medical Treatment of the HIV-Exposed Infant," *Pediatrics* (June 1997): 909–917.

10. CDC, "U.S. Public Health Service Recommendations for Human Immunodeficiency Virus Counseling and Voluntary Testing for Pregnant Women," *Morbidity and Mortality Weekly Report,* 28 July 1995, 3.

11. World Health Organization, "HIV and Infant Feeding: An Interim Statement," *World Health* 50 (March 1997): 30. It should be noted that these figures reflect worldwide vertical HIV transmission rates.

12. D. T. Dunn, M. L. Newell, A. E. Ades, and C. S. Peckham, "Risk of Human Immunodeficiency Virus Type 1 Transmission Through Breastfeeding," *Lancet* 340 (1992): 585–588.

13. United Nations AIDS officials finally started in 1998 to advise mothers in Africa, where AIDS is spreading rapidly, not to breastfeed their children, reversing policy that had advocated such feeding for decades. Michael Specter, "Breast-Feeding and HIV: Weighing the Health Risks," *New York Times,* 19 August 1998, A1.

14. Renna, "New York State's Proposal," 418.

15. Ibid., 417.

16. Some medical authorities, such as Catherine Wilfert, suggest that for HIV-positive mothers who did not receive AZT treatment during pregnancy and delivery, AZT therapy started shortly after birth may reduce the risk of transmission from mother to infant. She writes that "in women who have not received zidovudine [AZT] during pregnancy or labor, the postpartum com-

ponent of the regimen (six weeks of therapy for infants) should be offered if therapy can be started within 24 hours of birth." But she cautions that "in such situations, infants have not had zidovudine present in their bloodstream at the time of intense viral exposure during delivery; therefore, administration of zidovudine provides only post-exposure prophylaxis. . . . There are no data to suggest that initiation of zidovudine therapy after 24 hours of age will reduce perinatal HIV transmission"; Wilfert et al., "Evaluation and Medical Treatment of the HIV-Exposed Infant," 909–917. Although it is true that practical concerns may prevent many, if not most, newborns from receiving test results within twenty-four hours, these considerations at least present the possibility that early newborn testing could help prevent perinatal HIV transmission.

17. U.S. Department of Health and Human Services, *U.S. Public Health Service Recommendations for Use of Antiretroviral Drugs During Pregnancy for Maternal Health and Reduction of Perinatal Transmission of Human-Immunodeficiency Virus Type 1 in the United States; Request for Comment* (Washington, D.C.: HHS, 1997), 18.

18. Guthrie S. Birkhead et al., "Pathogenesis and Prevention of Vertical HIV Transmission," paper presented at the Institute of Medicine, Second Perinatal Transmission of HIV Committee Meeting, Washington, D.C., 11–12 February 1998.

19. According to one press report, the use of AZT and bottle-feeding cut the maternal HIV transmission rate by half. David Brown, "In Africa, Fear Makes HIV an Inheritance," *Washington Post*, 30 June 1998, A2.

20. Renna, "New York State's Proposal," 419.

21. New York State Department of Health, AIDS Institute, *HIV Medical Evaluation and Preventative Care for Children* (New York: New York State Department of Health, 1993), 520 (table 5).

22. Renna, "New York State's Proposal," 419.

23. Jim Dwyer, "A Silence That Kills Children," *Newsday*, city edition, 15 April 1994, 2; Nat Hentoff, "The New Tuskegee Experiment: Infected Has a Right to Be Told–No Matter What the ACLU Says," *Village Voice*, 1 October 1996, 8.

24. American Civil Liberties Union, "New York to Require All Mother[s] Be Tested for AIDS," *ACLU News Wire*, 6 June 1996.

25. Jeffrey L. Reynolds, "Keep Policy on Newborns' HIV Test," *Newsday* (Nassau and Suffolk edition), 6 January 1994, 105.

26. Catherine A. Lynch, "Don't Test Newborns for AIDS," *Newsday*, Nassau and Suffolk edition, 19 May 1991, 37.

27. Nat Hentoff, "Censuring the Right to Live: HIV Testing of Infants," *The Progressive* 59 (February 1995): 19.

28. CNN News, transcript 1504–3, 1 May 1996.

29. Helen Rodriguez-Trias and Ana O. Dumois, "Free for All," *Washington Post*, 17 June 1995, A15.

30. Office of Rep. Tom Coburn, private communication, 26 January 1998.

31. Ibid.; "U.S. House Bill Passed Requiring HIV Test for Infants," *AIDS Weekly Plus*, 13 May 1996, 17.

32. Anne Hamilton and Frank Spencer-Molloy, "Disclosure Battle Halts HIV Testing of Newborns," *Hartford Courant*, 21 June 1995, A1.

33. See Michael Chapman, "CDC Still Plays Politics While Babies Die," *Human Events*, 10 January 1997; CDC, *CDC Draft Guidelines for HIV Counseling and Voluntary Testing for Pregnant Women* (Atlanta: CDC, 21 February 1995); ACLU, *ACLU Position Statement on Prenatal and Newborn HIV Testing* (New York: ACLU, 1996); Gay Men's Health Crisis, *New York State Legislative Agenda* (New York: GMHC, 1996), 7.

34. Wilfert et al., "Evaluation and Medical Treatment of the HIV-Exposed Infant." It should be noted here that the study looked only at women whose HIV infection met very specific conditions.

35. HHS, *U.S. Public Health Service Recommendations.*

36. Sheryl Gay Stolberg, "A Revolution in AIDS Drugs Excludes the Tiniest Patients," *New York Times*, 8 September 1997, A14.

37. "30% to 50% of HIV-infected infants have detectable levels of virus in their blood within 48 hours of birth. Of the remainder, more than 90% have detectable virus within two weeks of birth. These facts suggest that most infected infants acquire infection around the time of delivery." Catherine Wilfert, "Preventing Vertical Transmission: A Wise Investment," *HIV Newsline* (August 1997): 85.

38. Renna, "New York State's Proposal," 430–431.

39. New York State Department of Health and the AIDS Institute, *HIV Medical Evaluation.*

40. Jim Dwyer, "Breakthroughs Damn HIV Rule," *Newsday*, 17 June 1994, A02.

41. Educational Broadcasting and GWETA, *The MacNeil/Lehrer News Hour*, transcript 5292, 15 August 1995.

42. New York State Department of Health, *Newborn HIV Testing* (Albany: New York State Department of Health, 1998).

43. Lynda Richardson, "Doctors Criticize Delays in Receiving Newborns' HIV Data," *New York Times*, 14 May 1998, B1. After nine months of the pro-

gram, sixty-nine babies born to mothers with unknown HIV status were identified; New York State Department of Health, *Newborn HIV Testing.*

44. Lawrence Altman, "Disease Control Agency Urges Wider Use of HIV Blood Test," *New York Times*, 27 March 1998, A16.

45. Statement made at Institute of Medicine, Second Perinatal Transmission of HIV Committee Meeting, Washington, D.C., 11–12 February 1998.

46. American Academy of Pediatrics, "Newborn Screening Fact Sheets," *Pediatrics* 98 (September 1996): 474.

47. Dr. Robert Janssen, letter to author, 20 February 1998.

48. Ibid.; Institute of Medicine, Second Perinatal Transmission of HIV Committee Meeting, 11–12 February 1998, Washington, D.C. Doctors in all states also routinely test infants for branched-chain ketonuria, homocystinuria, biotinidase deficiency, sickle-cell anemia, hepatitis, and syphilis; Nat Hentoff, "Sweet Land of Liberty—Privacy That Kills," *Washington Post*, final edition, 8 April 1995, A19; see also Crawford, "An Argument for Universal Pediatric HIV Testing," 33–34; American Academy of Pediatrics, "Newborn Screening Fact Sheets."

49. In 1993 the CDC recommended that hospitals with an AIDS diagnosis rate of more than one per 1,000 discharges or an HIV seroprevalence rate of at least 1 percent routinely counsel patients between the ages of fifteen and fifty-four about the benefits of an HIV test; "Cost Analysis Questions Value of Routine HIV Testing," *AIDS Alert* (August 1993): 120.

50. ACLU, *ACLU Position Statement on Prenatal and Newborn HIV Testing*, 2; see also Nina Lowenstein, "Mandatory Screening of Newborns for HIV: An Idea Whose Time Has Not Yet Come," *Cardozo Women's Law Journal* 3 (1996): 43, 46–47.

51. GMHC, *New York State Legislative Agenda*, 7.

52. Crawford, "An Argument for Universal Pediatric HIV Testing," 35.

53. Elizabeth Cooper, "Why Mandatory HIV Testing of Pregnant Women and Newborns Must Fail: A Legal, Historical, and Public Policy Analysis," *Cardozo Women's Law Journal* 3 (1996): 13, 28.

54. Nettie Mayersohn, "Capitol Offense" (letter to the editor), *Village Voice*, 18 July 1995, 4; Bill Viscovich, private communication, 12 February 1998.

55. Deborah Shelton, "Is It Time to Require HIV Testing? For Pregnant Women, It Just May Be," *Newsday*, 23 December 1996, B13.

56. CDC, "CDC Focuses on Preventing Perinatal Transmission," AIDS/HIV press release, 15 May 1995.

57. Ibid. Dennis Saffron, private communication, 6 May 1998.

58. "CDC to Stop Testing Newborns for HIV Virus," *Ridgway* [Penn.] *Record*, 12 May 1995.

59. Ibid.

60. Trilby DeJung, deputy director of policy at New York's AIDS Institute, interview with Colin Crawford, March 1995, in Crawford, "An Argument for Universal Pediatric HIV Testing," 35.

61. Janssen, letter to author, 20 February 1998.

62. It should be noted that the information about the value of providing AZT after birth had become available only very shortly before Dr. Janssen wrote his letter on 20 February 1998. However, the information about the dangers of breast-feeding by HIV-positive mothers has been available since 1992.

63. Crawford, "An Argument for Universal Pediatric HIV Testing," 34; Nat Hentoff, "When Good People Do Bad Things: Feminists, Gays, and the ACLU All Fought Nettie Mayersohn," *Village Voice*, 24 September 1996, 9.

64. Marcia Angell, "The Ethics of Clinical Research in the Third World," *New England Journal of Medicine* (18 September 1997).

65. Lowenstein, "Mandatory Screening of Newborns for HIV," 43–44; ACLU, *ACLU Position Statement on Prenatal and Newborn HIV Testing*.

66. Cooper, "Why Mandatory HIV Testing of Pregnant Women and Newborns Must Fail," 13.

67. Ibid.; Lowenstein, "Mandatory Screening of Newborns for HIV," 43.

68. Lowenstein, "Mandatory Screening of Newborns for HIV," 44.

69. In New York, under the new law, disclosure is permitted to the attending health care providers, third-party reimbursers or insurance companies authorized by the protected individual, and certain employees of correctional facilities; Renna, "New York State's Proposal," 424.

70. ACLU, *ACLU Position Statement on Prenatal and Newborn HIV Testing*.

71. Sofia Kwong and Randy Allgaier, "Letters to the Editor," *The Recorder*, 9 August 1996, 5.

72. Stephanie Armour, "Employers Work Around AIDS," *USA Today*, 24 September 1997.

73. Karen J. Rothenberg and Stephen J. Paskey, "The Risk of Domestic Violence and Women with HIV Infection: Implications of Partner Notification, Public Policy, and the Law," *American Journal of Public Health* 85 (November 1995): 1570.

74. Karen H. Rothenberg, Stephen J. Paskey, Melissa M. Reuland, Sheryl Itkin Zimmerman, and Richard L. North, "Domestic Violence and Partner Notification: Implications for Treatment and Counseling of HIV-Infected Women," *Journal of the American Medical Women's Association* 50 (1995): 87–93.

75. Renna, "New York State's Proposal," 443.

76. Ibid., 415; Crawford, "An Argument for Universal Pediatric HIV Testing," 39–40.

77. I am quite aware that these core values themselves require further examination; see Amitai Etzioni, *The New Golden Rule* (New York: Basic Books, 1996), chap. 8.

78. Marcia Angell, "The Ethics of Clinical Research in the Third World," *New England Journal of Medicine* (18 September 1997).

79. Suzanne Sangree, "Control of Childbearing by HIV-positive Women: Some Responses to Emerging Legal Policies," *Buffalo Law Review* 309 (1993): 374.

80. Renna, "New York State's Proposal," 426.

81. Marie-Jeanne Mayaux et al., "Neonatal Characteristics in Rapidly Progressive Perinatally Acquired HIV–1 Disease," *Journal of the American Medical Association* (28 February 1996): 606–610.

82. Story adapted from Dwyer, "Breakthroughs Damn HIV Rule," A02.

83. Jim Dwyer, "They Want to Know: Law Kept Women in Dark That Their Babies Had HIV," *Newsday*, 13 June 1994, A02; Dwyer, "A Silence That Kills Children," *Newsday*, 15 April 1994, 2.

84. Renna, "New York State's Proposal," 434, 435.

85. Quoted in Randall P. Bezanson, "*The Right to Privacy* Revisited: Privacy, News, and Social Change, 1890–1990," *California Law Review* 80 (1992): 1133, 1147.

86. Renna, "New York State's Proposal," 441.

87. "AIDS Among Children—United States, 1996," *American Health Association Journal of School Health* 67 (May 1997): 175.

88. Cooper, "Why Mandatory HIV Testing of Pregnant Women and Newborns Must Fail," 21.

CHAPTER TWO

1. Washington Institute for Public Policy, *Community Notification in Washington State* (Olympia: WIPP, November 1996).

2. See, for instance, the statement by Elizabeth Schroeder, associate director of the ACLU of Southern California, in Todd S. Purdum, "Death of Sex Offender Is Tied to Megan's Law," *New York Times*, 8 July 1998, A16.

3. John Leo, "Changing the Rules of a Deadly Game," *U.S. News & World Report*, 23 December 1996, 21; see also Blaine Harden, "HIV Outbreak in N.Y. Town Tied to One Man," *Washington Post*, 28 October 1997, A1.

4. Leo, "Changing the Rules," 21.

5. Larry Don McQuay, "The Case for Castration," part 1, "Punishment for Sex Offenses Against Children," *Washington Monthly* (May 1994): 26.

6. Linda Greenhouse, "Justices Sound Sympathetic but Troubled on Law to Confine Sex Offenders," *New York Times*, 11 December 1996, A24.

7. Jerry Adler and Peter Annin, "Too Dangerous to Set Free?" *Newsweek*, 9 December 1996, 39.

8. Michele L. Earl-Hubbard, "The Child Sex Offender Registration Laws: The Punishment, Liberty Deprivation, and Unintended Results Associated with the Scarlet Letter Laws of the 1990s," *Northwestern University Law Review* 90 (1996): 788, 789.

9. Ellen Bass and Laura Davis, *The Courage to Heal: A Guide for Women Survivors of Child Sexual Abuse* (New York: HarperCollins, 1992), 20.

10. Mark Weinrott and Maureen Saylor, "Self-Report of Sex Crimes Committed by Sex Offenders," *Journal of Interpersonal Violence* 6 (1996): 286, 291–292.

11. According to the study, "sex offense" entails rape and sexual assault, rape being defined as "forced sexual intercourse where the victim may be male or female and the offender may be of the same sex or a different sex from the victim." Sexual assault "includes a wide range of victimizations involving attacks in which unwanted sexual contact occurs between the victim and the offender. Threats and attempts to commit such offenses are included in the counts"; Bureau of Justice Statistics, U.S. Department of Justice, *Sex Offenses and Offenders* (Washington, D.C.: BOJS, 1997), v.

12. Ibid.; Bureau of Justice Statistics, U.S. Department of Justice, *Child Victimizers: Violent Offenders and Their Victims* (Washington, D.C.: BOJS, 1996), iv, 1.

13. Bureau of Justice Statistics, U.S. Department of Justice, *Correctional Populations in the United States, 1995* (Washington, D.C.: BOJS, 1997), 34.

14. Louise van der Does, private communication, 15 September 1997.

15. Corfu, 1973, cited in Lita Furby, Lyn Blackshaw, and Mark R. Weinrott, "Sex Offender Recidivism: A Review," *Psychological Bulletin* 105 (1989): 20.

16. Massachusetts Post Audit Bureau, *Report of the Committee on Post Audit and Oversight* (Bridgewater, Mass.: Massachusetts Post Audit Bureau, 1979), cited in Furby et al., "Sex Offender Recidivism," 18.

17. "A New Approach to Sex Offenders," *Responsive Community* 4 (Fall 1994): 13.

18. W. L. Jacks, "Sex Offenders Released on Parole," Pennsylvania Board of Parole (1962), cited in Furby, et al., "Sex Offender Recidivism," 18.

19. T.C.N. Gibbens, K. L. Soothill, and C. K. Way, "Sibling and Parent-Child Incest Offenders," *British Journal of Criminology* 18 (1978): 40–52, cited in Furby, et al., "Sex Offender Recidivism," 18.

20. Eric Lotke, "Issues and Answers—Sex Offenders: Does Treatment Work?" (Alexandria, Va.: National Center on Institutions and Alternatives), available from http://www.ncianet.org/ncia/sexo.html.

21. "Names Removed from Missouri Sex Offender List," ACLU press release, 28 August 1997, available from: http://www.aclu.org/news/n082897a.html.

22. Compare the recidivism rates found by L. V. Frisbie and E. H. Dondis for exhibitionists (40.7 percent), pedophiles (21.5 percent), and incest offenders (10.2 percent); cited in Furby et. al., "Sex Offender Recidivism," 13.

23. Compare the recidivism rates found by Broadhurst and Maller for sex offenders reincarcerated for another sex offense (8 percent) and those reincarcerated for any kind of offense (36 percent); R. G. Broadhurst and R. A. Maller, "The Recidivism of Sex Offenders in the Western Australian Prison Population," *British Journal of Criminology* 32 (1992): 63.

24. Compare the recidivism rates found by J. W. Mohr, R. E. Turner, and M. B. Jerry for first-time offenders (10 percent) and offenders with prior records (33 percent with a previous sex offense, 55 percent with both previous sex and non-sex offenses); Mohr, Turner, and Jerry, *Pedophilia: Exhibitionism: A Handbook* (Toronto: University of Toronto Press, 1964). Also, A. R. Pacht and L. M. Roberts found a significant discrepancy between first-timers (21 percent) and those with previous offenses (33 percent); Pacht and Roberts, "Factors Related to Parole Experience of the Sexual Offender: A Nine-Year Study," *Journal of Correctional Psychology* 3 (1968). Both studies cited in Furby et. al., "Sex Offender Recidivism," 14–15.

25. Compare the recidivism rates found by B. Grunfeld and K. Noreik for average offender follow-up of eleven years (13 percent) with K. L. Soothill, A. Jack, and T.C.N. Gibbens's offender follow-up of twenty-two years (48 percent); cited in Song and Lieb, *Adult Sex Offender Recidivism*, 6.

26. Compare the recidivism rates found by A. J. Beck and B. E. Shipley for rapists re-arrested for another offense of any kind (52 percent), reconvicted for another offense (36 percent), or reincarcerated for another offense (32 percent); Beck and Shipley for Bureau of Justice Statistics, U.S. Department of Justice, *Recidivism of Prisoners Released in 1983* (Washington, D.C.: BOJS, 1989), 2.

27. Compare the recidivism rates found by Joseph J. Romero and Linda Meyer Williams for sex offenders placed on probation (11 percent) with Broadhurst and Maller's rates for incarcerated offenders (51 percent);

Romero and Williams, "A Comparative Study of Group Psychotherapy and Intensive Probation Supervision with Sex Offenders," *Federal Probation* 47 (1985): 36–42; R. G. Broadhurst and R. A. Maller, "The Recidivism of Sex Offenders in the Western Australian Prison Population," 54–80; and Song and Lieb, *Adult Sex Offender Recidivism*, 14.

28. Compare W. L. Marshall and H. E. Barbaree's recidivism rates of treated offenders (13 percent) with those of untreated offenders (34 percent); Marshall and Barbaree, "The Long-term Evaluation of a Behavioral Treatment Program for Child Molesters," *Behavior Research Therapy* 26, no. 6, 499–511, cited in Song and Lieb, *Adult Sex Offender Recidivism*, 10.

29. Compare the rates found by R. K. Hanson, R. A. Steffy, and R. Gauthier for those receiving behavioral treatment (44 percent) with Hildebrand and Pither's rates for offenders receiving cognitive-behavioral treatment (6 percent); Hanson, Steffy, and Gauthier, "Long-term Follow-up of Child Molesters: Risk Predictors and Treatment Outcome," Corrections Branch, Ministry of the Solicitor General of Canada, no. 1992–02, cited in Song and Lieb, *Adult Sex Offender Recidivism*, 15; and Gordon C. Nagayama Hall, "Sexual Offender Recidivism Revisited: A Meta-Analysis of Recent Treatment Studies," *Journal of Consulting and Clinical Psychology* 63 (1995): 806.

30. Compare the rates found by Rice et al. for those treated in a psychiatric hospital (38 percent) with the state of Vermont's rates for outpatient programs (7 percent); M. E. Rice, V. L. Quinsey, and G. T. Harris, "Sexual Recidivism Among Child Molesters Released from a Maximum-Security Psychiatric Institution," *Journal of Consulting and Clinical Psychology* 59, no. 3 (1991): 381–386; State of Vermont, Center for the Prevention and Treatment of Sexual Abuse, "Vermont Treatment Program for Sexual Aggressors: Program Evaluation" (1992); both cited in Song and Lieb, *Adult Sex Offender Recidivism*, 15.

31. Furby et al., "Sex Offender Recidivism," 8.

32. Ibid., 27.

33. V. L. Quinsey, G. T. Harris, M. E. Rice, and M. L. Lalumiere, "Sexual Recidivism Among Child Molesters Released from a Maximum Security Psychiatric Institution," *Journal of Consulting and Clinical Psychology* 59 (1991): 519.

34. Hall, "Sexual Offender Recidivism Revisited," 806.

35. Margaret Alexander, "Sex Offender Treatment Efficacy Revisited" (Oshkosh: Oshkosh [Wisc.] Correctional Institution, 1996).

36. Beck and Shipley, *Recidivism of Prisoners Released in 1983*, 1.

37. Lotke, "Issues and Answers—Sex Offenders: Does Treatment Work?"

38. National Institute of Justice, U.S. Department of Justice, *Child Sexual Molestation: Research Issues* (Washington, D.C.: NIJ, June 1997).

39. Bureau of Justice Statistics, U.S. Department of Justice, *Criminal Victimization in the United States, 1994* (Washington, D.C.: BOJS, 1997), 88.

40. Lotke, "Issues and Answers—Sex Offenders: Does Treatment Work?"

41. Furby et al., "Sex Offender Recidivism," 8.

42. D. Finkelhor and J. Dziuba-Leatherman, "Children as Victims of Violence: A National Survey," *Pediatrics* 94 (1994): 413–420, cited in U.S. Department of Justice, *Child Sexual Molestation*, 1.

43. A. N. Groth, R. E. Longo, and J. B. McFadin, "Undetected Recidivism in Rapists and Child Molesters," *Crime and Delinquency* 28 (1982): 450.

44. Gene G. Abel, Judith V. Becker, Mary Mittelman, Jerry Cunningham-Rathner, Joanne L. Rouleau, and William D. Murphy, "Self-Reported Sex Crimes of Nonincarcerated Paraphiliacs," *Journal of Interpersonal Violence* 2 (1987): 3–25.

45. Mark Weinrott and Maureen Saylor, "Self-Report of Sex Crimes Committed by Sex Offenders," *Journal of Interpersonal Violence* 6 (1991): 291–292.

46. While self-report studies illustrate the true scope of sex offense, comparable self-report studies for other acts are scarce. However, we can use victimization surveys to gauge the underrepresentation of sex offenses relative to other violent felonies. Only 35.7 percent of sex offenses against those age twelve to nineteen are reported, but other crimes appear to have higher rates of reporting. In the same age group, 53.7 percent report robberies with injury, and 49.6 percent report assaults with injury; U.S. Department of Justice, *Criminal Victimization in the United States, 1994*, 88. It appears that sex offenses are reported significantly less than robberies and assaults.

47. ACLU (ACLU Media), "ACLU Answers: Megan's Law" (on excluding due process objection), received 3 December 1996.

48. Roberto Suro, "Town Faults Law, Not Boy in Sex Case," *Washington Post*, 11 May 1997, A1; see also ACLU, "California Legislators Seek to Narrow Megan's Law," press release, 4 April 1997.

49. For example, California's penal code includes as "habitual sexual offenders" those who have on their criminal record (which can date back to 1944) two arrests for a single sex offense, which can be consensual sodomy, categorized as a "crime against nature"; California Penal Codes 13885.4, 290.

50. Suro, "Town Faults Law, Not Boy, in Sex Case," A1.

51. ACLU, "ACLU Urges Congress to Curb Reach of Megan's Law to Exclude Consensual Sodomy," press release, 9 September 1997, available from: http://www.aclu.org/news/n090997b.html. However, this problem was

amended by a California law passed in October 1997 that allows gay men convicted of consensual sodomy both exemption from annual registration and the opportunity to expunge their names from the state registry; see ACLU, "ACLU Scores Win for Gay Men Swept up in California Sex Offender Law," press release, 12 November 1997.

52. For additional discussion and documentation, see Amitai Etzioni, "We Shouldn't Squander Our Moral Outrage," *Wall Street Journal*, December 27, 1994, A16; see also Amitai Etzioni, "We Should Focus Our Moral Voice," *Responsive Community* (Spring 1995): 13.

53. ACLU, "ACLU Urges Congress to Curb Reach of Megan's Law."

54. Scott Matson and Roxanne Lieb, *Community Notification in Washington State: 1996 Survey of Law Enforcement* (Olympia: Washington State Institute for Public Policy, November 1996), 3–5.

55. New Jersey's law has three levels of notification: (1) low risk of reoffense—only law enforcement agencies are notified; (2) moderate risk—community organizations (e.g., schools, churches, youth organizations) are notified; (3) high risk—the public is notified through channels most likely to reach those who will probably encounter the offender; New Jersey Statutes Annotate sect. 2C:7–8(c), cited by G. Scott Rafshoon, "Community Notification of Sex Offenders: Issues of Punishment, Privacy, and Due Process," *Emory Law Journal* 44 (1995): 1633, 1641.

56. Matson and Lieb, *Community Notification in Washington State*, 1.

57. Robert Hanley, "New Jersey, Megan's Home, Limits 'Her' Law," *New York Times*, 5 January 1998, B1.

58. Daniel L. Feldman, "The 'Scarlet Letter Laws' of the 1990s: A Response to Critics," *Albany Law Review* 60 (1997): 1081, 1085; see *Doe v. Poritz*, 662 A. 2d. 367, 439 [N.J. 1995].

59. E.B.V. Verniero, nos. 96–5132 and 96–5416, U.S. Third Circuit Court of Appeals, 119F3d 1077.

60. "Les Miserables and the Scarlet Letter All in One," *ACLU News Wire*, 10 July 1996.

61. Jennifer L. Couture, "An *Ex Post Facto* Analysis of Sex Offender Registration Statutes: Branding Criminals with a Scarlet Letter," *Suffolk University Law Review* 29 (1995): 1199, 1203.

62. Earl-Hubbard, "The Child Sex Offender Registration Laws," 829.

63. Lori N. Sabin, "*Doe v. Poritz:* A Constitutional Yield to an Angry Society," *California Law Review* 32 (1996): 331, 354; see also ACLU, "ACLU Answers: Megan's Law."

64. Earl-Hubbard, "The Child Sex Offender Registration Laws," 820–821.

65. Ibid., 821, citing *Harmelin v. Michigan* (501 U.S. 957 [1991]).

66. ACLU, "ACLU Answers: Megan's Law."

67. Quoted in ibid.

68. Quoted in ibid.

69. See Carl F. Horowitz, "The Shaming Sham," *American Prospect* (March-April 1997): 70.

70. "Public Humiliation for Crimes: Ain't That a Shame?" *ACLU News and Events*, 25 June 1996.

71. ABC News, *20/20*, 18 October 1996.

72. Tom Cahill, "Cruel and Unusual Punishment: Rape in Prison," *Victimology* 9, no. 1 (1984): 8–10.

73. Gordon Bazemore, "Communities, Victims, and Offender Reintegration: Restorative Justice and Earned Redemption," *American Behavioral Scientist* 41 (1998): 769; David Karp, "Judicial and Judicious Use of Shame Penalties," *Crime and Delinquency* (forthcoming); John Braithwaite, "Restorative Justice and a Better Future," paper presented at Dalhousie University, Halifax, Nova Scotia, 17 October 1996.

74. Sabin, "*Doe v. Poritz*," 354.

75. Earl Hubbard, "The Child Sex Offender Registration Laws," 851–852.

76. Weinrott and Saylor, "Self-Report of Sex Crimes Committed by Sex Offenders," 286, 291–292.

77. Earl-Hubbard, "The Child Sex Offender Registration Laws," 839.

78. Ibid., 812.

79. "Dealing with Sex Offenders" (editorial), *New York Times*, 15 August 1994, A14.

80. Sabin, "*Doe v. Poritz*," 354.

81. Lourdes-Medrano Leslie, "Sex-Offender Notification Debated," *Arizona Republic*, 29 August 1995, cited in Earl-Hubbard, "The Child Sex Offender Registration Laws," 824.

82. John T. McQuiston, "Sex Offender Is Suing His Neighbors over Protests," *New York Times*, 20 June 1997, B1.

83. Purdum, "Death of Sex Offender Is Tied to Megan's Law," A16.

84. Feldman, "The 'Scarlet Letter Laws' of the 1990s," 1114.

85. The 900 number, however, is presently unavailable owing to a court injunction; Kelly K. Haskin-Tenenini, New York State Division of Criminal Justice Services, private communication, 19 November 1997.

86. Todd S. Purdum, "State Registry Laws Tar All Convicted Sex Offenders with a Broad Brush," *New York Times*, 1 July 1997, A19.

87. Rebecca Fairley Rainey, "One Man's Crusade Against Sex Offenders," *New York Times/Cybertimes*, 16 September 1997.

88. "Education Urged to Prevent 'Megan's Law' Vigilantism," *New York Times*, 18 June 1998, A37. For instance, in Washington, as part of a tiered program, police went from door to door in three-fifths of the communities and half of the communities held community meetings. Such steps provide authorities an opportunity not only to inform citizens about a particular sex offender but also to educate people about different sexual crimes. In addition, people are reminded that vigilantism will not be condoned. "Sloppy 'Megan's Laws' Hinder Goal of Boosting Public Safety," *USA Today*, 12 May 1998, 12A.

89. Purdum, "Death of Sex Offender."

90. Mike Allen, "List of Sex Offenders Is Withheld After Girl's Killing in Connecticut," *New York Times*, 26 August 1998, B1.

91. Washington State Institute of Public Policy, *Community Notification of Sex Offenders in Washington State.*

92. In the six years between the law's implementation and 1996, only 33 acts of harassment have been reported (of 942 notifications), or in less than 4 percent of all cases; Scott Manson and Roxanne Lieb, *Community Notification in Washington State: 1996 Survey of Law Enforcement* (Olympia: Washington State Institute for Public Policy, 25 November 1996).

93. For more discussion of this equilibrium, see Amitai Etzioni, *The New Golden Rule: Community and Morality in a Democratic Society* (New York: Basic Books, 1996), 3–57.

94. This belief is largely a matter of conventional wisdom, supported only anecdotally by various therapists and other experts; U.S. Department of Justice, Bureau of Justice Statistics, *Child Victimizers*, iv.

95. Simeon Schopf, "'Megan's Law': Community Notification and the Constitution," *Columbia Journal of Law and Social Problems* 29 (1995): 117.

96. Detective Robert A. Shilling, Seattle Police Department., *Sex Offender Information Bulletin*, 8 May 1995.

97. "Education Urged to Prevent 'Megan's Law' Vigilantism," A37.

98. Center for the Common Interest, "New York Violent Felons to Serve More Time," *FridayFax*, 31 July 1998.

99. A.R.S. 13–4606 (1996), Washington Code RCW 71.09.060.

100. Wisconsin Statutes 980.02–06 (1996).

101. A.R.S. 13–4606, Wisconsin Statutes 980.06.

102. Adler and Annin, "Too Dangerous to Set Free?" 38, 41.

103. *State of Kansas v. Leroy Hendricks*, U.S. Supreme Court 95–1649 (1997).

104. Rael Jean Isaac, "Put Sex Predators Behind Bars, Not on the Couch," *Wall Street Journal*, 8 May 1998, A14.

105. Ibid.

106. National Public Radio, *Morning Edition*, 10 December 1996.

107. CBS, *60 Minutes*, 11 January 1997.

108. CNN, *TalkBack Live*, 24 June 1997.

109. CBS, *60 Minutes*, 11 January 1997.

110. Ibid.

111. Michael Jonathan Grinfeld, "Sexual Predator Ruling Raises Ethical, Moral Dilemma," *Psychiatric Times*, August 1997, available from: http://www.mhsource.com/edu/psytimes/p970801b.html.

112. Ibid.

113. Suzy Rotkiss, private communication, 7 August 1997.

114. Mireya Navarro, "Confining Tuberculosis Patients: Weighing Rights Versus Health Risks," *New York Times*, 21 November 1993, 1.

CHAPTER THREE

1. Yvette Butler, statement at the U.S. Department of Commerce, 23 June 1998.

2. Dorothy E. Denning and William E. Baugh Jr., "Encryption and Evolving Technologies as Tools of Organized Crime and Terrorism" (U.S. Working Group on Organized Crime, National Strategy Information Center, 1997).

3. Ibid.

4. Whitfield Diffie and Susan Landau, *Privacy on the Line: The Politics of Wiretapping and Encryption* (Cambridge, Mass.: MIT Press, 1998), 6ff.

5. A. Michael Froomkin invokes these two core images in his article "It Came from Planet Clipper: The Battle over Cryptographic Key 'Escrow,'" *University of Chicago Legal Forum* 15 (1996): 15.

6. For example, using homemade supercomputers and $250,000, researchers unscrambled the strong encryption on which the U.S. government was relying; John Markoff, "U.S. Data Code Is Unscrambled in 56 Hours," *New York Times*, 17 July 1998, D1. See also John Markoff, "New Method to Veil Data Could Upstage Export Policy," *New York Times*, 22 March 1998, 31.

7. Denning and Baugh, "Encryption and Evolving Technologies"; and "Encryption in Crime and Terrorism," in Alan D. Campen and Douglas H. Dearth, eds., *Cyberwar 2.0* (AFCEA International Press, June 1998). I benefited as well from Professor Denning's comments, and am grateful for permission to use these materials.

8. Denning and Baugh, "Encryption in Crime and Terrorism," 1.

9. House of Representatives, Committee on International Relations, *Hearings on Encryption*, testimony of FBI Director Louis J. Freeh, 26 June 1997, available from: http://www.netlynews.com.

10. Walter Pincus and Vernon Loeb, "CIA Blocked Two Attacks Last Year," *Washington Post*, 11 August 1998, A16.

11. Denning and Baugh, "Encryption in Crime and Terrorism," 1.

12. House Committee on International Relations, Freeh testimony, 26 June 1997; see also House of Representatives, Judiciary Committee, *Hearings on Encryption and H.R. 3011*, testimony of Deputy Attorney General Jamie S. Gorelick, 25 September 1996.

13. Steven Levy, "Battle of the Clipper Chip," *New York Times*, 12 June 1994, sect. 6, 46.

14. Compare to the view of G. A. Keyworth II, who believes that the United States would be better off if public authorities accepted some delays in access to encrypted communications; "Computer Security Doesn't Hamper U.S. Security," *Wall Street Journal*, 5 August 1998, A14.

15. Special Panel of the Association for Computing Machinery (ACM), U.S. Public Policy Committee, "Codes, Keys, and Conflicts: Issues in U.S. Crypto Policy," June 1994, available from: http://www.acm.org/reports/acm_crypto_study.html.

16. For a strong argument to this effect, see Electronic Privacy Information Center, *Cryptography and Liberty: An International Survey of Encryption Policy* (Washington, D.C.: Electronic Privacy Information Center, 1998).

17. Representative Bob Goodlatte, letter to the editor, *Washington Post*, 12 June 1997, A22.

18. For a recent survey of other countries' encryption policies, see Global Internet Liberty Campaign, "Cryptography and Liberty: An International Survey of Encryption Policy," 6 April 1998, available from: http://www.gilc.org/crypto/crypto-survey.html.

19. House Committee on International Relations, *Hearings on Encryption*, 26 June 1997, 34.

20. The American company Network Associates and its Dutch subsidiary, Network Associates International BV, have recently made available 128-bit PGP software (under the name "PGP Total Network Security Suite") for businesses around the world; see Network Associates, press release, 20 March 1998, available from: http://www.nai.com/about/news/press/1998/032098.asp.

21. Bruce J. McConnell and Edward J. Appel, "Enabling Privacy, Commerce, Security, and Public Safety in the Global Information Infrastructure," 20 May 1996, 2, available from: http://www.epic.org/crypto/key_escrow/white_paper.html.

22. The FBI seems to be moving closer and closer to supporting a mandatory key escrow system; Roberto Suro and Elizabeth Corcoran, "U.S. Law Enforcement Wants Keys to High-Tech Cover," *Washington Post*, 30 March

1998, A4. Additionally, Robert S. Litt of the Justice Department appears to leave the door open for a mandatory key escrow regime; see U.S. Senate, Judiciary Committee, Subcommittee on the Constitution, Federalism, and Property, *Privacy in a Digital Age: Encryption and Mandatory Access*, testimony of Principal Associate Deputy Attorney General Robert S. Litt, 17 March 1998, available from: http://www.computerprivacy.org/archive/03171998-4.html.

23. The term refers to classical liberals, contemporary classical liberals, laissez-faire conservatives, libertarians, and civil libertarians; for more discussion of the term, see Amitai Etzioni, *The New Golden Rule: Community and Morality in a Democratic Society* (New York: Basic Books, 1996), 8–9.

24. Levy, "Battle of the Clipper Chip," 46. The term also was used in Dorothy Denning, private communication, 4 March 1998.

25. Goodlatte, letter to the editor, *Washington Post*, 12 June 1997.

26. Note reports that the Clinton administration often compromised national security to satisfy commercial interests, especially Silicon Valley. Jeff Gerth and Eric Schmitt, "The Technology Trade: A Special Report; Chinese Said to Reap Gains in U.S. Export Policy Shift," *New York Times*, 19 October 1998, A1.

27. William Safire, "Sink the Clipper Chip," in Bruce Schneider and David Bunisar, eds., *The Electronic Privacy Papers: Documents on the Battle for Privacy in the Age of Surveillance* (New York: Wiley, 1997), 495–496.

28. Daniel P. Kahn, "French Law Governing Encryption Technology," and Wilson Wong, "Encryption Control and Policy in Singapore," papers presented at the Eighth Annual Conference on Computers, Freedom, and Privacy, Austin, Tex., 18–20 February 1998; see also Global Internet Liberty Campaign, "Cryptography and Liberty."

29. Philip Zimmermann, interview on WALE (Providence, R.I.), *High Tech Today* (radio show), 2 February 1996.

30. Ibid.

31. Ron Rivest, letter to Dorothy Denning, 25 February 1994.

32. A. Michael Froomkin, "The Metaphor Is the Key: Cryptography, the Clipper Chip, and the Constitution," *University of Pennsylvania Law Review* 143 (1995): 709–897; Froomkin, "It Came from Planet Clipper."

33. Froomkin, like this author, refers to public key recovery only for law enforcement purposes. Recovery for other reasons—for instance, if keys are lost—is not at issue. Froomkin, "It Came from Planet Clipper."

34. Froomkin, "The Metaphor Is the Key," 822, 833.

35. Lance J. Hoffman, "Encryption Policy for the Global Information Infrastructure," Eleventh International Conference on Information Security,

Cape Town, South Africa, 9–12 May 1995. The ACLU argues: "Export restrictions on cryptography are a prior restraint on protected speech, and are a content-based gag on Constitutionally protected speech"; available from: http://www.aclu.org/issues/cyber/priv/crypto.reg.comments.html.

36. ACLU, "Privacy in America: Computers, Phones, and Privacy," 1997, available from: http://www.aclu.org/library/ibpriv3.html.

37. "Law Professors' Letter Opposing Mandatory Key Escrow" (an open letter to the U.S. Congress), 23 September 1997, available from: http://www.law.miami.edu/~froomkin/lawprof-letter.htm.

38. Rick Henderson, in the libertarian publication *Reason*, bluntly states: "The Clinton Administration and its allies in law enforcement don't want your communications to be private"; see "Clipping Encryption: The White House Wants the Keys to Your Computer" *Reason* (May 1998): 7. In case it is not clear to whom "your" refers, Henderson elaborates: "The privacy of every law-abiding American will be left to the whims of regulators, cops, and spooks." Missing from this company are the courts—whose job is to determine when eavesdropping is legal. One may wonder whether the courts are strict enough or grant warrants too readily. The fact that only about 1,000 warrants are granted each year for phone taps all over the United States, including 568 for state and local governments and 581 for the federal government, suggests that they are rarely granted; House Committee on International Relations, Freeh testimony, 26 July 1997.

39. McConnell and Appel, "Enabling Privacy, Commerce, Security, and Public Safety."

40. Rivest, letter to Denning, 25 February 1994.

41. Ibid.

42. Levy, "Battle of the Clipper Chip."

43. Whitfield Diffie and Susan Landau, *Privacy on the Line* (Cambridge, Mass.: MIT Press, 1998), esp. 238.

44. Sameer Parekh, "Now What? Living with Perpetual Evolution," *Cato Policy Report* (January-February 1998): 8.

45. Tim May, "Cyphernomicon," 10 September 1994, available from: http://www.oberlin.edu/~brchkind/cyphernomicon.

46. Zimmermann, *High Tech Today* interview, 2 February 1996.

47. John Perry Barlow, "A Cyberspace Independence Declaration," 9 February 1996, available from: http://info.bris.ac.uk/~lwmdcg/DoI.html.

48. Subcommittee on Science, Space, and Technology, *Hearings on the Promotion of Commerce On-Line In the Digital Era Act of 1996, S. 1726*, testimony of Marc Rotenberg, 26 June 1996.

49. Levy, "Battle of the Clipper Chip."

50. John Perry Barlow, "Decrypting the Puzzle Palace," *Communications of the ACM*, June 1992, available from: http://english-server.hss.cmu.edu/cyber/clipper/bckgrnd.txt.

51. Dorothy Denning, "The Case for Clipper," *Technology Review* (July 1995): 53.

52. John Markoff, "Researchers Crack Code in Cell Phones," *New York Times*, 14 April 1998, D1.

53. Froomkin, "It Came from Planet Clipper," 17.

54. Deborah Russell and G. T. Gangemi Sr., "Encryption," in Lance Hoffman, ed., *Building in Big Brother* (New York: Springer, 1995), 11. In preparing this discussion of the history of cryptography, I benefited greatly from Kenneth Flamm, "Deciphering the Cryptography Debate," *Brookings Policy Brief* 21 (1997): 4–6; Graeme Browning, "Securing Cyberspace," *National Journal*, 16 March 1996, 621; Lance Hoffman, "Encryption Policy for the Global Information Infrastructure," Eleventh International Conference on Information Security, Capetown, South Africa, 9–12 May 1995; Kenneth W. Dam and Herbert S. Lin, eds., *Cryptography's Role in Securing the Information Society* (Washington, D.C.: National Academy Press, 1996); and Dorothy Denning, "Encryption Policy and Market Trends," 17 May 1997, available from: http://guru. gosc.georgetown.edu/~Denning/crypto/Trends.html.

55. For discussion, see Wendy M. Grossman, *net.wars* (New York: New York University Press, 1997), chap. 5.

56. Electronic Frontier Foundation, "EFF Analysis of Vice President Gore's letter on Cryptography Policy," 22 July 1994, available from: http://www.eff.org/pub/Privacy/Key_escrow/Clipper/gore_retreat_eff.analysis.

57. Jeri Clausing, "White House Yields a Bit on Encryption," *New York Times*, 8 July 1998, D1.

58. See, for instance, Browning, "Securing Cyberspace," and David E. Sanger, "Accord Near on Computer Security Codes," *New York Times*, 1 October 1996, A1.

59. Hoffman, "Encryption Policy for the Global Information Infrastructure," 5.

CHAPTER 4

1. Joseph W. Eaton, professor emeritus at the University of Pittsburgh, was one such advocate.

2. *ABC World News Tonight*, 18 December 1995.

3. U.S. Department of Justice, Federal Advisory Committee on False Identification, *The Criminal Use of False Identification* (Washington, D.C.: U.S. Government Printing Office, 1976), 36.

4. Gregory Gordon, "Computer Masterminds' Roundup of 249 Fugitives," UPI, 14 November 1988.

5. "Federal Fugitive Apprehension—Agencies Taking Action to Improve Coordination and Cooperation," report no. GAO/GGD–95–75, *GAO Reports*, 2 May 1995.

6. Ibid.

7. See, for example, Victoria Pope, "Day Care Dangers," *U.S. News & World Report*, 4 August 1997, 31–37.

8. U.S. Senate, Judiciary Committee, *Hearings on the National Child Protection Act*, "Protecting Children in Day Care: Building a National Background Check System," remarks by chairman Senator Joseph R. Biden Jr., 12 November 1991.

9. "Away from Politics" (editorial), *International Herald Tribune*, 17 August 1998, 3.

10. Senate Judiciary Committee, *Hearings on the National Child Protection Act.*

11. U.S. House of Representatives, Committee on Ways and Means, Subcommittee on Oversight, statement of Ronald K. Noble, undersecretary of the treasury for enforcement, 6 October 1994.

12. U.S. Department of Justice, *The Criminal Use of False Identification*, xii–xiv, 8.

13. GAO, "Identity Fraud: Information on Prevalence, Cost, and Internet Impact Is Limited," report no. GAO/GGD–98–100BR (Washington, D.C.: GAO, May 1998), 36.

14. U.S. Senate, Judiciary Committee, Subcommittee on Juvenile Justice, *Hearings on Criminal Penalty for Flight to Avoid Payment of Arrearages in Child Support*, remarks by chairman Senator Herbert Kohl, 29 July 1992.

15. Ibid., testimony of Senator Joseph R. Biden Jr., 29 July 1992.

16. U.S. Bureau of the Census, *Statistical Abstract of the United States: 1996*, 116th ed. (Washington, D.C.: Bureau of the Census, 1996), 386.

17. U.S. House of Representatives, Committee on Government Reform and Oversight, Subcommittee on Government Management, Information, and Technology, "Security of Government IDs and Documents," testimony of Richard W. Velde, 7 March 1995.

18. Jeffrey A. Roberts, "ID Cards Used to Buy Guns Illegally," *Denver Post*, 17 January 1994, A–01.

19. Sixty-one percent of illegal immigrants in the United States enter legally, through temporary tourist or student visas, according to the INS; cited in Karen Brandon, "Many Illegals Arrive Legally; INS Overlooks Millions Who Overstay Student, Tourist Visas," *Phoenix Gazette*, 4 August 1995, B4. One INS study of non-Hispanic illegal immigrants found that of those coming to the United States on tourist visas, approximately 37 percent of Poles, 17 percent of Haitians, 14 percent of Filipinos, and 10 percent of Soviets disappear into the population; cited in "Immigrants: INS Putting New Faces on Problems of Illegals," *Houston Chronicle*, 14 January 1996, 2. See also Mark Krikorian, "Who Deserves Asylum? Immigration Law," *Commentary* (June 1996): 52; and Miguel Perez, "Border Hype Creates Myth," *The Record* [Bergen, N.J.], 8 May 1996, N01.

20. Karen Bowers, "Crossing the Line: How Illegal Aliens with Criminal Records Come over the River—And Through the Cracks," *Denver Westword*, 10 May 1995, 15.

21. Federation for American Immigration Reform, "America Needs a Secure ID System," November 1997, available from: http://www.fairus.org/04116604.

22. Deborah Sontag, "Porous Deportation System Gives Criminals Little to Fear," *New York Times*, 13 September 1994, B1.

23. In fact, even some libertarians admit that "most immigration authorities worldwide base their estimates [of the costs of illegal immigration] on qualitative assessment." Their strongest critique is that "the impact of cards on illegal immigration has been patchy"; in other words, they still have a chance to make an important difference; Privacy International, "Identity Cards: Frequently Asked Questions," 24 August 1996, available from: http://www.privacy.org/pi/activities/idcard/idcard_faq.html.

24. Ibid.

25. Ibid.

26. Robert Kuttner, "Illegal Immigration: Would a National ID Card Help?" *Business Week*, 26 August 1991, 14.

27. John Commins, "Roundup Nabs Alleged Welfare Cheats," *Nashville Banner*, 9 July 1997, A1.

28. "Biometric Identifiers: Privacy Opportunities and Problems," *Privacy and American Business* 4 (1997–1998): 21; Commins, "Roundup Nabs Alleged Welfare Cheats"; Congressman Michael N. Castle, "Virtual Fingerprints, Iris Scans, Voice Recognition," *Congressional Press Releases*, 19 May 1998.

29. Castle, "Virtual Fingerprints, Iris Scans, Voice Recognition."

30. Toby Roth, "It's Time to Stop Welfare Fraud," *Congressional Press Releases*, 30 January 1995; Bureau of the Census, *Statistical Abstract of the United States: 1996*, 370.

31. Beth Givens and the Privacy Rights Clearinghouse with Dale Fetherling, *The Privacy Rights Handbook: How to Take Control of Your Personal Information* (New York: Avon Books, 1997), 227.

32. Ibid.

33. Givens and the Privacy Rights Clearinghouse, *The Privacy Rights Handbook*, 232.

34. Robert O'Harrow Jr. and John Schwartz, "A Case of Taken Identity," *Washington Post*, 26 May 1998, A9.

35. GAO, "Identity Fraud," 49.

36. Beth Givens, (director of the Privacy Rights Clearinghouse), personal communication, 11 August 1998.

37. Beth Givens, "Identity Theft: How It Happens, Its Impact on Victims, and Legislative Solutions," paper presented at the National Association of Consumer Agency Administrators' Annual Meeting, Dana Point, Calif., 19 May 1997, available from: http://www.privacyrights.org/ar/ id_theft_legis.html.

38. Givens, personal communication, 11 August 1998.

39. Givens, personal communication, 11 August 1998.

40. David Simcox, "The Need for a Secure National ID System," *USA Today: The Magazine of the American Scene* (January 1991): 15; Givens and the Privacy Rights Clearinghouse, *The Privacy Rights Handbook*, 228. Credit card fraud may involve misuse of another's lost or stolen card, use of a counterfeit card, or application for a credit card with criminal intent.

41. Gary T. Marx, "Fraudulent Identification and Biography," in Arizona State University School of Justice Studies, *New Directions in the Study of Justice, Law, and Social Control* (New York: Plenum Press, 1990), 143–144.

42. GAO, "Identity Fraud," 28.

43. See Raul Yzaguirre's discussion of a 1990 GAO survey on this topic, "Employer Sanctions Don't Work," *Washington Post*, 3 April 1990, A19. See also discussion of this report and the topic of discrimination later in this chapter.

44. Simcox, "The Need for a Secure National ID System," 14.

45. Ibid. In addition, in many states certified copies of real birth certificates—anyone's birth certificate, including those of infants who died at birth—may also be purchased by anyone for $5; see Glenn Garvin, "Bringing the Border War Home," *Reason* (October 1995): 5.

46. Available from: http://www.nic-inc.com.

47. Joseph W. Eaton, private communication, 16 April 1998.

48. For a thoughtful treatment of the principles and practices that should guide government collection and use of data, see George T. Duncan, Thomas B. Jabine, and Virginia A. de Wolf, eds., *Private Lives and Public Policies: Confidentiality and Accessibility of Government Statistics* (Washington, D.C.: National Academy Press, 1993).

49. William Branigin, "INS to Tighten Controls Against Immigration Fraud," *Washington Post*, 15 November 1997, A10. It should be noted, however, that experiences with private ID cards have proven so troublesome that the INS decided in 1997 to stop relying on private sources to fingerprint applicants for citizenship and chose instead to incorporate this function into its own offices.

50. "Biometric Identifiers: Privacy Opportunities and Problems," *Privacy and American Business* 4 (1997–1998): 20.

51. Ellen C. Greenblatt, "Massachusetts Uses Unisys to Track Criminals," *Datamation* (December 1996): 14; Aileen Crowley, "Me, Myself, and Eye," *PC Week*, 22 May 1995, E12; "Biometrics: The Measure of Man," *The Economist*, 19 September 1992, 102–103.

52. Saul Hansell, "Use of Recognition Technology Grows in Everyday Transactions," *New York Times*, 20 August 1997, D1.

53. The information in this paragraph is taken from Gerald Lazar, "Agencies Scan Biometrics for Potential Applications," *Federal Computer Week*, 20 January 1997, available from: http://www.fcw.com/pubs/fcw/1997/0120/feature.htm.

54. National Public Radio, "Vegas ATM," *Weekend All Things Considered*, transcript 98050903–216, 9 May 1998.

55. "Biometric Identifiers" (*Privacy and American Business*), 20.

56. Department of Health and Human Services, "Unique Health Identifier for Individuals: A White Paper," 2 July 1998.

57. Ibid.

58. Joseph R. Garber, "We Know Who You Are," *Forbes*, 10 August 1998, 110.

59. See, for example, Michael Conlon, "On the Move; Photo ID Requirement May Be Permanent for Air Travelers," *Los Angeles Times*, 11 September 1996, 4; Gary Scheets and Kristan Metzler, "Local Travelers Feel Security Pinch," *Washington Times*, 29 July 1996, C3.

60. Steven L. Nock, *The Costs of Privacy: Surveillance and Reputation in America* (New York: Aldine De Gruyter, 1993), 59.

61. Joseph W. Eaton, *Card-Carrying Americans: Privacy, Security, and the National ID Cards Debate* (Totowa, N.J.: Rowman & Littlefield, 1986), 175–177.

62. Susan Daniels, "Fraud Fighters Balance Privacy Rights," *National Underwriter*, 15 September 1997, 27.

63. National Center for Missing and Exploited Children, *DNA Databanks for Sex Offenders* (August 1996): 1.

64. National Public Radio, "Clinton Health Plan Card Could Alienate Supporters," *Morning Edition*, transcript 1240–7, 17 December 1993.

65. Judi Hasson, "Health Card Raises a Public Concern," *USA Today*, 16 December 1993, 8A. In a Louis Harris poll of 1,000 people, 85 percent of respondents believed "protecting people's medical records is essential in health reform." See also John Merline, "National Issue," *Investor's Business Daily*, 18 November 1993, 1; NPR, "Clinton Health Plan Card Could Alienate Supporters."

66. Princeton Survey Research Associates, "*Newsweek* Poll: Lifting Our Lamp (Immigration)," 31 July 1993.

67. Gallup/CNN/*USA Today* poll, 7 July 1995.

68. Equifax-Harris Consumer Privacy Survey, 1 February 1995 (survey conducted 17 August 1994 through 4 September 1994).

69. Gallup poll, 22 November 1984.

70. Eaton, *Card-Carrying Americans.*

71. "Talking Points: Welfare Reform, ID Cards, Religion, and More," *Libertarian Party News* (April 1995), reprinted from "Our View," *USA Today*, 15 July 1994, available from: http://www.lp.org/lp/lpn/9504-talking.html.

72. John J. Miller and Stephen Moore, "A National ID System: Big Brother's Solution to Illegal Immigration" (Washington, D.C.: Cato Institute, 7 September 1995), 3, 7.

73. ACLU, "The ACLU on . . . National Identification Cards," 1996, available from: http://www.aclu.org/library/aaidcard.html.

74. Robert Ellis Smith, "The True Terror Is in the Card," *New York Times Magazine*, 8 September 1996, 59.

75. ACLU, "National Identification Cards: 'Why Does the ACLU Oppose a National ID System?'" 1996, available from: http://www.aclu.org/library/aaidcard.html.

76. Uri Dowbenko, "Patriotic Gamble," *National Review*, 13 October 1997, 30.

77. Privacy International, "ID Cards: Some Personal Views from Around the World," July 1997, available from: http://www.privacy.org/pi/activities/idcard/personal.html.

78. Coalition for Constitutional Liberties, Open Letter to Newt Gingrich on National ID Card Regulations, 17 July 1998.

79. The Phyllis Schlafly Report, "Liberty vs. Totalitarianism, Clinton-Style," The Phyllis Schlafly Report, July 1998, 1–3.

80. Ibid.

81. Miller and Moore, "A National ID System," 3.

82. ACLU, "National Identification Cards."

83. Ron K. Unz, "Big Brother, Meet Big Sister," *Los Angeles Times*, 12 June 1995, B5.

84. Simon G. Davies, "Touching Big Brother: How Biometrics Will Fuse Flesh and Machine," *Information Technology & People* 7, no. 4 (1994).

85. Nojeim and Griswold quoted in Cato Institute Policy Forum, "Papers Please! National IDs in the '90s" (Washington, D.C.: Cato Institute, 1 October 1998).

86. See, for example, Miller and Moore, "A National ID System," 5, 6, 20.

87. Yzaguirre, "Employer Sanctions Don't Work," A19.

88. Senator Dianne Feinstein, "Feinstein: State-of-the-Art ID System Is Necessary to Help Identify Illegal Aliens," *Roll Call*, 22 May 1995.

89. "National ID Card: Still No," *Albany* [N.Y.] *Times Union*, 30 September 1995, A6.

90. Adriel Bettelheim, "Immigration Divides Nation," *Denver Post*, 21 December 1997, A01.

91. U.S. House of Representatives, Committee on Government Reform and Oversight, *Hearings on Campaign Finance Revisions*, testimony of Rep. Stephen Horn, 6 November 1997.

92. For additional discussion on inverse symbiosis, see Etzioni, *The New Golden Rule*, 35–45.

93. Frederick Schauer, "Slippery Slopes," *Harvard Law Review* 99 (1985): 379.

94. Brian Pendreigh, "Identity Parade," *Scotsman*, 25 May 1995, 17; see also Flynn, "Personal ID System Now Widespread," 8.

95. Flynn, "Personal ID System Now Widespread"; Eaton, *Card-Carrying Americans*, 23.

96. Eaton, *Card-Carrying Americans*, 23; Stephen Bates, "Commune of the Paper Forest," *Manchester Guardian*, 26 September 1995, 14.

97. Flynn, "Personal ID System Now Widespread," 8.

98. Barbara Green, "IDs: Don't Leave Home Without One," *Financial Times*, 3 November 1993, 18.

99. Pendreigh, "Identity Parade," 17.

100. Professor Beat Buergenmeier, dean at the Université de Genève, private communication, 3 March 1998.

101. Professor José Perez Adan, Universidad de Valencia, private communication, 20 February 1998.

102. Virginia G. Maurer and Robert E. Thomas, "Getting Credit Where Credit Is Due: Proposed Changes in the Fair Credit Reporting Act," *American Business Law Journal* 4 (1997): 607.

103. For discussion of the abundant electronic availability of personal data, see, among others, Joshua Quittner, "Invasion of Privacy," *Time*, 25 August 1997, 28; Joanna Smith Ber, "Secrets for Sale," *American Banker*, 4 August 1997, 38; Susan H. Nycum, "Protection of Electronic Databases," *Computer Lawyer* (August 1997).

104. Robert O'Harrow Jr., "For Sale on the Web: Your Financial Secrets," *Washington Post*, 11 June 1998, A1.

105. Robert O'Harrow Jr., "Banking Agency to Back Data Protection," *Washington Post*, 13 June 1998, D2.

106. See, for example, Electronic Privacy Information Center, "Surfer Beware: Personal Privacy and the Internet," 1997, available from: http://www.epic.org/reports/surfer-beware.html. See also U.S. House of Representatives, Judiciary Committee, Subcommittee on Courts and Intellectual Property, *Hearings on Communications Privacy*, testimony of Marc Rotenberg, 26 March 1998; Federal Trade Commission, "Privacy Online: A Report to Congress" (Washington, D.C.: U.S. Government Printing Office, June 1998), n. 4.

107. International Research Bureau, Inc., available from: http://www.irb-online.com/services.html; see also Nina Bernstein, "On Line, High-Tech Sleuths Find Private Facts," *New York Times*, 15 September 1997, A1; and Erin Moriarty, "Getting Personal," *48 Hours/CBS News Transcripts*, 9 April 1998. Generally, see Andrew L. Shapiro, "Privacy for Sale: Peddling Data on the Internet," *Nation*, 23 June 1997, 11–16.

108. Kimberly Blanton, "CVS Will Halt Drug Mailing; Customer Outcry Spurs Chain to Reverse Itself on Use of Woburn Manufacturer," *Boston Globe*, 19 February 1998, E1.

109. Bruce Horovitz, "AmEx Kills Database Deal After Privacy Outrage," *USA Today*, 15 July 1998, B1.

110. Joel Brinkley, "Web Site Agrees to Safeguards in First On-line Privacy Deal," *New York Times*, 14 August 1998, A15.

111. Available: http://www.edithroman.com.

112. See: http://www.directmedia.com

113. See http://www.listbrokers.com/home.htm.

114. See Robert O'Harrow Jr., "Plans' Access to Pharmacy Data Raises Privacy Issue," *Washington Post*, 27 September 1998, A1, A26, A27.

115. See http:// www.pcshs.com.

116. Saul Hansell, "Big Web Sites to Track Steps of Their Users," *New York Times*, 16 August 1998, section 1,1.

117. Jon G. Auerbach, Mark Maremont, and Gary Putka, "Prying Eyes: With These Operators, Your Bank Account Is Now An Open Book," *Wall Street Journal*, 5 November 1998, A1, A13.

118. John Markoff, "A Call for Digital Surveillance Is Delayed," *New York Times*, 14 September 1998, C10.

119. Privacy International, "Identity Cards."

120. Suzanne MacLachlan and David Mutch, "The News in Brief," *Christian Science Monitor*, 6 July 1995, 2; see also Maria Puente, "Immigrants Favor ID Card," *USA Today*, 4 July 1995, 1A.

121. It is worth noting here that any side effects will vary with the nature and format of the particular ID system that is adopted. A more targeted discussion of side effects would need to take place after an ID system was selected and implemented.

122. See, for example, Elizabeth MacDonald and Teresa Tritch, "Nosey IRS Employees May Be Peeking at Your Returns," *Money* (October 1993): 16–17; Lori Nitschke, "Bills Would Punish 'Browsing' of Returns by IRS Workers," *Congressional Quarterly Weekly Report*, 19 April 1997, 901.

123. For a recent perspective, see Samuel Dash, "Q. Are the Clinton White House Scandals Worthy of Comparison to Watergate?" *Washington Times*, 23 June 1997, 25.

124. "Passport to Scandal," *National Review*, 14 December 1992, 17; "Questions of a Wallower," *New Leader*, 30 November 1992, 4.

125. U.S. House of Representatives, Committee on Government Reform and Oversight, Subcommittee on Government Management, Information, and Technology, *Hearings on Integrity of Government Documents*, testimony of Joseph W. Eaton, 7 March 1995.

126. Maurer and Thomas, "Getting Credit Where Credit Is Due." "Not surprisingly, the instance of error rate in [the] databases [of credit reporting agencies] is significant, although the rate of error is hotly disputed. One study found an error rate in credit reports of about thirty-three percent by comparing the number of errors investigated and corrected with the number of consumers who saw copies of their reports in a given year; the error rate would be about one percent if one compared the number of errors investigated and corrected with the number of reports issued. Neither figure is satisfactory, of course, because consumers who seek access to reports are more likely to suspect error and the number of errors investigated and corrected must be some fraction of those that exist" (4).

127. Ibid.

128. Lynn M. LoPucki, "No Credit Where Credit Was Due," *New York Times*, 20 September 1997, 25.

129. Givens and the Privacy Rights Clearinghouse, *The Privacy Rights Handbook*, 2.

130. The Code of Fair Information Practices, enumerated in the Department of Health, Education, and Welfare's 1973 report of the Secretary's Advisory Committee on Automated Personal Data Systems, mandates that there must be channels by which individuals can find out what information about them is on record and how it is used. It also mandates that there be means by which individuals can correct or amend a record of personally identifiable information about themselves.

131. It is reasonable to assume that Congress would create such an ombudsperson, given its recent focus on issues of privacy and the common good. Recently, for example, the House of Representatives considered, among other bills, the Consumer Internet Privacy Protection Act of 1997; the Genetic Privacy and Nondiscrimination Act of 1997; the Background Security Records Act of 1997; the Taxpayer Browsing Protection Act; the Internal Revenue Service Accountability Act; the Social Security On-line Privacy Protection Act of 1996; the American Family Privacy Act of 1997; the Social Security Information Safeguards Act of 1997; the Federal Internet Privacy Protection Act of 1997; the Personal Information Privacy Act of 1997; the Medical Privacy in the Age of New Technologies Act of 1997; the Communications Privacy and Consumer Empowerment Act; and the Children's Privacy Protection and Parental Empowerment Act of 1997.

132. Eaton, *Card-Carrying Americans*, 189, 191.

133. For example, the Office of the Information and Privacy Commissioner in British Columbia. Information available from: http://www.oipcbc.org.

134. U.S. House of Representatives, Judiciary Committee, Subcommittee on Courts and Intellectual Property, *Oversight Hearings on Electronic Communications Privacy*, testimony of Marc Rotenberg, 26 March 1998, 11.

135. Ibid. For a very thorough article, see Colin J. Bennet and Charles D. Raab, "The Adequacy of Privacy: The European Union Data Protection Directive and the North American Response," *The Information Society* 13 (1997): 245–263. See also David Mirchin, "EU Database Directive Has Global Ramifications," *National Law Journal* (9 June 1997): B8; and M. F. Smith, "Data Protection, Health Care, and the New European Directive," *British Medical Journal* (27 January 1996): 197–198.

CHAPTER 5

1. Health Insurance Portability and Accountability Act, P.L. 104–191, sect. 264(c)(1).

2. "Patients' Bill of Rights Deserves Consideration," *National Underwriter*, 9 February 1998, 22; Peter H. Stone, "Ready for Round Two," *National Journal*, 3 January 1998, 14; Sandra Sobieraj, "Clinton, Health Insurers Debate Consumer Protection," *The Record* [Bergen County, N.J.], 21 November 1997, A12.

3. Booth Gunter, "It's No Secret: What You Tell Your Doctor—and What Medical Documents Reveal About You—May Be Open to the Scrutiny of Insurers, Employers, Lenders, Credit Bureaus, and Others," *Tampa Tribune*, 6 October 1996, 1.

4. Robert Davis, "Online Medical Records Raise Privacy Fears," *USA Today*, 22 March 1995, 1.

5. Donna E. Shalala, U.S. Secretary of Health and Human Services, speech delivered at National Press Club, Washington, D.C., 31 July 1997.

6. Matthew Brelis, "Patients' Files Allegedly Used for Obscene Calls," *Boston Globe*, 11 April 1995, 1.

7. Bill Siwicki, "Health Data Security: A New Priority," *Health Data Management* (September 1997): 11B; Doug Stanley and Craig S. Palosky, "HIV Tracked on Unauthorized Lists," *Tampa Tribune*, 3 October 1996, 1.

8. "How a Private Citizen Lost His Private Rights," *Maclean's*, 4 May 1992, 13; and Joan Ryan and Michael Kinsley, "The Greatest Tragedy Is That Ashe Didn't Have a Choice," *Sporting News*, 20 April 1992, 4.

9. Frank Deford, "Arthur Ashe's Secret," *Newsweek*, 20 April 1992, 62–63.

10. Christine Gorman, "Who's Looking at Your Files?" *Time*, 6 May 1996, reprinted in Robert Emmet Long, ed., *Rights to Privacy* (New York: H. W. Wilson Co., 1997), 81–84.

11. See, for example, "Privacy of Medical Records Is at Issue," *Richmond Times Dispatch*, 15 November 1995, A8; U.S. Senate, Labor and Human Resources Committee, *Hearings on Confidential Medical Information*, 28 October 1997; Christopher Snowbeck, "Patients at Mercy of Computer," *Pittsburgh Post-Gazette*, 11 January 1998, A1; Pamela A. Miya and Mary E. Megel, "Confidentiality and Electronic Medical Records," *MedSurg Nursing* (August 1997): 222; Craig S. Palosky and Doug Stanley, "Patients Can't Stop Leaks," *Tampa Tribune*, 16 February 1997, 1; Editorial, "Keep Medical Records from Prying Eyes," *St. Louis Post-Dispatch*, 7 October 1997, 6B.

12. Institute of Medicine, *Health Data in the Information Age: Use, Disclosure, and Privacy* (Washington, D.C.: National Academy Press, 1994), 140.

13. U.S. Senate, Committee on Labor and Human Resources, *Hearings on Confidential Medical Information*, statement of A. G. Breitenstein, director of

the JRI Health Law Institute, 28 October 1997; ibid., testimony of Senator Patrick J. Leahy (D-Vt.), 28 October 1997.

14. National Academy of Sciences, *For the Record: Protecting Electronic Health Information* (Washington, D.C.: National Academy Press, 1997), 22–23.

15. Carol Hymowitz, "Psychotherapy Patients Pay a Price for Privacy," *Wall Street Journal*, 22 January 1998, B1; John Riley, "When You Can't Keep a Secret/Insurers' Cost-Cutters Demand Your Medical Details," *Newsday*, 1 April 1996, 7A.

16. Hymowitz, "Psychotherapy Patients Pay a Price for Privacy," B1.

17. National Academy of Sciences, *For the Record*, is devoted to the subject.

18. IOM, *Health Data in the Information Age*, 89.

19. "I/T Sales to Soar Next Five Years," *Health Management Technology* (December 1995): 10.

20. Kenneth C. Laudon, in *Dossier Society: Value Choices in the Design of National Information Systems* (New York: Columbia University Press, 1986), was among the first to raise the specter of national databases.

21. U.S. Congress, Office of Technology Assessment, *Medical Monitoring and Screening in the Workplace: Results of a Survey* (Washington, D.C.: U.S. Government Printing Office, October 1991), 6.

22. "Medical Records: The Privacy Conundrum," *The Economist*, 29 April 1995, 92.

23. OTA, *Medical Monitoring and Screening in the Workplace*, 5.

24. Dr. David Korn of the Association of American Medical Colleges believes we cannot overemphasize that longitudinal record-keeping "offers enormous benefits to health care delivery and operations and is absolutely essential for a vast quantity of clinico-pathological, epidemiological, and health services research"; David Korn, private communication, 20 August 1998. Korn also notes, as does the National Academy of Sciences (*For the Record*, 82–126), that the same technological developments that may imperil privacy are also compatible with technologically advanced security capabilities. I discuss some of these technologies—such as access and audit trails—later in the chapter.

25. OTA, *Medical Monitoring and Screening in the Workplace*, 11. Critics of unique patient numbers (discussed in detail later in the chapter) cite the potential linkage of health care data to information in other databases (such as financial data or criminal background information) as cause to reject the introduction of UPNs; see Sheryl Gay Stolberg, "Health Identifier for All Americans Runs into Hurdles," *New York Times*, 20 July 1998, A1.

26. John Riley, "Know and Tell: Sharing Medical Data Becomes Prescription for Profit," *Newsday*, 2 April 1996, A06.

27. See chap. 4, n. 107.

28. IOM, *Health Data in the Information Age*, 3.

29. Workgroup for Electronic Data Interchange (WEDI), "Appendix 4: Confidentiality and Antitrust Issues," in *Report to Secretary of U.S. Department of Health and Human Services* (Reston, Va.: WEDI, July 1992), 19.

30. David F. Linowes, "A Research Survey of Privacy in the Workplace," unpublished paper, University of Illinois at Urbana-Champaign, April 1996.

31. Approximately 44 million individuals were enrolled in company self-insured plans in 1993, according to the General Accounting Office, and 48 million were so enrolled in 1995, according to the Employee Benefit Research Institute; Employee Benefit Research Institute, "Implications of ERISA for Health Benefits and the Number of Self-Funded ERISA Plans," summary of issue brief no. 193, January 1998, available from: http://www.ebri.org/ibex/ib193.htm.

32. OTA, *Medical Monitoring and Screening in the Workplace*, 2.

33. Siwicki, "Health Data Security"; Craig S. Palosky and Doug Stanley, "Privacy Lost," *Tampa Tribune*, 16 February 1997, 1.

34. Suzanne E. Stipe, "Genetic Testing Battle Pits Insurers Against Consumers," *Best's Review–Life/Health Insurance Edition* (August 1996): 38; National Academy of Sciences, *For the Record*, 77.

35. U.S. Senate, Labor and Human Resources Committee, *Hearings on Genetic Information Technology*, testimony of Senator Olympia Snowe (R-Maine), 21 May 1998. National Human Genome Research Institute, Department of Labor, Department or Health and Human Services, Equal Employment Opportunity Commission, Department of Justice, "Genetic Information and the Workplace," 20 January 1998. Available: http://www.nhgri.nih.gov/HGP/Reports/genetics_workplace.html.

36. Cited in Stipe, "Genetic Testing Battle Pits Insurers Against Consumers." E. Virginia Lapham, Chahira Kozma, Joan O. Weiss, "Genetic Discrimination: Perspectives of Consumers," *Science* 274 (1996): 621–624.

37. EEOC, *Cumulative ADA Charge Data for the 26 July 1992–30 September 1997 Reporting Period* (Washington, D.C.: U.S. Government Printing Office, 1997); Stephanie Armour, "Employers Work Around AIDS; Problems Arise Despite Efforts," *USA Today*, 24 September 1997, 4B.

38. EEOC, "Cumulative ADA Charge Data for the 26 July 1992–30 September 1997 Reporting Period."

39. Senate Labor and Human Resources Committee, *Hearings on Genetic Information Technology*, Snowe testimony, 21 May 1998.

40. Stolberg, "Health Identifier for All Americans," A11.

41. Samuel Greengard, "Genetic Testing: Should You Be Afraid?" *Workforce* (July 1997): 38.

42. "Note: Where the Public Peril Begins: A Survey of Psychotherapists to Determine the Effects of Tarasoff," *Stanford Law Review* 31 (1978), cited in American Psychiatric Association amicus brief no. 95–266, U.S. Supreme Court, *Jaffee v. Redmond* 95–266.

43. Jacob J. Lidenthal and Claudewell S. Thomas, "Psychiatrist, the Public, and Confidentiality," *Journal of Nervous and Mental Disease* 170 (1982), cited in APA amicus brief no. 95–266, U.S. Supreme Court.

44. "New Medical Privacy Law to Be Proposed," *Medical Industry Today*, 12 August 1997, cited in Robert Pear, "Clinton to Back a Law on Patient Privacy," *New York Times*, 10 August 1997, 22.

45. Gina Kolata, "When Patients' Records Are Commodities for Sale," *New York Times*, 15 November 1995, A1.

46. National Academy of Sciences, *For the Record*, 32.

47. Ibid., 77.

48. "Who's Reading Your Medical Records?" *Consumer Reports*, October 94, 628–632.

49. Robert O'Harrow Jr., "Prescription Sales, Privacy Fear," *Washington Post*, 15 February 1998, A1, A18; "CVS Also Cuts Ties to Marketing Service," *Washington Post*, 19 February 1998, E1, E5.

50. Riley, "Know and Tell."

51. Robert O'Harrow Jr., "Prescription Sales, Privacy Fears," *Washington Post*, 15 February 1998, A1, A18; O'Harrow, "CVS Also Cuts Ties to Marketing Service," *Washington Post*, 19 February 1998, E1, E5.

52. Sheryl Gay Stolberg, "The Numbering of America; Medical ID's and Privacy (or What's Left of It)," *New York Times*, 26 July 1998, sect. 4, 3.

53. National Academy of Sciences, *For the Record*, ix.

54. National Committee on Vital and Health Statistics, "Health Privacy and Confidentiality Recommendations," 25 June 1997, available from: http://aspe.os.hhs.gov/nchvs/privrecs.htm. See also National Academy of Sciences, *For the Record*, 101–127.

55. Louis Harris and Associates, Health Information Privacy Survey, poll conducted for Equifax, 1993.

56. *Consumer Reports*, "Who's Reading Your Medical Records?" 628–632, reprinted in Long, *Rights to Privacy*, 72. See also U.S. Congress, Office of Technology Assessment, *Protecting Privacy in Computerized Medical Information* (Washington, D.C.: U.S. Government Printing Office, 1993), 3.

57. "Patients' Bill of Rights Deserves Consideration," *National Underwriter*, 9 February 1998, 22.

58. Peter H. Stone, "Ready for Round Two," *National Journal*, 3 January 1998, 14.

59. Sobieraj, "Clinton, Health Insurers Debate Consumer Protection."

60. Brian J. Taylor, "The Screening of America: Crime, Cops, and Cameras," *Reason* (May 1997): 44.

61. Solveig Singleton, "Privacy as Censorship: A Skeptical View of Proposals to Regulate Privacy in the Private Sector," Cato Policy Analysis 295 (Washington, D.C.: Cato Institute, 22 January 1998), 1.

62. Sheryl Gay Stolberg, "Privacy Concerns Delay Medical IDs," *New York Times*, 1 August 1998, A10; Joel Brinkley, "Gore Outlines Privacy Measures, but Their Impact Is Small," *New York Times*, 1 August 1998, A10.

63. Robert Pear, "Plan Would Broaden Access of Police to Medical Records," *New York Times*, 10 September 1997, A15.

64. Both recommendations are outlined in "Confidentiality of Individually Identifiable Health Information," recommendations of the secretary of Health and Human Services to the Senate Committee on Labor and Human Resources, the Senate Committee on Finance, the House Committee on Commerce, and the House Committee on Ways and Means, 11 September 1997, available from: http://aspe.os.dhhs.gov/admnsimp/pvcrec0.htm.

65. *United States v. Santana*, 427 U.S. 38, 96 S.Ct. 2406 (1976).

66. L. Joseph Melton III, "The Threat to Medical-Records Research," *New England Journal of Medicine* 337 (1997): 1468.

67. Korn, private communication, 20 August 1998.

68. Ibid.

69. Robert H. Brook and Kathleen N. Lohr, "Will We Need to Ration Effective Health Care?" *Issues in Science and Technology* 3 (1986): 68–77, reprinted as RAND report N–3375–HHS; Barry Meier, "Rx for a System in Crisis," *New York Times*, 6 October 1991, 18; Stephen C. Schoenbaum, "Toward Fewer Procedures and Better Outcomes," *Journal of the American Medical Association* 269 (1993): 794–796. Schoenbaum states: "It should be disturbing to us as a profession that we have so few outcomes data and use so few in our practices. Most of us do not learn enough in our training to collect or analyze our own data or to interpret consistently the work of others" (796).

70. James E. Dalen, M.D., M.P.H., and Roger C. Bone, M.D., "Is It Time to Pull the Pulmonary Artery Catheter?" *Journal of the American Medical Association* 276 (1996): 916–918.

71. RAND Corporation, "Clinical Practice: Audit of Coronary Angiography and Bypass Surgery," Health-Related Research N–3370–HHS; also reported by David Gray, John R. Hampton, Steven J. Bernstein, Jacqueline

Kosecoff, and Robert H. Brook, "Audit of Coronary Angiography and Bypass Surgery," *The Lancet* (2 June 1990): 1317–1320.

72. Brook and Lohr, "Will We Need to Ration Effective Health Care?"

73. See, for example, Richard S. Dick and Elaine B. Steen, eds., *The Computer-Based Patient Record: Essential Technology for Health Care* (Washington, D.C.: National Academy Press, 1991): 13–19, 24; S. L. Yenney, "Solving the Health Data Management Puzzle," *Business Health* (September 1990): 41–49, cited in Lawrence O. Gostin et al., "Privacy and Security of Personal Information in a New Health Care System," *Journal of the American Medical Association* 270 (1993): 2488, 2493.

74. For an interesting recent examination of the concept of consent, see Jean Bethke Elshtain, "Beyond Consent," *New Republic*, 4 May 1998, 8–9.

75. See, for example, Len Doyal, "Journals Should Not Publish Research to Which Patients Have Not Given Fully Informed Consent—With Three Exceptions," *British Medical Journal* (12 April 1997): 1107; Arnold J. Rosoff, *Informed Consent: A Guide for Health Care Providers* (Rockville, Md.: Aspen Systems Corp., 1981), 1–32.

76. OTA, *Medical Monitoring and Screening in the Workplace*, 56; George J. Annas, *The Rights of Patients: The Basic ACLU Guide to Patient Rights*, 2d ed. (Carbondale and Edwardsville: Southern Illinois University Press, 1989), 163.

77. As in many discussions of this subject, these authors discuss all types of collection of information, not medical information in particular; Daniel Lin and Michael C. Loui, "Taking the Byte out of Cookies," *Computers and Society* (June 1998): 39.

78. OTA, *Medical Monitoring and Screening in the Workplace*, 56.

79. Ibid., 59; WEDI, "Appendix 4," 1.

80. IOM, *Health Data in the Information Age*, 150; see also Glenn McGee, "Subject to Payment? Cash and Informed Consent," *Penn Bioethics* 3 (1997): 3, 5.

81. McGee "Subject to Payment?" 1–2.

82. OTA, *Medical Monitoring and Screening in the Workplace*, 59.

83. IOM, *Health Data in the Information Age*, 150, 152, 158; see also McGee, "Subject to Payment?" 3, 5.

84. OTA, *Medical Monitoring and Screening in the Workplace*, 56.

85. IOM, *Health Data in the Information Age*, 150 (emphasis added).

86. OTA, *Medical Monitoring and Screening in the Workplace*, 60.

87. IOM, *Health Data in the Information Age*, 150 (emphasis in original).

88. OTA, *Medical Monitoring and Screening in the Workplace*, 60.

89. Janlori Goldman and Deirdre Mulligan, "Privacy and Health Information Systems: A Guide to Protecting Patient Confidentiality" (Washington, D.C.: Center for Democracy and Technology, 1996), 20–22; National Public Radio, "Health ID Numbers," *Morning Edition*, transcript 98072109– 210, 21 July 1998.

90. National Academy of Sciences, *For the Record*, 174–175.

91. Gorman, "Who's Looking at Your Files?" 82–83.

92. Melton, "The Threat to Medical-Records Research," 1467–1468.

93. Health Law Institute, *U.S. Health Information Privacy Policy*, June 1996, available from: http://www.jrihealth.org/programs/law.

94. Rosoff, *Informed Consent*, 5.

95. Melton, "The Threat to Medical-Records Research," 1467.

96. Robert M. Veatch, *The Patient as Partner: A Theory of Human-Experimentation Ethics* (Bloomington: Indiana University Press, 1987). For another perspective on the subject of consent, see Mark G. Kuczewski, "Reconceiving the Family: The Process of Consent in Medical Decision-making," *Hastings Center Report* 26 (1996): 30–37.

97. Esther Dyson, *Release 2.0: A Design for Living in the Digital Age* (New York: Broadway Books, 1997), 201; Ira Magaziner, "Self-Government on the Internet? Guidelines for the Private Sector," *The Responsive Community* 8 (1998): 37–42; Vice President Albert Gore Jr., "An Electronic Bill of Rights," remarks at the New York University commencement ceremony, 14 May 1998, reprinted in *Journal of Information Policy* 1 (1998): 29–30.

98. Dyson, *Release 2.0*, 194.

99. Federal Trade Commission, "Privacy Online: A Report to Congress" (Washington, D.C.: FTC, June 1998); Jeri Clausing, "Guidelines Are Sought for Internet Privacy," *New York Times*, 5 June 1998, D2.

100. FTC, "Privacy Online: A Report to Congress"; Goldman and Mulligan, "Privacy and Health Information Systems."

101. Case reported by Beth Givens of the Privacy Rights Clearinghouse to Department of Commerce Conference on Privacy, 23 June 1998.

102. See the Communitarian Network's position paper, "Opportuning Virtue: Lessons of the Louisiana Covenant Marriage Law," 1997, available from: Communitarian Network, (202) 994–7997, http://www.gwu/edu/~ccps.

103. Robert Bellah, Richard Madsden, William M. Sullivan, Steven M. Tipton, and Ann Swidler, *The Good Society* (New York: Alfred A. Knopf, 1991); Michael J. Sandel, *Liberalism and the Limits of Justice* (Cambridge: Cambridge University Press, 1982); Etzioni, *The New Golden Rule.*

104. Bellah et al., *The Good Society*, 40.

105. Many of these institutional reforms are discussed in National Academy of Science, *For the Record*, esp. 6–10, 93–106, 127–159.

106. U.S. House of Representatives, Committee on Commerce, Task Force on Health Records and Genetic Privacy, statement of Yank D. Coble Jr., M.D., for the American Medical Association, on privacy, confidentiality, and discrimination in genetics, 22 July 1997. Dr. Coble states: "Physicians and other entities regularly deal with categories of extra-sensitive information which have been afforded specific legislative protections above and beyond that applicable to more generalized records (e.g., HIV/AIDS information)."

107. National Academy of Sciences, *For the Record*, 8, 93–97.

108. Lynne Brakeman, "A Physician Leads the Technology Team," *Health Data Management* (February 1997): 36.

109. Ibid., 36.

110. OTA, *Medical Monitoring and Screening in the Workplace*, 48–49.

111. For a more complete discussion of smart card technology and its potential benefits and problems, see ibid., 46–51, and "Appendix B–Box 3-A," 116–119.

112. Stolberg, "Health Identifiers for All Americans," A1.

113. Office of the Vice President, "Vice President Gore Announces New Steps Toward an Electronic Bill of Rights," press release, 31 July 1998; see also Robert O'Harrow Jr., "White House to Delay Health ID Plan on Privacy Concerns," *Washington Post*, 30 July 1998, A2.

114. Korn, private communication, 20 August 1998.

115. See State of Maryland, Department of Health and Mental Hygiene, "Preventive Medicine," *Maryland Register*, 17 September 1993, 1485–1486; 4 February 1994, 201–202; 11 April 1994, 616–617; 17 January 1997, 124–125.

116. Lawrence O. Gostin, John W. Ward, and A. Cornelius Baker, "National HIV Case Reporting for the United States," *New England Journal of Medicine* (16 October 1997): 1162–1167.

117. Computer-Based Patient Record Institute, "Action Plan for Implementing a Unique Health Identifier" (position paper), November 1996, available from: http://www.cpri.org/summit/uhi.html. On the feasibility of UPNs, see Lynda Richardson, "State's List of HIV Patients Raises Privacy Issues," *New York Times*, 29 May 1998, A1.

118. Gay Men's Health Crisis, "Gay Men's Health Crisis Calls for Monitoring of HIV Infections," press release, 13 January 1998, available from: http://www.gmhc.org/press/980113.html; Jim Yardley, "Breaking the HIV Chain," *New York Times*, 25 January 1998, 27.

119. Thomas S. Bodenheimer, M.D., M.P.H., and Kevin Grumbach, M.D., "Capitation or Decapitation: Keeping Your Head in Changing Times," *Journal of the American Medical Association* 276 (1996): 1025, 1029.

120. FTC, "Privacy Online," 7–10. Additional sources include: Federal Trade Commission, "Public Workshop on Consumer Privacy on the Global Information Infrastructure" (staff report), December 1996, available from: http://www.ftc.gov/reports/privacy/privacy1.htm; Organization for Economic Cooperation and Development, *OECD Guidelines on the Protection of Privacy and Transborder Flows of Personal Data*, 1980, available from: http://www.oecd.org//dsti/sti/it/secur/prod/PRIV-EN.HTM; U.S. Department of Health, Education, and Welfare, *Records, Computers, and the Rights of Citizens* (Washington, D.C.: U.S. Government Printing Office, 1973); Privacy Protection Study Committee, *Personal Privacy in an Information Society* (Washington, D.C.: U.S. Government Printing Office, July 1977); Information Infrastructure Task Force, Information Policy Committee, Privacy Working Group, *Privacy and the National Information Infrastructure: Principles for Providing and Using Personal Information* (staff report), 1995, available from: http://www.iitf.nist.gov/ipc/ipc-pubs/niiprivprin_final.html; Canadian Standards Association, *Model Code for the Protection of Personal Information: A National Standard of Canada* (Ann Arbor, Mich.: CSS, 1996); Federal Trade Commission, *Individual Reference Services* (report to Congress), December 1997, available from: http://www.ftc.gov/bcp/privacy/wkshp97/index.html; Fair Credit Reporting Act 15 U.S.C.; European Union, *Directive on the Protection of Personal Data* (Brussels: Eur-Op, 1995). See also Goldman and Mulligan, "Privacy and Health Information Systems"; U.S. House of Representatives, Judiciary Committee, Subcommittee on Courts and Intellectual Property, *Hearings on Communications Policy*, testimony of Marc Rotenberg, 26 March 1998.

Similar principles are enumerated in Privacy Protection Study Committee, *Personal Privacy in an Information Society*, including the establishment of an independent privacy agency within the federal government and legally enforceable "expectations of confidentiality" to minimize intrusiveness and maximize fairness in record-keeping.

Likewise, similar principles of fair information practices are outlined in U.S. Department of Commerce, National Telecommunications and Information Administration, "Elements of Effective Self-Regulation for Protection of Privacy," discussion draft, January 1998, available from: http://www.ntia.doc.gov/privacydraft/198dftprin.htm.

The OECD's 1980 *Guidelines on the Protection of Privacy and Transborder Flows of Personal Data* outline eight principles: (1) putting limits on collection (there must be limits on the collection of personal data that may be lawfully obtained; (2) obtaining the knowledge or consent of the data subject (when appropriate); (3) ensuring data quality (keeping data relevant to the collecting agency's purpose, accurate, and up-to-date) and specifying purpose (data uses should be specified no later than at the time of collection, and the specified uses only should be made, unless specified on each occasion of change of purpose); (4) limiting use (personal data should not be disclosed without the consent of the data subject or authority of law); (5) safeguarding security (reasonable security safety protections must be taken to prevent unauthorized access or disclosure); (6) facilitating openness (it should be easy for data subjects to establish the existence and nature of personal data, the purposes of their use, and the identity and location of the data controller); (7) facilitating the data subject's participation (individuals should have access to data relating to themselves and be able to challenge denials of such access and/or to correct data about themselves), and (8) guaranteeing accountability (data controllers should be held accountable to these standards).

121. HEW, *Records, Computers, and the Rights of Citizens;* see also National Academy of Sciences, *For the Record,* 182.

122. HEW, *Records, Computers, and the Rights of Citizens;* IOM, *Health Data in the Information Age,* 177–179.

123. Goldman and Mulligan, "Privacy and Health Information Systems."

124. WEDI, "Appendix 4," 5; for a detailed discussion of statutory and common law protections for the privacy of medical records, see pp. 6–17.

125. IOM, *Health Data in the Information Age,* 151; OTA, *Medical Monitoring and Screening in the Workplace,* 10.

126. Center for Democracy and Technology, *Privacy and Health Information Systems: A Guide to Protecting Patient Confidentiality* (Seattle: Foundation for Health Care Quality, 1996), 5.

127. IOM, *Health Data in the Information Age,* 151.

128. OTA, *Medical Monitoring and Screening in the Workplace,* 10.

129. IOM, *Health Data in the Information Age,* 190–194; WEDI, "Appendix 4," 42.

130. U.S. Secretary of Health and Human Services Donna E. Shalala, speech at the National Press Club, Washington, D.C., 31 July 1997.

131. IOM, *Health Data in the Information Age,* 176.

132. Ibid., 177.

133. OTA, *Medical Monitoring and Screening in the Workplace,* 15.

134. IOM, *Health Data in the Information Age,* 177.

135. Dana Hawkins, "A Bloody Mess at One Federal Lab," *U.S. News & World Report,* 23 June 1997, 26–27.

136. OTA, *Medical Monitoring and Screening in the Workplace,* 15–16.

137. Shalala, National Press Club speech, 31 July 1997. For Vice President Al Gore's position, see Gore, "An Electronic Bill of Rights."

138. For details and documentation, see Amitai Etzioni, "The U.S. Sentencing Commission on Corporate Crime: A Critique," *Annals: American Academy of Political and Social Science* 525 (1993): 147–156.

139. For additional discussion, see Etzioni, *The New Golden Rule*, 161–188.

CHAPTER SIX

1. For discussions of these matters by legal scholars, see Richard G. Wilkins, "Defining the 'Reasonable Expectation of Privacy': An Emerging Tripartite Analysis," *Vanderbilt Law Review* 40 (1987): 1077–1130; Stephen P. Jones, "Reasonable Expectation of Privacy: Searches, Seizures, and the Concept of Fourth Amendment Standing," *Memphis State University Law Review* 27 (1997): 907; Anthony Amsterdam, "Perspectives on the Fourth Amendment," *Minnesota Law Review* 58 (1973–1974): 349–984; Lewis R. Katz, "In Search of a Fourth Amendment for the Twenty-first Century," *Indiana Law Journal* 65 (1989–1990): 549–590; Daniel B. Yeager, "Criminal Law: Search, Seizure, and the Positive Law: Expectations of Privacy Outside the Fourth Amendment," *Journal of Criminal Law and Criminology* 84 (1993): 249.

2. Frederick Schauer, "Slippery Slopes," *Harvard Law Review* 99 (1985): 361–383.

3. Amitai Etzioni, *The Active Society: A Theory of Societal and Political Process* (New York: Free Press, 1968).

4. For a discussion of self-regulation by companies on the Internet, see Esther Dyson, "Governance," in *Release 2.0: A Design for Living in the Digital Age* (New York: Broadway Books, 1997), 103–130.

5. *Osborn v. United States*, 385 U.S. (1966) Douglas is still quoted to that effect today.

6. Jeri Clausing, "Group Proposes Voluntary Guidelines for Internet Privacy," *New York Times*, 21 July 1998, D4; Electronic Privacy Information Center, "Self-Regulation Gets Low Marks at Privacy Summit," *EPIC Alert*, 25 June 1998.

7. Barrington Moore Jr., *Privacy: Studies in Social and Cultural History* (New York: M. E. Sharpe, 1984); Arnold Simmel, "Privacy," *International Encyclopedia of the Social Sciences*, vol. 12, 481–487. For a masterful essay on the historical contingency of the concept of privacy, see Randall P. Bezanson, "*The Right to Privacy* Revisited: Privacy, News, and Social Change, 1890–1990," *California Law Review* 80 (1992): 1133–1175.

8. For an early book that laid important groundwork for this way of thinking, see Alan Westin, *Privacy and Freedom* (New York: Atheneum, 1967).

9. Ferdinand David Schoeman, *Privacy and Social Freedom* (New York: Cambridge University Press, 1992), 1–10.

10. Samuel H. Hofstadter and George Horowitz label the right of privacy a "parasite," stating that it developed "annexed to or as a part of property or contract rights or some relationship of confidence"; *The Right of Privacy* (New York: Central Book Co., 1964), 5. See also Richard F. Hixson, *Privacy in a Public Society: Human Rights in Conflict* (New York: Oxford University Press, 1987), 62.

11. A pivotal case in this regard was *Olmstead v. United States* (1928), in which the Supreme Court explicitly rejected the idea that privacy was a separate *constitutional* right protected by the Fourth Amendment's prohibition of unreasonable searches and seizures but instead reasoned that protection of privacy is embedded in, and legitimated by, protection of property rights. The case involved the wiretapping of a phone by the FBI without a warrant so that federal agents could gain evidence of violations of Prohibition laws. The Court ruled that since wiretapping did not involve trespassing on private property, the evidence was not gained through unreasonable search and seizure; see Edward J. Bloustein, "Privacy as an Aspect of Human Dignity: An Answer to Dean Prosser," *New York University Law Review* 39 (1964): 975.

12. John Locke, *The Second Treatise of Civil Government* (New York: Hafner Publishing Co., 1956), 135; see also Mary Ann Glendon, *Rights Talk: The Impoverishment of Political Discourse* (New York: Free Press, 1991), 20–25; Barbara C. Jordan, "Individual Rights, Social Responsibility," in *Rights and Responsibilities: International, Social, and Individual Dimensions* (Los Angeles: University of Southern California Press, 1980), 10–11.

13. Samuel Warren and Louis D. Brandeis, "The Right to Privacy," *Harvard Law Review* 4 (1890): 289–320.

14. Charles O. Gregory and Harry Kalven Jr., *Cases on Torts* (Boston: Little, Brown, 1969), 883. Hixson states that owing to the publication of Warren and Brandeis's article, "the legalization of privacy moved like a brush fire through this [the twentieth] century"; *Privacy in a Public Society*, 50.

15. Bloustein, "Privacy as an Aspect of Human Dignity," 970; see also Hixson, *Privacy in a Public Society*, 49–51.

16. Warren and Brandeis, "The Right to Privacy," 196.

17. See, for instance, Center for Public Integrity, *Nothing Sacred: The Politics of Privacy* (Washington, D.C.: Center for Public Integrity, 1998); and Roger Scruton, *An Intelligent Person's Guide to Philosophy* (New York: Penguin, 1996), 112.

18. Warren and Brandeis's privileging of privacy is highlighted toward the end of their seminal essay, ironically, in a section devoted to outlining six conditions under which competing concerns should be accommodated. While the two scholars first observe that privacy may have to be curbed for purposes such as allowing the "publication of matter which is of public or general interest" and "meeting the communicative need of courts and legislative bodies" ("The Right to Privacy," 196), the fifth condition on their list establishes that privacy is not only violated by false statements but can be transgressed even by truthful publications. And the sixth condition notes that the absence of malice by a publisher who violates privacy is insufficient to afford him legal defense. Even as they seek to curb privacy, they end up extending it. Under the third condition, oral communication, as distinct from written or published communication, cannot be construed to be an invasion of privacy—unless there is "special damage," which Warren and Brandeis do not define. And under the fourth condition, the right of privacy cannot be asserted after an individual explicitly consents to a disclosure or publishes private things himself; this condition does not, of course, diminish the claim the right lays on others but only notes that it does not bind the acting self.

19. U.S. Office of Science and Technology, *Privacy and Behavioral Research* (Washington, D.C.: U.S. Government Printing Office, 1967), 3.

20. William R. Lund, "Politics, Virtue, and the Right to Do Wrong: Assessing the Communitarian Critique of Rights," *Journal of Social Philosophy* 91 (1997): 103; see also Mary Ann Glendon, *Rights Talk: The Impoverishment of Political Discourse* (New York: Free Press, 1991).

21. Lund, "Politics, Virtue, and the Right to Do Wrong," 104.

22. Ibid.

23. Louis Henkin, "Privacy and Autonomy," *Columbia Law Review* 74 (1974): 1429–1430.

24. Charles Fried discusses privacy as an "intrinsic" value, as distinct from an instrumental one ("Privacy," *Yale Law Journal* 77 [1968]: 475). To suggest that a value is unbounded puts a higher claim on it; a value can be inherently or intrinsically good, such as public safety, but not unbounded.

25. Bloustein, "Privacy as an Aspect of Human Dignity," 973.

26. Jean L. Cohen, "Rethinking Privacy: The Abortion Controversy," in Jeff Weintraub and Krishan Kumar, eds., *Public and Private in Thought and Practice: Perspectives on a Grand Dichotomy* (Chicago: University of Chicago Press, 1997), 137.

27. Avishai Margalit, *The Decent Society* (Cambridge, Mass.: Harvard University Press, 1996), 201.

28. Glen O. Robinson, "Communities," *Virginia Law Review* 83 (1997): 294.

29. Stanley I. Benn, "Privacy, Freedom, and Respect for Persons," in Ferdinand David Schoeman, ed., *Philosophical Dimensions of Privacy* (New York: Cambridge University Press, 1984), 239–241.

30. Lawrence Mitchell has suggested that "*Griswold* was not that broad, and in fact, although the language (I think especially of Douglas's opinion) left room for mushrooming, the case can be read fairly narrowly in terms of establishing privacy rights"; Lawrence Mitchell, private communication, 4 May 1998. I am confident that Mitchell's observation is on the mark as far as the letter of the law is concerned. However, I would suggest that the societal consequences, as well as the legal mushrooming, have been rather broad and extensive.

I have been asked by a colleague (private communication, 9 February 1998) how the Court could have limited the new right; she wondered whether it may be one of those rights that cannot be "notched" to begin with. I responded that the Court could, for instance, limit the legal use of contraception to couples who have at least one child, on public interest grounds. I hardly recommend such a rule but only note that notching is possible.

31. See Michael Sandel's discussion of this case and the general development of privacy rights in American jurisprudence, "Moral Argument and Liberal Toleration: Abortion and Homosexuality," in Amitai Etzioni, ed., *New Communitarian Thinking: Persons, Virtues, Institutions, and Communities* (Charlottesville: University Press of Virginia, 1995), 78.

32. Henkin, "Privacy and Autonomy," 1430.

33. Cf. Michael Sandel, who sees *Griswold v. Connecticut* as distinct from later opinions asserting the right of privacy in that its basis was not the expansion of individual choice or autonomy; "Moral Argument and Liberal Toleration," 71–87.

34. *Roe v. Wade* 410 U.S. 113 (1973).

35. The right to an abortion, as Justice Blackmun wrote, is "not unqualified and must be considered against important state interests in regulation" (*Roe v. Wade* 410 U.S. 113 [1973]).

36. Warren and Brandeis, "The Right to Privacy," 194. They then provide a long list of prior instances when the common law accommodated changing social arrangements by establishing new rights. For example, they point out that early on people were secured only from physical intrusions, such as harm to their bodies. This protection was then extended to include their property and eventually grew to encompass their very feelings and intellects.

37. T. H. Marshall, *Citizenship and Social Class* (London: Cambridge University Press, 1950).

38. Benn, "Privacy, Freedom, and Respect for Persons," 239; Calvin C. Gotlieb, "Privacy: A Concept Whose Time Has Come and Gone," in David Lyon and Elia Zureik, eds., *Computers, Surveillance, and Privacy* (Minneapolis: University of Minnesota Press, 1996), 156.

39. Robert N. Bellah, William M. Sullivan, Ann Swindler, and Steven M. Tipton, *Habits of the Heart: Individualism and Commitment in American Life* (Berkeley: University of California Press, 1985); Glendon, *Rights Talk;* Amitai Etzioni, *An Immodest Agenda: Rebuilding America Before the Twenty-first Century* (New York: McGraw-Hill, 1983); Etzioni, *The New Golden Rule*, 58–84.

40. Marshall, *Citizenship and Social Class;* Benn, "Privacy, Freedom, and Respect for Persons," 239–241; and Gotlieb, "Privacy," 156.

41. Jeff Weintraub and others have stressed the role of scrutiny, in terms of not being visible or audible to the community, in their formulations of privacy, while leaving the question of its normative standing in society—how much and in what social territories privacy is appropriate—largely unexamined; see Weintraub's "The Theory and Politics of the Public/Private Distinction," in Weintraub and Kumar, *Public and Private in Thought and Practice.* I aim to address not only the role of scrutiny but also the question of the *legitimacy* of a given society's commitment to and desired level of privacy.

42. Others have used location, private versus public, for their differentiation of privacy and publicness. For reasons that will become obvious shortly, I focus on action.

43. Amitai Etzioni, "The Good Society," *Journal of Political Philosophy*, 6 (1998): 395–410.

44. For a remarkable and groundbreaking article on the topic, see Robert C. Post, "The Social Foundations of Privacy: Community and Self in the Common Law Tort," *California Law Review* 77 (1989): 957–1010.

45. Richard A. Posner's analysis ("The Right of Privacy," *Georgia Law Review* 12 [1978]: 393–422) ignores the inherently normative dimension in the concept of privacy. He explicitly states that he will "avoid the definitional problem" in his inquiry by focusing on "the withholding or concealment of information" (393). Thus, he de facto defines privacy while skirting any assessment of whether society, or the law, deems the concealment at the core of his definition to be legitimate. Another example is provided by Richard Parker, who states that "privacy is control over who can sense us"—again without any reference to the legitimacy of that control ("A Definition of Privacy," *New York University Law Review* 42 [1967]: 35). Charles Fried also limits the definition of privacy to the ability to be free from scrutiny and neglects the notion of a legitimate exemption from such scrutiny when he defines privacy as "not sim-

ply an absence of information about us in the minds of others; rather it is the control we have over information about ourselves" ("Privacy," 482).

Cf. Carl J. Friedrich, who does keep a clear distinction between secrecy, as an empirically determined notion, and privacy, as a normative one; "Secrecy Versus Privacy: The Democratic Dilemma," in J. Roland Pennock and John W. Chapman, eds., *Nomos XIII: Privacy* (New York: Atherton Press, 1971), 105–120.

46. The legal literature draws a similar distinction between informational and decisional privacy. We shall see that referring to the decisional sphere as privacy has confused the matter; I will be suggesting that the second realm be viewed as a realm of private choice.

47. Amitai Etzioni, "The Responsive Communitarian Platform: Rights and Responsibilities," in *The Spirit of Community* (New York: Crown, 1993), 251–267.

48. See, for instance, Bilahari Kausikan, "Asian Versus 'Universal' Human Rights," *The Responsive Community* 7 (1997): 9–21.

49. Etzioni, *The New Golden Rule*, 34–44.

50. Glendon, *Rights Talk;* Etzioni, *The Spirit of Community.*

51. See Amitai Etzioni, Introduction to Amitai Etzioni, ed., *The Essential Communitarian Reader* (Lanham, Md.: Rowman and Littlefield, 1998).

52. The idea is gradually gaining some currency. My first stab at it was published in *The Responsive Community* and later reprinted in *Legal Times.* Steven L. Nock reached a similar conclusion, following his own considerations. Amitai Etzioni, "Less Privacy Is Good for Us (and You)," *The Responsive Community* 6 (1996): 11–13; Steven L. Nock, "Too Much Privacy?" *Journal of Family Values* 19 (1998): 101–118.

53. Fred H. Cate, *Privacy in the Information Age* (Washington, D.C.: Brookings Institution Press, 1997), 31.

54. Alan Westin, *Privacy and Freedom* (New York: Atheneum, 1967) 42. Another book that leans in this direction is David Brin, *The Transparent Society: Will Technology Force Us to Choose Between Privacy and Freedom?* (Reading, Mass.: Perseus Books, 1998). See also William G. Staples, *The Culture of Surveillance: Discipline and Social Control in the United States* (New York: St. Martin's Press, 1997).

55. Talcott Parsons, *The Structure of Social Action: A Study in Social Theory and Special Reference to a Group of Recent European Writers* (New York: Free Press, 1968); see also Philip Selznick, *The Moral Commonwealth: Social Theory and the Promise of Community* (Berkeley: University of California Press, 1992); John Gray, *Isaiah Berlin* (Princeton, N.J.: Princeton University Press, 1997);

and Steven Lukes, "Berlin's Dilemma: The distinction between relativism and pluralism," *Times Literary Supplement*, 27 March 1998, 8–9.

56. Cf. Ronald Dworkin, *Taking Rights Seriously* (Cambridge, Mass: Harvard University Press, 1977).

57. In the section "Of Property" in his *Second Treatise of Civil Government*, Locke makes the claim that ownership of property derives from, and is legitimated by, the individual's expenditure of labor to acquire or transform some natural or physical entity: "Whatsoever then he removes out of the state that nature hath provided and left it in, he hath mixed his labor with, and joined it to something that is his own, and thereby makes it his property" (134). As a direct consequence, legitimate ownership—a right of property—is not dependent on social formulations, collective agreements, or other contextual factors: "Thus the grass my horse has bit, the turfs my servant has cut, and the ore I have digged in any place where I have a right to them in common with others," he states, "become my property without the assignation or consent of anybody" (135). In this way Locke asserts a natural right to property while at the same time denying that it is a social construct or grounded in collective commitment; *Two Treatises of Government* (New York: Hafner, 1956), 134–135.

58. Alon Kaplan, ed., *Israeli Business Law: An Essential Guide* (Boston: Kluwer Law International, 1997), pt. 2, chap. 11.

59. Some may argue that the concept of private property no longer plays a role in current conceptions of privacy. However, Morgan Cloud shows that a close overlap between property rights and privacy still exists; "The Fourth Amendment During the *Lochner* Era: Privacy, Property, and Liberty in Constitutional Theory," *Stanford Law Review* 48 (1996): 555.

60. James K. Weeks, "Comparative Law of Privacy," *Cleveland Marshall Law Review* 12 (1963): 485–486.

61. Henkin, "Privacy and Autonomy," 1421; see also June Aline Eichbaum, "Towards an Autonomy-Based Theory of Constitutional Privacy: Beyond the Ideology of Familial Privacy," *Harvard Civil Rights-Civil Liberties Law Review* 14 (1979): 361; and Sandel, "Moral Argument and Liberal Toleration," 71–87.

62. Carl E. Schneider, "Moral Discourse and the Transformation of American Family Law," *Michigan Law Review* 83 (1985): 1864–1865.

63. Hyman Gross, "The Concept of Privacy," *New York University Law Review* 42 (1967): 35. Robert Bork echoed the sentiments of a fair number of conservatives when he wrote unabashedly about the Supreme Court's creation "out of thin air, of a general and undefined right of privacy"; *Slouching Towards Gomorrah: Modern Liberalism and American Decline* (New York: Regan Books, 1996), 103.

64. Jeffrey Rosen, "Breyer Restraint," *New Republic*, 11 July 1994, 20.

65. Herbert J. Spiro, "Privacy in Comparative Perspective," in Pennock and Chapman, *Privacy: Nomos XIII*, 121–148; see also Weeks, "Comparative Law of Privacy," 485–486. Cf. Westin, *Privacy and Freedom*.

66. For a rather informal but insightful account by a prominent British attorney, see Geoffrey Robertson, "Privacy Matters," *New Yorker*, 8 September 1997, 38–40.

67. For further discussion, see Moore, *Privacy*, 267–288. Note that these observations do not necessarily point to relativism, a social philosophy that I have critiqued in some detail in an earlier publication (Etzioni, *The New Golden Rule*, 217–257). Even though societies vary greatly in the scope of what they consider covered by the mores of privacy, this is not to deny the standing of privacy as a basic value, or at least as a facet of another fundamental value—most likely autonomy—respected in one way or another by most, if not all, societies; see J. Roland Pennock, "Introduction," in Pennock and Chapman, *Privacy: Nomos XIII*, xiii.

68. See Alan Ehrenhalt, *The Lost City: The Forgotten Virtues of Community in America* (New York: Basic Books, 1996).

69. For further examples of such warrantless, suspicionless searches that have been ruled permissible under the Fourth Amendment, see Michael Froomkin, "The Metaphor Is the Key: Cryptography, the Clipper Chip, and the Constitution," *University of Pennsylvania Law Review* 143 (1995): 824–825.

70. See, for instance, Priscilla M. Regan, *Legislating Privacy: Technology, Social Values, and Public Policy* (Chapel Hill: University of North Carolina Press, 1995); Richard F. Hixson, *Privacy in a Public Society* (New York: Oxford University Press, 1967), 26–51. Hixson devotes a scant three pages, which are not even indexed, to the role of the Fourth Amendment in the development of privacy (48–50), while devoting almost entire chapters to Warren and Brandeis's article, William Prosser's reformulations of privacy protections in tort law, and the concept of privacy articulated in *Griswold v. Connecticut* and *Roe v. Wade*. See William L. Prosser, "Privacy," *California Law Review* 48 (1960): 383–423.

71. See, for instance, Eichbaum, "Towards an Autonomy-Based Theory of Constitutional Privacy," 361–384; Henkin, "Privacy and Autonomy," 1410–1433; Ruth Gavison, "Privacy and the Limits of Law," *Yale Law Journal* 89 (1980): 421–471; and Sandel, "Moral Argument and Liberal Toleration."

72. There is much debate among scholars even today as to whether privacy is a unitary right or just a name for a bundle of other rights. We shall not join this discussion here. See Prosser, "Privacy," 383–423; and Bloustein, "Privacy as an Aspect of Human Dignity."

Privacy has been considered an aspect of the Fifth Amendment's protections (particularly against self-incrimination), free speech in the right to anonymity in public expression, and freedom of association.

73. See also *Gilbert v. Minnesota* (1920), in which the Court ruled that, under the First and Fourth Amendments, parents were free to teach their children the doctrine of pacifism in the privacy of their homes, and also *National Association for the Advancement of Colored People v. Alabama* (1964), in which the Court found that Alabama could not require the NAACP to publicize its membership lists under the First and Fourteenth Amendments' protection of freedom of association.

74. I discuss searches and not seizures precisely because the latter are often concerned with primary control rather than with scrutiny. Although seizures are sometimes used to obtain and preserve evidence, often they are the means of transferring property rights from the current actor to the state, especially in the so-called zero-tolerance cases in which the assets of drug dealers are seized and turned over to the police for their own use.

75. Patrick Henry, for instance, argued in favor of the Fourth Amendment, stating, "The officers of congress may come upon you now, fortified with all the terrors of paramount federal authority. . . . They ought to be restrained within proper bounds"; quoted in Regan, *Legislating Privacy*, 35. Henry saw a balance expressed in the notion of "proper bounds" and would not have ruled such interventions completely out of bounds or demanded that those seeking to allow them pass a strict security test.

76. See, for example, Scott E. Sundby, "Everyman's Fourth Amendment: Privacy or Mutual Trust Between Government and Citizen?" *Columbia Law Review* 94 (1994): 1751; Brian J. Serr, "Great Expectations of Privacy: A New Model for Fourth Amendment Protection," *Minnesota Law Review* 73 (1989): 583–642; Mary I. Coombs, "Shared Privacy and the Fourth Amendment, or the Rights of Relationships," *California Law Review* 75 (1987): 1593–1664; Christopher Slobogin and Joseph E. Schumacher, "Reasonable Expectations of Privacy and Autonomy in Fourth Amendment Cases: An Empirical Look at 'Understandings Recognized and Permitted by Society,'" *Duke Law Journal* 42 (1993): 727; Robert J. Liebovich, "Privacy Goes Camping: Staking a Claim on the Fourth Amendment," *Memphis State University Law Review* 26 (1995): 293; and Cloud, "The Fourth Amendment During the *Lochner* Era."

77. One may suggest that the Fourth Amendment does not treat privacy as a trump but does privilege it. Even such an interpretation would serve many of the points that need to be made; other amendments tend to leave them open to more absolutist reading. However, the Fourth Amendment can be read as not privileging if one notes that prohibition on unreasonable searches

is not accorded more weight than the permission to conduct reasonable searches.

78. For additional discussion, see Marc Stanislauczyk, "An Even-handed Approach to Diminishing Student Privacy Rights Under the Fourth Amendment: *Vernonia School District v. Acton*," *Catholic University Law Review* 45 (1996): 1041. Although the author refers to administrative searches, the same point may be extended further.

79. Michael A. Riccardi, "Duty to Warn Weighed by Pennsylvania Justices," *Legal Intelligencer*, 13 December 1996, 1.

80. See discussion of *Jaffee v. Redmond* in Daniel J. Capra, "Communications with Psychotherapists and Social Workers," *New York Law Journal*, 12 July 1996, 3.

81. For an example of the argument that America is a Lockean nation, see especially Louis Hartz, *The Liberal Tradition in America: An Interpretation of American Political Thought Since the Revolution* (New York: Harcourt Brace, 1955). In response to Hart, see, among others, J.G.A. Pocock, *The Machiavellian Moment: Florentine Political Thought and the Atlantic Political Tradition* (Princeton, N.J.: Princeton University Press, 1975); Isaac Kramnick, *Republicanism and Bourgeois Radicalism: Political Ideology in Late Eighteenth Century England and America* (Ithaca, N.Y.: Cornell University Press, 1990); and Rogers M. Smith, "Beyond Tocqueville, Myrdal, and Hartz: The Multiple Traditions in America," *American Political Science Review* 87 (1993): 549–566.

On the other side, Robert Bellah explains that "in Alexis de Tocqueville's *Democracy in America*, individualism was treated as a destructive tendency that needed firm restraint if American democracy was to flourish"; Robert N. Bellah, "Individualism, Community, and Ethics in the United States and Japan," *Moral Education* 4 (1995): 1–2.

82. For additional discussion, see Etzioni, *The New Golden Rule*, 85–118.

83. This important distinction has been highlighted by Michael Sandel ("Moral Argument and Liberal Toleration"). I am not arguing that establishing exemption from state control was the intent of the Court; it may well have been bound by doctrinal considerations like *stare decisis*, or perhaps it was looking for ways to legalize behaviors that, up to that point, had been considered criminal.

84. Weintraub, "The Theory and Politics of the Public/Private Distinction," 5. Cf. Cohen, "Rethinking Privacy," 144–146. See also Gross, "The Concept of Privacy," and Bork, *Slouching Towards Gomorrah*. For a powerful feminist criticism of the private/public distinction see Catharine A. MacKinnon, *Feminism Unmodified: Discourses on Life and Law* (Cambridge, Mass.: Harvard University Press, 1987) and Elizabeth Frazer and Nicola Lacey, *The Pol-*

itics of Community: A Feminist Critique of the Liberal-Comunitarian Debate (Toronto: University of Toronto Press, 1993).

85. Gerald Gunther, *Constitutional Law* (Westbury, N.Y.: Foundation Press, 1991), 491–571; John Hart Ely, "The Wages of Crying Wolf: A Comment on *Roe v. Wade*," *Yale Law Journal* 82 (1973): 920.

86. Henkin, "Privacy and Autonomy," 1424.

87. See also Sandel ("Moral Argument and Liberal Toleration"), who accepts this argument.

88. Henkin, "Privacy and Autonomy," 1424.

89. *Griswold v. Connecticut*, 381 U.S. 479 (1965), 485–486.

90. Prosser, "Privacy," 383.

91. For more discussion on this point, see Etzioni, *The New Golden Rule*, esp. 138–149.

92. I will not go into the many issues raised by the fact that this distinction is much more problematic and blurred than is often assumed. Alan Wolfe also addresses the slippery nature of the distinction between the public and the private; see "Public and Private in Theory and Practice: Some Implications of an Uncertain Boundary," in Weintraub and Kumar, *Public and Private in Thought and Practice*, 182.

Using privacy as an all-encompassing concept often results in confusion and conceptual vagueness, such as Henkin's attempt to refer to freedom from scrutiny as distinct from freedom from control with the circumlocution "private right of privacy"; "Privacy and Autonomy," 1419. See also Jeff Weintraub's discussion of the line between private and public, "The Theory and Politics of the Public/Private Distinction."

93. Michael Sandel in effect suggests that we should talk about two kinds of privacy that have been recognized in American jurisprudence. The first, freedom from surveillance, was the dominant understanding of privacy up to and including *Griswold v. Connecticut.* Beginning in 1972 with *Eisenstadt v. Baird*, the Court shifted to what Sandel terms a "voluntarist," or autonomy-based, conception of privacy. In short, Sandel's thesis is that the pre-*Eisenstadt* conception was freedom from surveillance (including *Griswold*, which is often interpreted to advance a notion of autonomy), and afterwards it shifted to encompass freedom from control. While it does not matter much which words are used as long as the distinction is clearly maintained, the established term for freedom from public control seems to be "private" choices or acts, as implied in phrases such as "the private sector."

94. *Autonomy* does not have one precise, agreed-on definition. I suggest, though, that it tends to evoke the right to choose, while privacy evokes the right to be exempt from scrutiny. Both might be seen as elements of the right

to be let alone. If this distinction is accepted, one can use this pair of concepts—autonomy and privacy—to denote the important difference between choice and exception from scrutiny.

95. For a discussion of a third perspective, see Wolfe, *Whose Keeper*, 188, 220. See also Hillary Rodham Clinton, *It Takes a Village: And Other Lessons Children Teach Us* (New York: Simon & Schuster, 1996), and Bill Bradley, "Rebuilding Urban Communities," *The Responsive Community* 3 (1993): 12–21.

96. In a similar discussion, Steven Nock frames the issue in terms of *reputation:* "Reputation, I will argue, is a necessary and basic component of the trust that lies at the heart of social order. To establish and maintain reputations in the face of privacy, social mechanisms of *surveillance* have been elaborated or developed. In particular, various forms of credentials and modern ordeals produce reputations that are widely accessible, impersonal, and portable from one location to another. *A society of strangers is one of immense personal privacy. Surveillance is the cost of that privacy*"; Steven L. Nock, *The Costs of Privacy: Surveillance and Reputation in America* (New York: Walter de Gruyter, 1993, 1 (emphasis in original). For additional discussion of this issue, see also Schoeman, *Privacy and Social Freedom*.

97. Robert J. Sampson, "The Community," in James Q. Wilson and Joan Petersilia, eds., *Crime* (San Francisco: Institute for Contemporary Studies Press, 1995), 193–216.

98. For relevant data, see Robert J. Sampson, Stephen W. Raudenbush, and Felton Earls, "Neighborhoods and Violent Crime: A Multilevel Study of Collective Efficacy," *Science*, 15 August 1997, 918–924.

99. See discussion above in Chapter 3.

100. William A. Donahue, "Culture Wars Against the Boy Scouts," *Society* (May-June 1994): 59–68.

101. Cf. Ernest van den Haag, "On Privacy," in Pennock and Chapman, *Privacy: Nomos XIII*, 149.

102. On the question of how communities make such formulations, see Etzioni, *The New Golden Rule*, 85–159. The basic idea is that social and public decision-making is substantive, not merely procedural.

103. I am referring to a society-wide rise in permissiveness rather than to the relaxation of mores in one limited area of behavior.

ACKNOWLEDGMENTS

Several staff members of the George Washington University Institute for Communitarian Policy Studies served as research assistants on the communitarian privacy project that yielded this book. Most of them also commented on, and made editorial suggestions for, all the chapters as they took special responsibility for specific chapters. Barbara Fusco nourished the chapters on ID cards and medical records privacy and also helped coordinate the project. Nora Pollock and Peter Rubin worked on encryption, Tim Bloser on infant HIV testing, and Peter Rubin on Megan's Laws. Jennifer Ambrosino patiently made many corrections in several drafts of the text. Jacquelyn Bareford helped greatly to put the book to press.

In addition, I am grateful for the work of Michael Bocian and Judith Lurie, who provided some preliminary research assistance for the chapter on ID cards. I am indebted to Joseph W. Eaton and David Simcox for critical comments on a draft of this chapter.

Research assistance on medical privacy was provided by Zubin Khambatta as well as Rachel Mears. I am also indebted to Molla Donaldson, Scott D. Ramsey, and Ruth Etzioni for comments on a previous draft of this chapter. I am especially indebted to Dr. David Korn for a very detailed, profound, and judicious criticism of an early draft.

In drafting the chapter dealing with encryption, I benefited from discussions with Dorothy Denning, Lance Hoffman, Priscilla Regan, and Marc Rotenberg. In composing the chapter on Megan's Laws, I learned much from the comments of David Karp. I am also grateful for discussions with Ernie Allen and Suzy Rotkiss.

The conclusion benefited greatly from the extensive comments of Professors Robert Park, Scott Sundby, Mary Coombs, and some by

Louis Henkin. My staff, who were no less critical, included Zubin Khambatta and Andrew Wilmar. I am indebted to Professor Elizabeth Cavendish and Clifton Kellogg for their suggestions, and I also benefited from the editorial suggestions of Daniel Doherty and the research assistance of Micah Schwartzman.

The scholars who commented on parts of early drafts of the book did not necessarily agree with my conclusions.

Tim Bartlett, my editor at Basic Books, made several very fine and helpful suggestions.

A.E.

INDEX